To Linda
with best wishes
from Valrie Gordon.

The Magician's Daughter

A modern mystic's journey of discovery

THE MAGICIAN'S DAUGHTER

A modern mystic's journey of discovery

VALERIE GORDON

*A true account of one woman's extraordinary
paranormal adventures*

Boudicca Press of Norfolk

First published in July 2006 by
Boudicca Press of Norfolk
21b High Street Heacham
King's Lynn Norfolk PE31 7ER

A catalogue record for this book is available from the British Library.

ISBN 0-9553377-0-4   978-0-9553377-0-3

Cover illustration: Jason Holt

Last draft edit: Amanda Burfoot

Produced by John Saunders Design & Production

Printed and bound by Biddles Ltd. King's Lynn

ACKNOWLEDGEMENTS

To Kent Landimore, who was so patient with my incomprehensions regarding computer technology, constantly coming to my rescue. For his love and support.

To my late father, Gordon Anckorn, and my mother, Margery – for setting my path.

To Ailsa Fraser, who scrutinised and amended early drafts making me aware of grammar, punctuation and apostrophes. Her excellent memory reminded me of some prophesies and other data I had forgotten over the years.For assisting with the crucial text wording for the cover.

To authors Dr. Margaret Gullan-Whur, Susannah Campbell, and Michael Putegnat for helpful advice, encouragement and friendship.

To my talented children, Lucinda and Leigh, who suffered an eccentric and, at times neurotic, mother during their childhood.

To my grandchildren, Tatiana and Zachary – for just being wonderful.

To Martin Goodsell, who put up with me during our married years.

To Jason Holt, the gifted artist who designed the beautiful cover illustration for me in the style of Mucha, the French art nouveau artist.

To Carol Hopwood, who explained to me many aspects of clairvoyance.

To Margaret Maynard, for her constant support and keen interest.

To Wendy Rodley, gifted astrology teacher, charismatic friend.

To Shirley Pearce, Penny Dowen, Brenda Harry, Barbara Sonnex, Johanna Sonnex, Regina Lee, Trixie and John Gillard, and all my friends who have remained constant, despite my peculiarities.

To the wonderful universe which lets secrets slip every now and again and provides answers when we need them.

Finally, to all the Spirit Guides, Angels and Spirit Animals who look after each and every one of us.

CONTENTS

CONTENTS

Part Two

CONTENTS

Part Three

Part Four

CONTENTS

CONTENTS

INTRODUCTION

NOVEMBER 1958
A WARNING FROM THE ETHER

There was the most terrible sound of screeching brakes just around the corner – then an explosive bang as cars impacted. My blood ran cold and I felt the hackles rise on the back of my neck. Then came that intense sound of silence – which always seems to stop time and dent the atmosphere after accidents – until the rattle of a rolling hubcap filled the air with metallic rumbles across the tarmac, intensifying in sound with its ever-quickening clatter to culmination. Time then readjusted and a solitary bird yakked out its alarm.

Horrified to hear the crash, I felt full of phobic dread. My stomach tightened with apprehension and my throat began to constrict. I had stopped working in London to avoid panic attacks after witnessing daily gory accidents, and now, supposedly safe in the country, I was to encounter yet another – my bête noire still snapping and snarling at my heels. Plucking up my courage, I began to walk tentatively around the fateful curve of the path to see what carnage awaited me.

Not one, but *three* cars had crashed into the high wall against the pavement. Steam hissed from radiators, screams and groans came from the injured, bloodied glass crunched underfoot as people rushed to help. My limbs trembling, I edged my way around the mangled vehicles trying to ignore the sounds of distress, and thankfully my assistance was not necessary. Dazed and in shock – not so much because of the disaster, but because I knew with absolute certainty that if I had not stopped a few minutes earlier, I would have been at that *exact* spot when the accident happened, and undoubtedly be a bloodied corpse pinned against the wall. Tremulously, I continued walking to the station, my thoughts whirling.

Once seated in the safety of the train, I still felt very shaken as it clickity-clacked its way homeward bound, the recent scenario going over and over in my mind. What was so shocking, you see, was that there was far more to my numbed reaction than the crash itself – something far more awesome. *The reason I had waited for those few minutes earlier was because a man had called out, "Stop! There's going to be an accident!"*

The rain lashed against the train windows. I shivered even though it was warm in the carriage. As I sat, rocking with the rhythm of the train, I stared with sightless introversion, seeing nothing in the darkness outside the windows, as I tried to recall exactly what had taken place. I had to make sense of what had happened.

Recalling my incomprehensible panic attacks in crowded places, I wished I knew what caused them and often wondered if I were a little mad – at that time there was no medical understanding or treatment of phobias. I would walk long distances to avoid using crowded public transport, hence my perambulations on that wet winter's evening to avoid using the bus. I had been walking to the station from the office where I worked as a secretary. The trains at this time of evening were empty and where I knew I would find solace from my irrational fears.

Holding an umbrella in front of me to protect me from the buffeting wind and lashing rain, I had been startled when the man's voice rang urgently in my ears – "Stop! There's going to be an accident!" Swinging around to see who had spoken to me with such emphasis, I was shocked to realise there was not a soul in sight. How awful – added to the panics I suffered, I was now hearing voices! Was I going insane? What should I do?

On hearing the voice of command, I had been rooted to the spot – too numb with bewilderment to do anything other than heed the warning. I moved a few paces to a shop window and pretended to find interest in its display – an uninspiring bathroom suite in a lurid shade of pink. With the self-conscious thoughts of a shy teenager – I was eighteen at the time – I felt embarrassed staring at a toilet, even though there was nobody around to witness my confused blushes. Still shocked, I had wondered if the warning voice was some kind of madness and felt so indecisive. Should I stand there getting soaked by the rain, staring like an idiot at porcelain indefinitely? But if the voice was *'real'* – and it had certainly sounded so – how long should I wait for the accident to happen?

The voice had halted me just as I was approaching the last shop where a wide pavement narrowed and then curved round a sharp bend in the road. A high stone wall flanked a narrow pavement that was directly next to the road, leaving pedestrians vulnerable to the closeness of passing vehicles. Just at the very moment I decided that I would wait no longer, I heard the disconcerting cacophony of vehicles crashing, setting my heart racing and my thoughts full of dread.

As the train rattled along, I contemplatively wished I could dismiss the voice as imagination; but I could not – it had been so very real and if I had ignored it I would certainly have been dead, not homeward bound trying to unravel such a puzzling riddle. Clearly, if I had not imagined the warning then I had been saved from death *by a disembodied voice from the ether*! I groaned inwardly, thoughts racing around in my head. Where had the voice come from? It had seemed so very real. I just could not get over what had happened – a situation where logic could not be applied – then wondered all over again if I *was* actually crazy – but I could not ignore the fact that I *had* heard a voice, an accident *did* occur and the voice *definitely* saved me from death. But how, and why?

Understandably, my mind was in a complete whirl. Still confused when I reached home, I told my parents what had happened. "Have a nice cup of tea dear," advised Mother. "Put it out of your head," said Father. But how could I?

ONE WEEK LATER
A DREAM COMES TRUE

A few nights later, I had a particularly vivid dream in which my boss dismissed one of the girls at work. The dream, still fresh in my mind when I woke, made me smile – it was unlikely this would ever happen – she was far too conscientious. Later that morning when I saw her, I warned with a grin, "You'd better be careful, I dreamt last night that you got the sack!" We both laughed at the improbability, got on with our work, and forgot the incident. Surprisingly, the girl did not turn up for work on the following day. My boss called me into his office ready for dictation. I collected my shorthand pad and sat with pencil poised ready for him to begin. To my astonishment, he dictated a letter of dismissal to the girl I had dreamt about – a young widow with small children. Although shy, I was bold enough to query his decision, pointing out that something extreme must have happened. He replied curtly that, as she had not telephoned to explain why she had taken the day off, then she would have to suffer the consequences – remarking that if she had wanted to keep her job, then she should have informed him, come what may. As I typed out the letter, I could not help thinking about the coincidence of having dreamt about this only the night before. How very strange.

THE SAME NIGHT

That night, maybe because of the previous dream, I dreamt of another girl I had worked with in my last job and had not seen for months. In the dream, she told me that her sister-in-law – about whom I had completely forgotten – had just had a miscarriage. In reality, a few days later, this same girl visited me unexpectedly, so during our conversation – remembering my dream – I enquired about her sister-in-law. I was informed that, sadly, she was terribly ill. She was pregnant, but it was feared she would miscarry. I thought how odd it was that two recent dreams I'd had were so true. At a later date, I found out that thankfully the expected baby was born safely and survived – so my dream was not entirely correct, but unusual enough for me to feel puzzled at the odd coincidences of both dreams.

THREE DAYS AFTERWARDS
GYPSY MUSIC

We did not have central heating in those days so rooms were never warm, except for the sitting room in the evenings, where a coal fire battled to keep the chill at bay. After particularly cold nights, we would awaken to find our windows white with rime, etched with wondrous forests of fern across each pane that glittered and twinkled as if diamond studded. Jack Frost had passed by while we slept and it was worth chattering teeth and shivering limbs to view his artwork. Winters were colder then, before global warming.

The weather had been cold all day. After our evening meal, my parents and I sat by the fire and I toasted my toes for a while, eventually retiring to my bedroom to listen to records and read a book. I curled up in bed with a couple of hot water bottles to keep me warm. I had turned the volume of my record player high, enjoying Bill Haley and the Comets and the scandalous Elvis Presley, but I eventually began to feel a bit drowsy. Putting down my book, I turned off the record player and then the light and snuggled back into bed, but as soon as my head touched the pillow, I heard the most wonderful music filling the room. I had never heard anything like it before – fast tunes from a multitude of gypsy violins – tumultuous, totally exhilarating and exciting. I was swept into the passion of the throbbing beat until, suddenly and disappointingly, it stopped in mid bar.

I leapt out of bed and burst into the sitting room like a whirling dervish. "Why did you switch the radio off?" I queried frantically as I twiddled the knobs trying, without success, to locate the source of the violins. Looking at me in astonishment, my puzzled parents told me the radio had not been on, nor had the television. My mother looked bewildered. My father, mildly rustling his newspaper, remarked, "You must be hearing things."

Impatiently, I stomped back to bed wondering what was wrong with my parents – telling me there had been no music playing – of course there had been and how could they not have heard it? It had been so loud. I was puzzled at their reaction but did not dwell on it, assuming they had just not been listening properly; nor did I stop to consider that I might have imagined the music because those violins had been so wonderful, so *real*, there was no reason for me to doubt their existence. Having made such an impression on me, the incredible sound remained at the centre of my thoughts.

I searched the record shops the next day and for ages afterwards in the hope I could find a recording, but without success. I could not forget the music, feeling sure that I would eventually hear it again at some time in the future.

I was yet to realise that I had heard clairaudient music and that I would hear those gypsy violins again many years later when mysterious forces would be at work in the most astonishing way.

Little did I know that I was also to receive well over two hundred precognitive dreams during the following years – the first being the dream of the woman who had been dismissed at work – all of which could be amply verified by the people concerned or by news reports in the media. Neither was I aware that this was the beginning of a lifetime of extraordinary supernatural experiences, or that I was destined to become a seer and eventually a healer.

Clairaudience: *the alleged power of hearing things beyond the range of the normal sense of hearing.*
Prescience, Presentient, Precognition: *foreknowledge, foresight.*
Clairvoyance: *the alleged power of discerning things beyond the normal range of sense or perception.*
Seer: *a person who sees into the future.*

These words had not yet entered my vocabulary. I had led quite an insular life and knew nothing about such things, so did not link my strange experiences to anything 'supernatural'. To me, they were just weird events of a coincidental nature. This was just as well, because in that era anyone or anything that smacked of the occult was viewed with deep suspicion. Imprisonment was a threat to anybody 'dabbling' until the mediaeval witchcraft laws were repealed by Parliament in the late 1950s. If people were clairvoyant they seldom broadcast it for fear of ridicule, ostracism and more sinister repercussions.

FOREWORD

When I was a child, I planned to be a witch when I grew up. I spent hours in the back garden wearing a tall pointy hat and black cloak, stirring noxious brews that I hoped would be of magical content. I plucked weeds and flowers and boiled them in a billycan over campfires I had expertly constructed – courtesy of the Brownies. I would have preferred to be a magician like my father, but realised that, because of my gender, the lesser job description would have to do. My father, you see, as well as being a journalist by profession, was a part-time stage magician and a member of The Magic Circle. His prowess was such that 'magic' to me was quite natural. To have a bunch of brightly coloured flowers produced out of my ear was very exciting and when I was allowed to use his wand and say the magic words 'Abracadabra' to make something amazing happen – well, no wonder I wanted to be a witch. Dad's brother was also a magician, belonging to the Inner Sanctum of The Magic Circle, so you can imagine that when the two men were together and comparing their 'magic' it was very exciting for me. Top hats produced rabbits, white mice peeped out of pockets, colourful scarves arrived endlessly from the magicians' mouths, knots in ropes disappeared before my eyes and packs of cards were shuffled with the speed of light.

I really must have annoyed the other children at my primary school with constant boasts that "My daddy's a magician! He's a wizard and can do *real magic* – and so can my uncle." My fascination with magic was fuelled by reading fairy stories by torchlight under the sheets – the Brothers Grimm, Norse Fairy Tales, Hans Christian Andersen. An avid reader from a young age, I could never get enough.

The eventual realisation that *sleight of hand* was my father's forte and that he did not actually have supernatural powers made little difference to me. I suppose my perceptions had been ingrained so that magic, for me, was viable and all things were possible. I therefore continued to view him as a magical person. In addition, the fact that my mother told me strange things, such as her ability as a child to view her sister and herself lying asleep in their beds from a position high on the ceiling, backed up my notion that as a family, 'Magic Was Us'.

As I grew older, my childhood career decision to become a witch had been sensibly abandoned for the more practical one of secretary. I left school at the age of fifteen – as the majority of children did in those days – to launch myself enthusiastically at shorthand pads and various sit-up-and-beg typewriters. I was quite useless and could seldom read back my shorthand, yet I always retained my employment – something to do, perhaps, with blonde hair and tight pencil skirts. My childish belief in magic still lurked, but I did not connect my perceptions with the curious experiences – the voice, the dreams or the violins – that happened to me when I was eighteen. Unaware of what the forces of destiny intended for my future, my only desire was to become a wife and mother, and that part of my life happened quite happily without the intervention of anything paranormal. Marriage and motherhood rescued me from the office work that I disliked and where I certainly did not excel.

★ ★ ★

The contents of this book are true accounts of my paranormal adventures. The writing of this journal was not a task I would ever have considered had I not been commanded to do so, when I was in my forties, by a *Native American brave* who astonishingly manifested before my eyes – more of which I will reveal later on. I have taken care not to allow myself any creative embellishments to exaggerate the truths for more exciting reading, and maybe at times I have erred in over-simplification in my narration as I have found it impossible to convey the terrifying fear I felt when faced with other-worldly horrors.

Not everything is in chronological order because I have 'fast forwarded' in places to tie in the precognitions with their eventual conclusions – sometimes years afterwards – thus saving the necessity for cross-reference. I have also inserted, in italics, comments and conclusions that have come from the retrospective understanding of what was, effectively, tuition that I was receiving from a non-physical plane.

I had not realised the full extent of my extraordinary experiences until I had received my instruction to write this book. When I dutifully sat down with pen and paper to compile a list of dreams and events in preparation for such an undertaking, I was really surprised that there was, in fact, enough to fill a journal. I did not want this task, nor did I look forward to doing it. I wondered who would want to read the finished work, written by an ordinary woman such as I – and would anyone believe my story as it unfolded? But I felt this was a quest I could not shirk from, especially having been given the command for such work from a stern individual from another dimension.

It has taken me a long time to bring the book to fulfilment, but after my initial worry at the slow pace, I realised that time between the physical and non-physical world is very different, and that when I eventually finished the journal it would be the right time to be presented.

Forced to confront the extent and content of my many varied experiences from the world of spirit, I began to feel overawed as I worked on the project, realising that the book's content would be unusual by showing an extraordinary wide range of data that happened to *just one person*, rather than a spectrum of events experienced by a number of different people. While writings from professional psychics and mediums indicate that they have huge success with their given genre, which they can harness at will – i.e. they can give readings to clients when they wish, proving that they can 'tap into' the spirit world at any given time – what I have received, it seems, is a broader variety of experiences and 'realities' beyond that kind of range. Everything that I have been given has come out of the blue when I least expected it. I did nothing to summon up any of these experiences from beyond the veil – no rituals, no requests. They were unwanted and unasked for, but are now a welcome part of my life. I cannot 'perform' at will – though, nowadays, I do seem able to harness healing energies, which work in an amazing manner, but they are of a different nature to precognition, clairvoyance, clairaudience etc.

Because I feel that my non-physical, non-verbal spiritual tuition is not yet over, it will be interesting to find out where the extensive training is leading me. I do know that whatever and whenever assistance for myself and other people is needed, it will come for the right reason. I trust my guides totally.

I wondered *why* the Indian brave wanted me to write this journal of my varied experiences and realised that it is in order to demonstrate to readers the many different ways in which the spirit world comes through to teach and guide us along our spiritual paths, to show us that there is life beyond our own physical world, to encourage us to look for the various clues we are given, to live a more fulfilling life on this plane and be more tolerant and helpful to those around us.

I am not suggesting that all people will run the whole gamut of paranormal experiences as I have done, but this journal gives examples of many of the subtleties that arrive from the ether and which, after having read this work, can be more easily identified in readers' own lives. The ways of spirit can be very subtle, obtuse, coincidental, in riddle form and, at times, downright frightening. Their gift to us is probably more easily understood as 'The Sixth Sense' – a natural sense that we all have, once essential for survival and sadly lost over the years, but now ready for re-emergence in this 'New Age of Aquarius' in which such matters can be more readily understood by our more scientific brains once the shrouds of mystery have been ripped asunder.

In the vastness of our universe each one of us is but a tiny dot or atom, and yet from the improbable hugeness of the unknown, there are, miraculously, unseen guides to assist every one of us in our minuteness and to show that each of us has a purpose, a meaning. That there are such spirits keeping an eye on us (and my own experiences have given me that proof) then there must be some purpose to our mortal lives – which should embrace the probability that there are also other non-physical worlds awaiting us when we 'pop our clogs'.

* * *

My mystical journey began, as you have already read, at the age of eighteen when I heard the voice warning me of the car crash, and this is how it continued....

PART ONE

JUNE 1962
A DREAM OF DEATH

I was thrilled with my newborn daughter, Lucinda, bonding with such an enormous rush of love when she was first placed in my arms. I was twenty-two years old and had so looked forward to her arrival. Amazingly, during the pregnancy I had cast aside my phobias by facing my fears of public transport for the well being of my unborn child. I forced myself to board buses for hospital checkups, finding my panics lessen each time. After the birth, the frightening knowledge that such a tiny, jaundiced baby was reliant on me for survival was immense – I forgot to worry about my own insecurities and phobias while trying to cope. I did not even know how to put her nappy on and was completely unprepared for all the problems that arose. She did not feed well, lost weight and cried all the time. It seemed to take all hours of the day and night to get her to take one feed, then to wind her and try and stop her screams – by which time I had to begin all over again. I was constantly exhausted. One afternoon after a gruelling time, I badly needed sleep. Little Lucinda would not stop crying, so tucking her in my arm to comfort her and stop her tears, I wearily flopped into bed, immediately falling into a deep and exhausted sleep.

I dreamt that I was having a cup of tea with my mother. We were seated in my sitting room that had a highly polished floor. Turning to my mother, I asked her conversationally, "And how did she die?" She replied – equally nonchalantly, "Oh, she suffocated." Just as she spoke, tiny ghostly footprints appeared towards and around us leaving small dusty marks on the polished tiles. Then, I realised with horror that we were talking about my own baby who had died!

In my exhausted sleep I knew that the dream was a warning and that I must wake up. Feeling leaden and so deeply asleep I just could not rouse myself. My weary, sleeping self knew how vital it was for me to awaken or my newborn infant really would be dead. One more effort and I forced myself from the deep sleep – only to realise that little Lucinda was not in my arms and nowhere to be

23

seen! Panicking, I snatched at the sheets and looked under the blankets until I found her, somehow wriggled towards the bottom of the bed – not suffocated yet, thank goodness!

I dwelt for some time on what had happened. The dream had certainly saved my baby's life, but I wondered how much my subconscious had played its part? I guessed that probably my sleeping awareness knew she was in difficulties, at risk of suffocation. There was no doubt, however, that if the dream had not forced me into action, I would undoubtedly have slept on. I remembered the voice that had saved my own life, and now the dream that had saved my baby – was I being fanciful to think it was more than coincidence?

FEBRUARY 1966
DEMONS

Four years went by – happy days with my sweet little daughter. During this time she was 'discovered' by the royal photographer, Lisa Sheriden, who was so smitten by my baby's forming character that she took regular photographs of her from the age of six months to include in a book she was writing. Together, Lucinda and I were given modelling assignments and it was strange to see posters of us both all over London. This was a new part-time career for me, which gave me a lot more confidence, and I was relieved to be able to face London again without the panic attacks. I was also proud to see images of my little girl amongst photographs of the royal children in Lisa's various books, and some of me as well.

I was delighted when I became pregnant again. I felt my growing baby kick for the first time when I was on a set at Pinewood Studios doing my first television commercial. It was heady stuff!

Unfortunately, towards the end of the pregnancy I became ill with high blood pressure, causing toxaemia, a dangerous condition that can induce fits, endangering the child. I was rushed to hospital and had to lie totally inert in bed, not even allowed to read a magazine as even this small exertion could make the condition worse. Because I was so poorly, I was given a quiet room to myself.

In the stillness of one particular night, I could hear footsteps in the room and looked to see if it was the nurse. Nobody was there. I did not worry about it, turned over and went back to sleep. Later on, when the nurse popped her head around the door to check on me, I joked that I must have a ghost in the room as I had heard someone walking around. She looked at me quizzically and asked if I had been frightened. No, I wasn't, I told her quite truthfully, wondering why she had asked.

I was soon to find out. "There *is* a ghost in this ward," the nurse whispered conspiratorially, looking over her shoulders with a theatrical gesture. I grimaced to myself as I really did not want to know that, but could see she had anecdotes to tell. "I have been in a ward of sleeping children, when one by one, each child woke up, as if someone were touching them as they walked by."

Pausing in her narration to make sure she had my attention, she continued, "Another time, a nurse ran screaming along one of the passages after she had seen a ghostly apparition." After elaborating on those anecdotes she said, "My parents go to a lot of séances and you would be surprised at what goes on there." The nurse settled down in the chair by my bed to relate spine-chillingly spooky stories.

When my blood pressure was taken in the morning, it was higher than ever. Clearly, ghost stories had a worse effect than reading a magazine! I felt terrible.

I had to go into the sluice room and as soon as I entered it, noticed a fearsome atmosphere. It was as if an evil, brooding presence were waiting for me. I felt a sickening compulsion to walk over to the long window and throw myself out to the ground far below. I was really scared.

Logically, I knew that the nurse's ghost stories must have been playing on my mind, but I really could not believe that my imagination could conjure up such a tangible evil in this way. I was very frightened, so kept close to the wall, away from the lure of the window and death, then carefully backed out of the door to return to the safety of my bed as quickly as I could. To my relief, the 'presence' did not follow me.

The next time my blood pressure was taken, the nurse said that it had reached a dangerous level, which meant I would have to be strapped into a padded bed. This did not bode well and I was carried vertically on a stretcher down a spiral staircase, clutching a vase of tulips – I felt almost ready for the grave – which made me chuckle.

Wheeled into another room, I was tied into the padded bed. It was a horrible experience. I was so frightened for my baby. Determined to show no fear, I was annoyed that my lips quivered uncontrollably. The foreign nurse left in charge of me seemed to take pleasure in informing me that my baby would die and that women like me made her sick – she did not explain why. She shouted at me, then ignored me and sat down to read a novel – which she quickly hid when a doctor entered the room, by which time she was bent over me with insincere and caring smiles.

Luckily, despite that nurse, my blood pressure went down and the immediate danger had passed, but I was told that it would be necessary to have my baby induced. After this was done – another dreadful experience, with a pack of students watching intently – I slept for a few hours to awaken when the contractions began.

Rushed to the theatre, I was soon prepared for the birth and a reassuringly kind Asian doctor helped me through the ordeal, which was touch and go because the cord was round my baby's neck. There was no cry and I thought he had been born dead, but the doctor was wonderful, acting quickly and saving the little boy's life. As my baby was premature – a tiny scrap of only four pounds – he was whisked out of my sight and into an incubator. The doctor and nurses left me alone in the theatre, assuring me that someone else would be in shortly to stitch me up – but nobody came.

I felt myself haemorrhaging badly – a ghastly sensation. I was very weak and called for help when the occasional nurse passed by, but they ignored me. It was ages before anybody came to my aid. When they did, they told me that I had lost an horrendous amount of blood – only an armful left – and that I looked like a slab of marble. Even though I felt like death was approaching, I raised a wan smile at the description.

I was sorted out and stitched up and a cheerful nurse was left to watch over me. I was trying to keep my senses but found myself drifting down into a lovely deep, soft pit, rather like falling gently into a never-ending feather bed. I knew that I was dying and fought hard against it. Eventually, I just could not 'fight' any more. I weakly gasped to the nice little nurse, "I don't think I can hold on (to life) any longer." I was ready to let myself drift into the cosy pit of oblivion. With a cheeky smile she replied, "Oh, go on! Just hang on a little longer, until we can find you some blood!"

I believe my quirky sense of humour saved me from death because I laughed, and this seemed to give me the extra strength I needed to hang on until, eventually, the drip was wheeled in. The one good thing that came of that near-death experience is that I am not afraid of dying now – it felt far too cosy for fear or worry.

THE NIGHTMARES REALLY BEGIN

I did not realise it at the time, but because I was very weak from loss of blood and had been so near death, as well as having been filled with various prescribed drugs – which may have caused some of the hallucinogenic effects I was to experience – I was in the very vulnerable condition ideal for 'low plane spirits' that can invade a person and take control when their defences are down. This can lead to all manner of strange behaviour – madness, schizophrenia and suicide attempts – as the entity takes control of the host's mind. As there is light, there is also darkness, and this is how the darkness came to me.

★ ★ ★

The danger caused by the haemorrhaging had passed. Moved to another ward with a saline drip attached to the back of my hand, I had been told that my baby – glimpsed for only a short moment – was surviving in his incubator. I gave a sigh of relief and tried to get comfortable in the narrow bed. The pillows were incredibly uncomfortable, my head ached intolerably and the noise in the ward was awful. Outside, doors banged continuously, cars revved up outside loudly, driving to and fro, deliverymen shouted and, in general, a cacophony ensued – *a cacophony that, I was to later realise, was not an actuality.*

A nurse came to check me and to change the saline drip. As she opened the cellophane covering, I winced, amazed at the deafening noise the wrapping made. She noticed my discomfort and queried the problem. I told her the noise really hurt my head and she reassured me that it was a medical condition and not to worry. However, she moved me into a quieter ward and introduced me to the other occupant.

Apart from the pillows that seemed filled with concrete lumps and did not help my headache, I felt much better. Time dragged by slowly, as it does in such places, until I heard voices in the corridor outside. I recognised the voice of the Asian doctor who had delivered my baby. Wanting to thank him for his kindness to me and for saving my baby's life, I was about to ring the bell for attention when I realised that what I was hearing *was the exact communication exchanged between the doctor and nurses during the birth of my child!* Horrified, I realised I was listening to a repetition of something that had happened hours ago! To make sure, I asked my room mate if she could hear people talking outside.

"No," she said. "There's nobody there."

"Oh dear," I wailed in distress. "Then I must be hearing things!" Was I going mad?

I settled down again, trying to get comfortable and checked on the time. The hands of my bedside clock had not moved since I had last looked at them. Maybe it had stopped. I picked it up and held it to my ear. It was still ticking merrily. I tried not to panic, and deliberately lay back for a while before I checked the time again. When I did, the hands were in the same position. Perhaps the clock needed rewinding. No, it was fully wound and still ticking loudly. I sighed in bewilderment, and then noticed with amazement that the hands of the clock were moving *backwards*, gathering momentum until they were almost whirring. I watched in horror, until they came to a stop at six thirty – the time of my baby's birth. Oh, I wondered, what is happening? Bewildered, I peered through the small gap in the window by my bed to distract myself from the mysteries of the clock. Through the window's narrow confines, I could see a man on a Vespa Scooter driving away from a parking bay. Then I saw him go backwards, like a film rewound. He then drove forward again, then whizzed back. This scene repeated itself endlessly, sound effects included, until I could look no longer.

I realised that my brain was doing strange things and was 'on the blink' and told the girl in the other bed. "Oh dear," she said kindly, at a loss. Throughout the day, I kept checking with her as to what was real and what was not. If she was worried about being in the same room as a mad woman, she did not show it and was very sympathetic.

During the night, I could not sleep. The loud noises had calmed down and the ward was now peaceful. I could hear the nurse getting babies' bottles ready and I found this reassuring. I wondered how my little baby was getting on.

The peaceful silence was soon shattered when I heard a bedside bell ring urgently and the sounds of a nurse as she ran down the corridor, her rubber soles squeaking on the polished floor, towards a woman who was screaming out, "I am going to kill my baby!" I heard the nurse soothing her and saying, "Mothers don't do that kind of thing."

The woman was hysterical and the nurse was having trouble trying to calm her. Eventually, the woman quietened apart from an occasional soft sob. I could hear the nurse's footsteps as she returned to the bottle bay. I settled down again in the quiet, then heard a car drive slowly along the tarmac outside the windows, heard the crash of glass breaking as the woman threw her baby out, heard the little body thud onto the ground and the terrible sound of the car scrunching over it – I knew the baby was dead. I was transfixed with horror at the surreal scenario.

Bells rang, nurses panicked, the mother was screaming and confusion reigned for some time until, eventually, an eerie quiet returned. All I could hear then was the sound of muffled sobbing.

While all this was going on, I was sitting in bed gripping onto my sheets, quite horror-struck, wondering if what I had heard was real or if my mind had been playing tricks again. When it was silent once more, I breathed more easily until I heard the outer door down the corridor swing open and a Catholic Priest enter, whose footsteps echoed as he walked along the empty corridor to the murdering mother. I could hear quiet murmurs as they spoke together in her room. I did not question how I knew it was a Catholic priest – I just knew.

In retrospect, as my own religion was Church of England, I found my certainty rather odd, feeling that if my mind was playing tricks, it would move along a path it knew and conjure up a vicar of my own denomination.

As I was still feeling horrified by the bizarre events I had heard during the night, I wanted to find out what had really happened – if it were real or imagined, that I was either sane or insane – so when the night nurse came round to check on me before going off duty, I asked her, "Am I going crazy, or did I *really* hear a woman kill her baby during the night?" She looked at me sharply, a perplexed look passing over her face. I realised by her reaction that nothing had happened at all, so when the nurse asked me to elaborate, I refused to say more. It was clear to me that I must be going very mad and I did not want to be sent to a mental home!

Next, I was entering the realms of a House Of Hammer Horror film.

The nurse's face changed. It turned blotchy and mauve, looked sly and evil and her movements became uncoordinated. I noticed that as she left the room, her gait was like a robot, jerky, disjointed. All colour disappeared. Everything was in shades of grey. The worst thing of all was the atmosphere. My nostrils filled with the smell of must and dust – like unopened tombs that had received no fresh air for aeons. I gasped for air but there was none.

I could see through the glass partitions two nurses changing sheets on a bed in the next room. I could hear their voices amplified through the glass, spiteful and squeaky – they sounded as if they had been inhaling helium gas! They were talking about one of the patients who had gone mad (me, perhaps). Their tittered laughter was shrill and demonic. Every movement they made was jerky, but worse than anything was the timeless feeling of my existence. I was think-ing, feeling and seeing, but in the midst of an 'eternity' quality that was quite horrible. I believed that I was locked into timelessness in this dusty, musty, grey and airless zone forever. If there is such a place as hell, I was in it then.

I lay in my bed trying to understand what I was doing in this terrible place. I knew that I had given birth to a child, but was it a boy? I was unsure and in my confusion believed that it must have been Lucinda, my little girl – but she was four years old now – I felt so bewildered – why was I here in this timeless, musty, forever-zone, and where was she?

The door to my room opened and two nurses entered, one with huge exag-gerated wart-like protuberances on her nose. This woman held in her hands the most enormous hypodermic syringe I had ever seen. It was the size of a drainpipe – about six feet long – and she was going to inject me with it! I screamed furiously as I fought with the nurse, believing her to be some kind of demon, and tried to stop her, but was too weak and soon overcome. I remem-ber wondering why I was going through this kind of hell as I had not been a bad person during my life. They held me down while the huge syringe was lunged at me and I screamed again with terror as the enormous needle found its mark and oblivion engulfed me.

★ ★ ★

I woke up in a different room, this time alone. I did not know who I was or where I was. I looked down at a stranger's hands and arms. I noticed some moles, and thought dispassionately, I used to have moles on my arms like that.

29

I looked up at the ceiling and noticed some large cracks. As I traced the cracks with my eyes, they disappeared from view. Oh well, it did not matter, I was getting used to all the strangeness.

The musty, fusty, airless atmosphere was still prevalent in this horrible time-less place, so I made the decision to attempt an escape from the hell in which I was incarcerated. It was worth a try. I climbed carefully from the bed and put on my satin quilted dressing gown – a lovely shade of turquoise – and looked around for my purse as I hoped to catch a bus. Alas, it had disappeared along with the ceiling cracks, so I sighed and reasoned that I was clearly dead and a ghost. I concluded that I must be the ghost that haunted the corridors that the nurse had told me about so many aeons ago. That problem solved, I resolved to wander around and see if there were any means of escape from this dreadful place.

The suffocating smell of dust and must filled my nostrils and the grey shades and timelessness of another dimension was still with me as I furtively tiptoed along the corridors until I came to some double-doors, which led to the gardens. I tried to push the doors open, but they would not budge. Oh, of course! I was a *ghost* and, therefore, had no substance, so naturally I would not be able to open a door. What I ought to do is to *waft through it as ghosts do!*

I was very nervous about doing this – I knew I was a ghost, but could not remember attempting this kind of thing before. I drew in a deep breath and boldly attempted to walk through the closed door, expecting to dissolve through it. Oh the pain! Clearly, it did not work because I was not through and my nose hurt badly.

As I stood, confused, nurses came running. I was annoyed as I knew they were going to thwart my escape! I started to run but they grabbed hold of me and I noticed that blood was flying everywhere and was splattered down the front of my dressing gown. Then, most surprisingly, the blood disappeared. How strange. Next, it appeared again. I was more interested in watching the blood as it flashed on and off – now you see it, now you don't – rather like a flickering neon light. Fascinated, I watched as the sparkling ruby-red globules disappeared and reappeared on my turquoise gown, barely caring as the women led me back to my room.

I did not bother to talk to them, trusting no one, though I did allow the nurses to plaster my nose back into position – I was beyond pain now. Everything was so confusing.

MORE CONFUSION

After the nurses had left my room, I decided I would try to phone home. I wanted to get out of that awful place. Once more I climbed out of bed to wander the corridor where I had noticed a telephone. I did not have any money to operate it but, as nothing seemed real, that small problem was not important. What was so confusing, however, was that once I had found the phone and reached out to pick up the receiver, it disappeared! This kept happening – there it was – like the blood on my dressing gown – there it wasn't, disappearing just like the Cheshire cat in Alice in Wonderland and far too difficult for me to comprehend.

Disappointed, I gave up that project to meander in confusion back along the corridors in the timeless dimension, loathing the dusty, musty smell, hating the eternity feel, bereft of colour. I trailed into other mothers' rooms and looked at their babies in the cribs. The babies meant nothing to me – I was so dispassionate.

Tired, I shuffled back to my room on leaden limbs and struggled back into bed to lie down. Suddenly, and with horror, I could feel myself haemorrhaging again. Oh no! Gushes of clotted blood were pumping down my legs, just as they had in the operating theatre. Not only that, I could also feel the contractions beginning again as if I were about to give birth. Oh no! It could not be happening again!

I lifted the sheets and was confused to discover that there were no signs of bleeding but, as I lay there, I could still feel those horrible sensations, which went on for a long time. How frighteningly weird it all was.

When the nurse came in to check me she told me my baby was getting on all right. "What baby?" I queried. "I don't believe I've had one." She disappeared and came back later with another nurse, who cradled a baby wrapped in a shawl. "That's not mine," I said, not recognising it as the baby I had given birth to those aeons ago. I turned away from them to stare at the wall. To this day, I suspect they bundled up a bigger baby just to pacify me. Nothing was real. I did not believe anything or trust anyone. I checked constantly, every few minutes, on my belongings to make sure they were still in place and felt relieved when they did not disappear but stayed put.

My hair felt horribly greasy. It had not been washed for ages and I knew that somewhere I had some dry shampoo. I had not used it before, but it was in powder form to shake over the hair and clean it. I rifled through the bedside cabinet until the shampoo 'appeared', then walked over to the wall mirror. At that time I was an attractive twenty-four-year-old without a wrinkle on my face, yet what I saw in the mirror was a hideous, wrinkled, ancient old crone looking back at me!

Her face was furrowed, her cheeks drawn and her hair was wispy and grey. As the reflection of that old woman stared back at me, I became more confused than ever.

"Oh well," I eventually reasoned, "perhaps I am an old lady after all." The way time had stopped still and the 'eternity' place in which I had been entrapped was probably some kind of hell; maybe I had died in old age, doomed to stay here forever, my memories erased. Past caring by now, I ceased trying to understand. With the container in my hand, I reasoned I might as well continue my task, so began to sprinkle it over my hair, except the powder would not come out. Perplexed, I tried hard but was incapable of figuring out how it worked, so gave up, dragged myself back across the room and climbed laboriously into bed.

What next? I looked around, keen to do something to pass the time in a place where time stood still. I picked up a library book about Nell Gwynn that I had chosen some time ago. Although I read that book from beginning to end, not one word of it made sense.

★ ★ ★

THE DEMON HOUND FROM HELL

Something woke me in the dark of the night. I heard a strong wind that flung open the distant main door then travelled with howling ferocity along the corridor outside my room, swirling dried leaves along in its wake, rattling furiously against the walls and thudding against my door. It was an unearthly and terrifying sound, chilling me to the core. In the midst of the howling gale and the clattering of storm-swept leaves, I could hear the pounding paws of some fearsome hound from hell as it loped along the corridor, its long nails clitter-clattering, its panting breath heavy, its nose sniffing out its prey – which I knew with certainty was me.

Terrified, I lay with bated breath, sheets clutched under my chin, hoping the creature would not find me. My heart accelerated with fear. There seemed to be so much evil that it was tangible. With some new kind of perception, I could see the creature snuffling at the base of the door while the tornado howled by it, leaves swirling, rattling, thudding. I was bathed in a hot sweat of terror, believing the evil creature would soon burst in and drag me from my bed. As I prayed for help, I made the sign of the cross in front of me to protect me from this evil – maybe it helped, for after sniffing noisily a little longer at the base of my door, the creature moved on, still panting, puffing, sniffing for its prey. As it prowled off out of view I could hear the shaking of its head, hear its collar chinking. I could even hear its ears flapping and its nails clicking on the floor. The gale, after thudding angrily against my door a few more times in a vain attempt at entry, resumed its noisy course behind the creature, drawing rattling leaves in its wake until the sounds faded into the distance. I hardly dared to believe it had gone.

When there was an eventual eerie quiet, I let out my breath hoping that the danger had passed for good. That was the most frightening thing I had ever encountered and so very 'real'.

I did not know what to believe once things settled down to normal again. That I was trapped in some terrible dimension was a reasonable assumption for me at the time, but in view of my total experiences to the present day, I feel sure that this had been some kind of psychic manifestation – not just something my tortured mind had imagined. [1]

SATAN'S LURE

I must have slept for a while for I awoke suddenly, instantly alert. I sensed someone in the room, then heard a soft voice behind my left shoulder. Prickles of icy fear ran over me because I knew it was the devil. He spoke to me softly, kindly, beguilingly.

"You *know* you're going mad, don't you?"

I was scared, despite his soothing manner. I was also angry. I had gone through enough. So much never-ending horror, locked into a grey and stinking eternity, tended by robotic, malicious, mauve-faced nurses on helium gas, jabbed by six foot long syringes, seeing and hearing things that were not there, terrorised by hounds from hell – and now the Devil was making a personal appearance. I was so, so frightened but I was not going to give in now. Despite inward terror, my anger gave me bravado. I replied, "Yes, I know."

The devil continued, his voice smooth and tempting. "There is one way that will take away the madness, make you sane again, and it's so *easy*. All you have to do is to pretend to go through the birth again. Just push, like you did before, and then everything will be fine – no more confusion, no more madness, everything back to normal, and such a *simple* solution."

I thought about this. I did want to be normal again, but I did not want to 'sell my soul to the devil'. Maybe his suggestion would do me no bodily harm,

[1] *While compiling this work, I 'coincidentally' came across a book called 'Dancing with the Devil as you Channel in the Light!' by David Ashworth, 2001 (a book for healers about psychic attack and how to resist it) in which, under the heading DEMONS, it makes reference to 'Griffin-featured dog/s that cause as much discomfort to other spirits as they do humans...such creatures have been seen prowling around and over the occupied beds of patients in hospital. Not my imagination after all then!*

but at what cost to my mind? I reasoned I would go properly over the edge if I succumbed. I seemed to be locked into some kind of awful hell, but I was not going to be sweet-talked into anything by the Devil, who would probably be lying anyway. Without turning round to look at him – what would happen if I did? – I told him I'd rather stay mad – and meant it. His presence did not have the frightening horror of the hound in the corridor but I was still terrified, even though the room was calm and quiet and he was being so soothing.

Without another word, he just disappeared from the room. I was surprised that he had not tried to persuade me – I had expected a struggle and a whiff of brimstone at the very least. Phew! I felt a lot better, lighter somehow.

The musty, fusty smell had lessened and the timelessness did not seem so bad. The cracks in the ceiling – which had been continuously coming and going – stabilized. I got up feeling invigorated after such a brush with the Devil and hoped he had left for good and was not planning to send any monstrous minions to feed my insanity.

★ ★ ★

OFF TO THE FUNNY FARM?

In a thoughtful mood, I decided to search for something to do. As I wandered along the corridors, I found a sluice room filled with empty flower vases rimmed with green slime. I spent a long while washing them until they were clean and sparkling, and nobody disturbed me at all. I considered my experience with the Devil. Although I had not turned round to look at him, I knew who he was, and although I was terrified, it did not seem that he was some kind of cloven-hoofed monster with horns protruding from his widow's peak. Without seeing him, I knew with intuitive perception – that is now commonplace with me – that he was not garbed in the fancy-dress red tights and black cape that we associate with him, nor carrying a pitchfork. I concluded he came in many guises and that he had visited me as an ordinary man.

I desperately felt the need to visit the hospital's chapel and get nearer to God and pray at his altar for help, but unfortunately the matron refused permission – why I will never know – the short walk to the chapel would have done me no harm, after all, I had been walking around the corridors for long enough. To my muddled mind, this seemed like more conspiracy and collusion against me.

Although things had definitely improved, my mind was still confused; I was still in another dimension of time and half of me believed I was a ghost. A nurse informed me that a psychiatrist was coming to assess me. My strange behaviour must have been noted even though I had kept all the horrors to myself. Oh no! I did not want to be sent off to the funny farm! I dreaded that the 'shrink' would be wearing a white coat. I did not want to be taken away to a mental home and be wired up to electrodes – I did not think I would survive such archaic treatment. I knew my brain was not functioning correctly, but certainly did not want part of it destroyed. Thankfully, when the consultant arrived, he was dressed in a suit and not the white coat of which I was so curiously fearful. He was pleasant, kind and courteous.

I knew it was very important that I gave all the right answers to his questions as well as creating a good impression, so I smiled at him and shook his hand politely, remarking how kind it was of him to come and visit me. I used all the charm and communication skills that I believed were needed to dupe him.

My mind really worked hard with cunning to ensure I appeared sane. For every question, I agonised inside for the correct answer. What was the date? What day had I had my baby? What was my name? On and on he questioned and I fought to get the details right, telling him what I knew he wanted to hear. I learned from that exercise what a devious, clever, cunning creature the insane could be! I certainly did not tell him about pursuit from the demon hound from hell, the encounter with the Devil, the way time was standing still, nor about the woman who had killed her baby, or the way I heard and saw the same things happening over and over again and how telephones kept disappearing. I certainly was not going to tell him that I now knew that I was dead and the ghost of the hospital. If I had, I knew that I would be whisked away to the asylum, wired up to those electrodes and my brain fried in next to no time.

Clicking his pen and putting it back into his top pocket, he closed his notepad and said kindly, "I can see that you don't need my help – there is nothing wrong with you and you can go home shortly."

I smiled at him, thanking him nicely, giving my goodbyes sincerely as I once again shook his hand, but as soon as he had left the room, I collapsed back onto my pillows in exhausted elation. Thank goodness, I had fooled him completely! I was not going to be taken off to a lunatic asylum, even though I knew I was dead, living in a timeless zone, having hallucinations, talking to the Devil, and totally mad into the bargain!

★ ★ ★

GOING HOME

For my next foray – with time standing still I felt I had to do something – I decided that I would venture upstairs to find the baby I was supposed to have given birth to. I found my way to the lift but could not work out how to use it, so toiled up the stairs and wandered around until I saw a room containing what I reasoned were incubators. I asked the nurse on duty if I could see my baby (still not sure if I really had given birth), so she showed me over to an incubator where I thankfully did recognise him as he lay vulnerable and naked, except for a nappy. He had tubes thrust up his nose and wires attached. My heart went out to the poor little boy, looking more like a skinned rabbit than a baby. He was so tiny and looked so lonely and cold. To the consternation of the nurse, I lifted the incubator lid so I could make contact with the tiny infant. The nurse said I was not to touch the little scrap, but I took no notice of her whatsoever. I realised that I must not try and pick him up, but took his wee hand in my own and sat there holding it and whispering sweet nothings to him so that he would know I was there. Maybe I was as mad as a coot, but my maternal instincts were strong enough and I wanted my baby to know I was there. I suppose the nurse soon realised I was not going to do anything silly – even though she must have been aware of my strange state of mind. She left me to communicate with my tiny child, eventually telling me I must go back to my bed. I returned to my room a happier person, knowing that I really had got an infant, that he was surviving and that we had had some contact with each other.

It is curious that during all the time that I existed in the colourless, dusty, timeless zone, when my husband visited me he appeared in normal colour while everyone else was still in shades of grey. He brought with him the smells I recognised, of home and normality, even though nothing he said made sense to me, it gave me some feelings of reality.

When the ward sister told my husband he could take me home, she emphasised that I had been seriously ill, had nearly died and was by no means better yet. She made it plain that because of my poor condition it was critical that I was to stay in bed, do nothing, and have twenty-four hour supervision. She asked him if he could arrange for all this and he agreed that he would. I could not wait to get home. I was still on my best behaviour, smiling politely and thanking sister, but convinced I was dead, so thankful that I would be able to go home instead of staying in the dreadful hospital for eternity as the resident ghost.

When I returned home, I felt very strange. I touched everything – all seemed familiar yet at the same time unfamiliar. My husband was very upset because he had built a bench-seat and table in the kitchen as a surprise for me, but I had not noticed or commented on it; but how could I make him understand my confusion?

I was feeling a sense of relief through my muddled mind; perhaps it was because I had thwarted the Devil. Being dead was really not so bad after all – it was good to be home – I did not expect to be able to return. It was very surprising as I had supposed that when dead I would either 'go on' to some heavenly realm, or just 'not be' any more. Although a pleasant surprise, I still needed to re-establish my bearings. I felt exhausted, so was relieved to be able to climb into my own comfy bed – so good after the ones at the hospital. Within a short time my four-year-old daughter came running in, back from her granny's, and glad to see me after such a long time. It was good to cuddle her – things were definitely getting so much better! It was true, then, I did have a daughter. Apparently, she had exhausted my mother who was weak herself after a hysterectomy and needed to take to her own bed and gain strength after looking after the boisterous child for the five weeks I had been hospitalised.

When my husband left for work the next day, he must have forgotten the strict advice given by the ward sister. I was left alone with only my little girl to look after me. She buttered lumps of bread and spread them with Marmite for me and brought me glasses of water. Poor child! No doubt my husband thought I looked all right and would be able to cope. He could have had no idea what I had gone through, how very weak I was, or my state of mind.

I lay in bed, nursed by a four year old, to find myself at one stage revolving with the stars in the universe, rolling round and round so gracefully, and changing – one moment a Roman lady with black coiffured hair, the next a Roman centurion, then someone playing with a kitten. The universe was a lovely place in which to float, an inky blue-black peaceful hugeness sequinned with twinkling stars and I was at one with it all.

My doctor came round and let himself in. He boomed, "Well, you've had a bad old time of it. No more babies for you, my girl – the next one *will* kill you." He bristled with good humour, tweed and fresh air. He could see that I was alive but had no idea of the state of my mind so, satisfied, he left.

Lucinda brought me some more water. She must have dragged a chair to the sink to get it and presumably fed herself with bread as well.

For two weeks I still believed I was a ghost. As I gained strength, I coped better at looking after my daughter and myself. I had become more familiar with the situation and believed myself lucky to be able to 'live' at home while I was dead. Up until this time, nobody had visited me – presumably my husband had forgotten to tell friends I was home.

One day the phone rang – it had been silent up to now – and I was so pleased that telephones were allowed to a ghost as well. Picking up the phone, wondering who would be on the other end was a weird experience, so I was really pleased to hear a friend's voice. *I felt a click in my head, and my brain switched back to normal in an instant.* Time began again for me and I realised I was not dead as I had believed, but very much alive, knew I had been very ill and was now back to normal. I was so pleased to hear the friendly voice asking how I was and replied happily, knowing it to be true, "I'm absolutely fine!" If I had been likened to a computer, it was if some loose wires had been crossed, scrambling the works, then when the computer was jolted, it was up and running once more.

* * *

It was good to realise that I was not dead after all. I did a lot of thinking about the 'hows and whys' of my experiences. I believed that the many drugs I had been given caused a lot of the hallucinations – but even so, it made me realise that the brain is capable of enormous trickery. I was also forced to wonder what 'reality' actually is! I was not so sure, however, that what happened to me was all down to drugs – the sense of evil, the Devil, the woman killing her baby, the Catholic Priest – they seemed so 'real' in what had been a very unreal and frightening situation. Had chemical reactions from drugs altered my senses, enabling my brain to transport me to other realms, had other dimensions intertwined somehow? Of course, there were no logical conclusions to my varied theories.

I was very aware of the fragile instability into which my mind had been placed and very much believed that if I had complied with what 'The Devil' had suggested, this would have tipped the balance and I would, indeed, have become one of the statistics in a mental home with whom I can now so readily empathise.

I theorised that vulnerable people, such as I had been, could perhaps be possessed by some kind of evil entity, which confuses the host brain as it tries to take over, causing the state that we call insanity. I had been very close to the line and was thankful that everything was back to normality – or so I believed.

* * *

MARCH 1966
SEEING RED

My baby boy, whom I named Leigh, was kept in the hospital for a month, during which time I regained my strength. It so was difficult for me, having a child but not being able to look after him. He was too small and vulnerable to come out of the incubator so I could not even cuddle him, nor did I have the opportunity to visit him very often.

I did not forget anything that happened to me during my stay in hospital. Everything was still very vivid in my mind – and still is, forty years later – and it gave me a great deal to think about.

I had believed my problems were over but I was wrong. They were only just beginning!

When I collected my son from the hospital, I was so relieved that all was well with him. He had weighed only four pounds at birth and was still extremely tiny. I worried about him, but he was a good little baby, never giving any problems, and because of hospital regime, fitted well into routine. He smiled a lot and it would have been difficult not to love such a cute little scrap. So why was it that sometimes, when I was cuddling him, I was aware of a red mist around us? It was horrible. I had heard the expression 'seeing red' but had not known that it could be so tangible.

With a terrifying red cloud shimmering around us and almost filling the room, I felt the most terrible urge to kill the defenceless little child I was holding. *I* did not want to kill my baby, but the red cloud surrounding us did. I cannot describe how frightened I was.

I tried to psychoanalyse the situation. I knew that sub-consciously I was probably blaming the baby for all the fear and problems I had gone through because of his birth, but if that were so, how could it actually manifest this red cloud and the terrible thoughts of murder?

I badly needed help. Thankfully, I did not succumb to the urge to kill my child, but I desperately wanted to confide in somebody, yet did not dare as I thought my baby would be taken away from me – I could not have borne that – and the threat of being carted off to an asylum was too close for comfort.

It was a terrifying experience and I dreaded that it might happen again. I prayed for help.

★ ★ ★

AUTOMATIC WRITING

I was absentmindedly doodling on a piece of paper at the kitchen table one cold March morning when, to my surprise, the pen began to write without my aid. I was still holding it but it seemed to have a life of its own. *I did not realise at the time that this is what is known as automatic writing, when a spirit can 'come through' in this manner to give messages.*

To my alarm, as words formed on the paper it became apparent that they came from the woman in hospital who had killed her baby. She was attempting to give me a message but seemed undecided on how to go about it. I was not sure what to do either, so I asked her questions out loud, which seemed to make the process easier for her.

The woman, through the automatic writing, told me that she hated her baby as it screamed all the time and that although she had killed it, the infant was still with her, constantly screaming. She also said that she hated everyone, especially me. She said her baby was driving her insane and she did not know what to do. I suggested that perhaps it was hungry and she should try feeding it –

maybe that would help. "What, in *this place*?" she asked, indicating that she was locked into some kind of void with nothing except her screaming child and no means of feeding it.

I asked her what her name was and where she used to live when she was alive, and was given a name and address that was very near to the hospital. The writing was heavy, written angrily and with venom. When it stopped, I felt bemused and very troubled.

I wondered if my mind was playing tricks again and had been dredging up my own inner darkness. If not, then had the lost spirit of that woman somehow come through and was now trying to influence me to kill my own child and join her in a similar kind of hell?

I looked at the piece of paper and re-read the name and address. I became faced with yet another dilemma. Should I make a journey to find out if the address she had given me actually existed? I was sure that it did. I could then make discreet enquiries about the woman to find out if she were alive or dead, had borne a baby and whether she had killed it.

But how was I going to feel if I discovered that there *had* been a woman of that name at that address who had murdered her baby? If she *had* existed then I would have to believe that all the horrors in the hospital were real and not my imagination, and that there *was* a mad woman in spirit trying to make me kill my own baby. I did not think I could face up to that possibility.

Alternatively, if there was no evidence of a house at that address then the whole thing *would* have been a figment of my imagination – and I would know that I really *was* insane.

I eventually concluded that I did not want to find out. Ignorance seemed the best option.

I tried to tell my husband what was happening to me, hoping that he could somehow reassure me, but I could see he thought I was mad, so the less said, I thought, the better. It must have been difficult for him, believing that his wife was crazy, and I certainly must have been behaving oddly. He did, in fact, make psychiatric appointments for me after suggestions from a friend who worked at a top London hospital. I felt a lot saner after my attendances, purely because the psychiatrists to whom I was referred seemed madder than me! One of them actually sneered at me and, in derisive tones, told a colleague that I thought I was a clairvoyant – which was the conclusion I had arrived at to explain away the phenomenon I had experienced. Another psychiatrist, an unattractive man with thick glasses, informed me what he would like to do to me sexually, and the third, a Japanese woman whose English was minimal, would not let a question go unless I answered it the way she wanted me to – untruthfully. I remember looking out of the window staring at the stark branches of a winter tree. She wanted to complete the form in front of her, and until I told her what she wanted to hear she would not listen to me. I stared at the tree for a second longer, sighed, turned to her and gave her the lie. Satisfied, she completed her form and I was dismissed. This was at London's top psychiatric unit. I wondered what harm these so-called experts would have done to me if my mind truly had been unbalanced. Thank goodness for my indomitable spirit! I returned home happy in the knowledge that there was little wrong with me apart from a gremlin or two!

June 2005: a nursing friend told me that there is a condition named 'puerperal psychosis' that happens to some mothers after the birth of a child. I searched the web for case histories and, while there was nothing as horrendous as my own experiences, I think the medical term probably applied to my condition. Apparently, in old China there were various conditions, one named 'Chan Hou Wang Yan Jian Gui Fa Kuang' meaning 'absurd speaking, seeing ghosts and manic behaviour after child-birth' and it indicates incoherent speech, visual and acoustic hallucination and hypo-mania. I do have an open mind and it is a relief for me to know, after all these years, that this is a condition that can happen to a few women (it is rare, apparently) – but it still does not explain the reality of my experiences or the automatic writing, the 'possession' or the fact that entities or attachments can enter into the vulnerable mind of a medically weak person causing the problems, or the madness.

I also recently discovered a series of channelled books – messages from a Dr. Karl Nowotny in the Fourth Dimension. During his lifetime the Doctor was a specialist and professor of psychiatry and neurology. After his death he made contact with the medium, Grete Schroeder, to dictate many documents explaining the correlations with the world beyond – subjects include possession and ways to overcome it.

The book, previously mentioned, titled 'Dancing with the Devil as you Channel in the Light' by David Ashworth (Crucible Publishers) also includes astounding cases of possession by entities. So, whatever the cause, whatever the condition is named, whatever chemical imbalance takes place, something more sinister than 'merely a medical condition' can happen.

* * *

1967
DIVINE INTERVENTION

One day, I took my pre-school daughter to meet an older friend from his school. We were walking towards the coach drop-off point by a busy main road. I was holding my baby son in one arm while grasping Lucinda with my other hand – but not tight enough – she wriggled free and was away like a ferret, running so fast and close to the road. To my horror, I saw her trip and begin to fall into the road. Time for me did that strange change into slow motion with the utmost detail and clarity. Hampered by the baby, I knew I could not reach her in time. I also noticed that a car was hurtling towards her and that the driver had not noticed her. It would impact with her as she hit the road in front of it. There was no way she would not be killed. All this knowledge in a few swift seconds that felt like a lifetime – it felt like being in a bubble of a different time span where I was powerless to intervene.

Lucinda had fallen past the stage where she could right herself and the car was nearly upon her. To my amazement, she was picked up by invisible hands and set down safely on the grass verge! Like myself so many years ago, she'd had her life saved by paranormal means – clearly she also had a vigilant guardian angel. By now I had reached her side and, like many mothers after a near disaster, I grabbed her and yelled and shrieked, relief releasing my horror as anger at what had so nearly been. My distress at nearly losing my child momentarily took away the wonder of her miraculous rescue, but when I thought about it again, I did wonder if my own eyes could be believed.

I do not know what the term is for being placed out of danger by invisible forces. Over the years, I often wondered if I had imagined it, but years later was to discover another such incident, illustrated in my section about astrology, so now realise that this kind of rescue can be an actuality.

* * *

I believe Lucinda saw her guardian angel in a vision not long after this incident. The two children and I were both resting in the afternoon. I was lying on the bed in the baby's room and she was asleep in her bed next door. She called across, urgently saying, "Mummy, I have just seen Jesus!" She looked shocked so to diffuse the situation, I asked her why she thought he was Jesus. "Well, Mummy, he looked very kind and smiled at me, but then I felt shy, so hid under the sheets." I asked her what he looked like, wondering if her description would be like Jesus depicted on the Sunday school posters, but although she told me he was wearing a long white robe it was not the typical stereotype. It was clear to me that she had seen a Spiritual Being, her reaction and description being very believable.

THE BEGINNING OF A PLETHORA OF PRECOGNITIVE DREAMS

March 1968: a murder

One night, I had a very vivid, upsetting dream. I saw a man lurking in a field, then noticed a young girl, unaware of him, walking in his direction. I tried to warn the young girl to run away as I was sure that the man's intention was to sexually abuse and then murder her, but she did not see me or hear my warning. The dream left me with a very real sense of fear, despite the sketchy content.

The dream was still vivid when I awoke and with me for the rest of the day, so when the evening television news reported that a young girl had been sexually assaulted and left dead in a field, I gasped at the screen in confusion.

The field, briefly shown in the news report, looked very similar to the field of my dream and I could not help but remember my previous two dreams of a similar, vivid nature – the suffocating baby, the girl getting sacked and the woman with the threatened miscarriage. I hoped it was just coincidence, but could not truthfully believe that it was.

This was the first of hundreds of precognitive dreams I had of national events later verified in newspapers and on television. Without exception, they were very vivid and I always knew that they were 'one of those dreams', even if I did not understand the content. The majority of them happened during 1968 and 1969 – they came at me rather like ack-ack fire – disturbing and something I could not ignore. I can still recall the dreams forty years later while real events in my life have become hazy. The dreams were mainly what should be termed as 'disaster dreams'. The often-shocking content made it impossible for me to forget or ignore them. After I had reached an understanding of why I was receiving them, they did change in content, but they still came – but until that understanding I did become neurotic. Understandably, I was frightened, but I also became burdened by a sense that I should be 'saving the world somehow' – that I was missing important data and that if I took the B road instead of an A road I would crash my car! I must have been very difficult to live with.

A shipwreck

Soon after that, I had another vivid dream where I was standing on a beach looking at the calm sea as it swished lazily at the shoreline. Suddenly, from out of nowhere, huge crashing waves appeared. Lots of flotsam and jetsam were soon washed up on the tide. I realised that it had come from a shipwreck. Just as that information was manifested, a fisherman came running along the sand dunes. It looked as if he was racing to gain help and I began to run with him. "Where is this place?" I asked him as we ran together. "Between Devon and Cornwall," he replied in a panting breath. Then I woke up.

When I bought a paper in the morning, there was a short report about freak waves, which had suddenly risen from a calm sea and broken up a fishing vessel at a location 'between Devon and Cornwall'. I was struck by the curious description – instead of a place name – used by both the fisherman in my dream and the newspaper report.

March 17th 1968: another murder

I had a dream in which I saw a woman sitting under the sign of a government secret munitions area in Kent. I then saw an ambulance arrive and a covered body being carried away on a stretcher.

I was sure that a murder would take place at that location. I scanned the papers and television screen for a week until the news broke that a girl was missing from that place. She was later found murdered.

A disappearance

I had another dream about the same place. I dreamt that my father was going away to Russia and I would never see him again. I was very upset and cried in my dream.

After awakening, I was relieved to realise that my journalist father had not disappeared and told him about the dream. Viewing me quizzically, he mentioned that he had just written a story for his newspaper about a woman who lived there, whose father had actually gone to Russia, never to be heard of again. Some kind of foul play was suspected. Yet another strong 'coincidence'.

A ghost

I used to baby-sit for a friend and on a few occasions heard footsteps upstairs. I knew nobody was walking around because the baby was only a few months old. Strangely, although I thought it was a ghost, I was not frightened. My friend divorced her husband and he employed a young housekeeper with whom I also became friendly. She confided to me that she often heard footsteps upstairs, but she too did not find it frightening. I had not told her about my own experiences, so I knew her remarks were genuine.

I was away on holiday and dreamt that we were sitting around the kitchen table at that house and all heard the footsteps together. I decided to go and find out who it was. A sad and mild man was coming down the stairs dressed in a demob suit.

When I returned from holiday, before I had a chance to tell my friend about the dream, she told me that she had had a very strange experience. She had been sitting on the loo daydreaming when she saw a man coming towards her from the landing. Embarrassed at being seen on the toilet, she kicked the door close. Her description of the man fitted the one I had seen in my dream. After making local enquiries, she discovered that the original house owner had lost his wife in the war. He employed a housekeeper whom he later married.

*As you can imagine, my mind seldom strayed from the strange things that had happened to me. I had, out of necessity, to question the religion in which I had been brought up. A religion where such things only happen to witches. Already people were crossing the road to avoid me and friends, while admitting the accuracy of my dream predictions, were wary of me and put them down to neurosis and openly called me mad – and a witch. But I had to keep probing my mind for answers. I still wondered if I **had** gone mad in hospital and that all these unexplainable things were part of insanity, as my friends and husband believed. This kind of speculation was unpleasant and my only source of comfort was the adage that really insane people never questioned their own sanity.*

I could not explain the hospital horrors but could speculate on the dreams. Looking to find a logical answer, I realised that as the disaster dreams seemed to happen at around the time the actual events took place in reality, telepathy could be the answer. Perhaps I had somehow linked into the mind of a journalist who was reporting or writing up the story while I was dreaming. This seemed feasible and I could cope with that explanation. Telepathy seemed so much more benign that precognition – though at that time I would have preferred to be without it!

November 25th 1968: a disastrous fire

This time I was in a small and dingy room, with children sitting at desks drawing. One little girl caught hold of my sleeve and said to me earnestly, "We're not mental or retarded, you know, we are just a little backward." A woman then came into the room with two men. The little girl, looking very frightened, whispered to me, "She killed us, you know." I then smelled smoke and woke up.

When I turned on the radio later that day to listen to the news, sure enough, there was a report that fitted my dream. Apparently, there had been a fire in a home for 'retarded' children in Beauvais, France. Foul play was not suspected, but a lot of children had been burned to death. On the television news that night, the report mentioned that the home was for *backward* children. I remembered how the little girl was insistent that I realised that.

I could not help wondering whether there had been some kind of foul play, perhaps for an insurance claim. What should I do? Go to the police and tell them about my dream and my suspicions? I had nothing tangible to report and would only look foolish, so did nothing – well, what could I do?

A boy or a girl?

A friend of mine had told me she was pregnant, during the years before modern technology showed the sex of a child prior to birth. I had a dream in which I found myself in a huge warehouse with shelves stacked with blue baby clothes. There was one miniscule pink jumper, abandoned on the floor, too small to fit even the smallest baby. Baby fashion was not imaginative at that time – baby boys wore blue and little girls were dressed in pink. In the dream, I was aware that I was being shown that my friend's baby would be a boy because of the shelves overflowing with blue outfits and that it would be most unlikely to be a girl because of the one tiny pink jumper thrown away. She gave birth to a boy.

* * *

ROMANY GYPSIES, PSYCHOMETRY, A SPIRITUALIST CHURCH, AN AMULET AND AN EXORCISM

The dreams – more examples of which will be given later – were not the only disturbing things that happened to me during this time.

After my paternal grandfather died, I visited my grandmother who told me to help myself to some of granddad's books. His study was a joy to me, the walls being lined with shelves tightly packed with leather-bound books, many of them first editions and worth a fortune. But I was overcome with shyness and did not want to plunder his library by taking away armfuls.

I took three books at random. To my surprise and pleasure, one of them was a history of Romany Gypsies with lots of photographs taken in the early days of photography. To me, this could not have been a better treasure because I had only recently discovered that my maternal grandfather was of Romany descent and I was keen to find out more about Romany ways. I wondered if my clairvoyance – if that is what it was – had been handed down in my genes from him. As I looked through the book, there were sepia photographs of Romanies, some looking so similar to my mother's family that it gave me goose bumps to see such familiar faces looking out of the pages. I also noted with surprise, and no little excitement, that the most famous of Romany palmists was a Gypsy named Lucy Lee. I had called my daughter Lucinda Lee – Lucy Lee for short. Another of those amazing 'coincidences'.

I could not believe that it was just coincidence that I should, so randomly, pick out a book that was the perfect choice for me. Were my hands guided to select it? I am sure they were.

Not long after this time, a friend wanted me to go with her to a psychometry meeting. I had never heard of such a thing, but she explained to me that the medium is given small, often-used items to hold, like a ring or watch, from which she would receive knowledge or visions appropriate to the owner.

By now I was very curious about all things metaphysical even though I was very nervous, having had such bad experiences. Even though I did not like it, psychic encounters were happening to me and I wanted to find out why. The meeting was held at a local Spiritualist Church. I had never heard of such a place either, but was ready to learn.

The meeting was in a gloomy side hall behind the church. At the front of the hall was a table upon which lay a wooden tray containing many small individual compartments or boxes. People who had arrived before us had already put their possessions into the containers, so I took off my watch and placed it in one. There were probably about twenty people gathered, seated in rows, waiting for the medium. I was feeling rather apprehensive when at last the door opened and a small lady entered the room. She wore thick glasses and brown clothes and had a pallid complexion. She settled down in her chair, asking us to join her in a little prayer. I was pleased about this, still wary of hell and damnation and felt prayer kept all the dark forces at bay.

The medium then chose a ring out of one of the compartments in the tray, and began to give a reading. The owner of the ring looked puzzled and shook her head when the medium asked her, "Do you understand?" I felt sorry for the medium. Each time she did a reading, people looked puzzled because nothing rang true to them. I must admit that I got a bit bored, thought the medium was useless and drifted off with my own thoughts, absentmindedly doodling on my jeans with a biro pen.

As I completed the doodled design, I came out of a trancelike state with a start, wondering why I had ruined my jeans by scribbling on them. Just as I turned my attention back to the medium, I heard her say to yet another disappointed person "You have been in hospital where you nearly died. You had a lot of terrifying things happen to you and you thought you were mad. You still think you may be. Is this correct?" The man she had been addressing said, "No, it means nothing to me." The medium looked puzzled and the audience shuffled their feet.

However, the message was relevant to me, so I listened carefully to what she said to the next person. "I can see a Gypsy lady standing in the aisle. She is very striking. She is telling me that she is Romany and that she is here for you. Does this mean anything to you?"

"I'm afraid not," she replied with disappointment.

I was getting excited, for I knew that the Gypsy was for me, especially after having so recently acquired the Gypsy book.

47

After that, everything the medium said did not apply to anyone but me. I did not like to own up, but waited until she picked up my wristwatch which, unfortunately for all the others, was the last item in the tray. As the medium picked it up, she let out a large sigh. "Oh, no wonder!" she said, in amazement. "There is so much energy in this watch that I'm quite sure everything I have been saying has been directed to the owner. The vibrations I am getting from this are *so strong*," she said, almost in awe, "that they've completely overruled everyone else in the room. Whose is it?" I felt really embarrassed when everybody turned to stare at me. I realised I had unwittingly ruined their readings.

The medium asked me to stay behind after everyone had left. She was very excited about me, telling me that I had so much 'power' and must certainly attend the next meeting at the Spiritualist Church, which I agreed to do. She also wanted me to join their circle but it was not something I wanted to do, as I did not want to encourage more strange and upsetting supernatural experiences. I felt I had had enough for one lifetime!

I had a great deal to think about as I drove home, but it was not until I sat down with a cup of coffee that I noticed the detail of the doodle on my jeans. I had drawn some kind of amulet, which I *knew* I must have made in silver as protection from dark forces. This, even to me, seemed rather dramatic, but nevertheless I took immediate steps to get the design made up for me by a silversmith friend. The amulet's shape resembled a kite with a central cross, which was encased on the outside by curved, thin strips. On the end of each tip of the cross was a ball, and from the bottom ball hung a small crescent moon on a chain. I became almost obsessive in my desire to wear it for protection.

I had not thought it necessary to wear a crucifix, as some people do, for protection up to this time, but I did feel the necessity for my silver amulet.

Feeling the need to investigate as fully as I could in the hope I would understand the strange things that were happening to me, I decided to visit the Spiritualist Church one evening. I dressed in bright red – a colour that always gave me courage – and set forth armed with a drawing of my amulet for protection. I was very frightened of all the metaphysical things I had been experiencing and therefore wanted to eliminate the possibility that I could be insane by gaining hard evidence that the paranormal existed. The amulet, having been subconsciously delivered to me, now seemed vital to my safety from supernatural forces. I trusted nobody but was determined to obtain facts and clarifications and, hopefully, help.

The Spiritualist Church was very peaceful, if rather gloomy, with a lingering damp and fusty smell. It had a stage at one end with a table and chair placed centrally. In front of the stage ranks of chairs were set out with already a few people seated.

I was feeling very nervous as I found a place for myself. Although I did not suffer phobic panic attacks any more, I did not like going out very much and mingling with strangers, especially on my own, and felt quite brave as I looked around to check the kind of people who were there. I was half expecting Dennis Wheatley types – witches and warlocks; sinister dark eyes in reptilian faces – but no, I saw little old ladies with gentle smiles, moth-eaten fur tippets around their thin shoulders, and ancient felt hats attached to their buns with long hatpins. They had obviously all made an effort to be well presented and, without exception, clutched their well-worn handbags tight to their breasts. There were a few elderly gentlemen too, who looked quite benign and pleasant. I must have stood out, so young and alien amongst the elderly, wearing brilliant red, with long blonde hair escaping from my black 'monk's' hat – a Carnaby Street fashion accessory at the time.

I did not know what to expect, so felt reassured when a cord was struck on an ancient upright piano and the congregation launched into hymn singing with warbled gusto. After this, a prayer was read, which reassured me that God was involved and that the prayers would ward off the intrusion of his dark counterpart, of whom I was so fearful.

A speaker was introduced and she came forward and smiled at us all. She informed us that she was going to start with a little talk, then pass on any messages she received from the spirit world, and that when her Guide came through, her voice would change and we would then know that it was his message that we were receiving.

Suddenly, she pointed to one of the little old ladies. "Dear," she began, "I've got someone with me who says her name is Vera. Does that mean anything to you?"

"Oh, yes," said the old lady, "that's my sister, over in spirit."

"Well, dear. She says that you mustn't wear those shoes any more. They are too small for you and will do your feet a lot of damage. Does that mean anything to you, dear?"

"Oh yes," replied the little old lady, very happily, "these shoes have been hurting me. I'll not wear them any more."

"Oh, and there is a little dog here as well, dear," continued the medium, going on to describe a dog that the lady was pleased to acknowledge as her pet who had also 'passed over'. Clearly, she was overwhelmed with pleasure with the medium's reading.

Similar messages were passed to other members of the audience. I thought it was lovely for these old people who probably were all alone in life, their loved ones having been long gone to the after-world; these messages were giving them comfort and strength. It also gave them a positive belief in an afterlife where they would, no doubt, soon be reunited with their loved ones.

I could see only good in what the speaker was doing, but realised it was not for me. I did not want to communicate with the departed, nor did I want any of my demised relatives and friends to feel obliged to hang around waiting to advise me about my footwear when they should be getting on with their own progress. I have to admit I was amused by what now seemed to be an army of Chinese and Native American guides who were invisibly filling the hall, according to the medium, and wondered why all the people who liked communicating with the dead looked half dead themselves. I did not think I belonged with them at all, though I had been very interested in the proceedings.

Just as I was thinking this, and getting rather fidgety and ready for home, I noticed that the medium's face looked different. It seemed to be turning into that of an elderly Native American Indian. I rubbed my eyes and thought the shadows were playing tricks – but no – the face was still there. I looked away and viewed the lights. Were they causing the strange effect? I did not think so, and when I concentrated on the speaker once more, I continued to see the different face, superimposed over the lady's features. Her voice *had* changed and she was giving an interesting talk. I do not remember what she said now – it was a long time ago – but I do remember that she talked about small acorns and how they grew into large oaks. I wondered if this was a little message to me; because of my surname, Anckorn, my nickname at school had always been Acorn. Maybe I could grow spiritually somehow.

When the meeting was over, I wanted to stay and have a word with the medium, curious at how her image had changed and needing verification whether or not this could happen. I waited my turn, and when I confided in her, she was absolutely delighted. "That was my Guide, dear. I'm so glad that you saw him."

Like the psychometry medium, she was very excited by me and took me into a back room where we could talk privately.

I told her about all my grim experiences in the hospital and how I thought I must have gone mad, having a visitation from the Devil, seeing things that were not there, believing I was dead and so on. She looked very concerned and told me that no, I had not been mad. She also told me that there was no such person as 'The Devil', although there was certainly a dark side with evil at the fore. Because I had been brought up as a Christian, I would believe in what I had been taught, therefore, 'The Devil' was what I perceived. Nonetheless, the threat was just as real and that was the way in which 'they' on the dark side were trying to influence and get to me.

This kind lady spent a long while talking to me and gave me a lot of comfort. I now understood what had been happening to me. She convinced me that I *was* clairvoyant, that I emanated very strong psychic 'powers' and therefore, put simply, was being lured by the dark side as well as being called towards the light. She suggested that I joined her Circle to learn how to control and harness the power I had been given, but I was not keen on that. I was having enough trouble without looking for it and did not want to conjure up the spirits of the dead as well. If being lured by the dark side meant being frightened almost to death, I wanted none of it. I felt far too vulnerable to delve into such potentially dangerous waters. However, she gave me the telephone number of another lady whom she thought would be able to give me more support and advice. I drove home (by this time I had my own car) feeling very relieved that at last someone was taking me seriously and that maybe my sanity was not in question after all.

The next day, with no little trepidation – I was still very scared of all this 'mumbo jumbo' – I phoned the number that I had been given, making an appointment to visit the lady, feeling anything was worth a try. I was still very frightened by all the things that had happened to me and so the thought of a quiet and helpful chat with someone who understood metaphysics was encouraging.

I took my small son with me when I visited the lady but, to my surprise, there was a small group waiting for me. They told me a blind priest would be arriving shortly and then they would begin. Begin what? I wondered to myself. What *am* I doing here, for goodness' sake – what are they going to do? I felt rather bewildered.

The doorbell rang and twittering ladies ushered in the blind man, who tapped his way into the house with a white cane while his friend, who had driven him there, guided him round the chairs in the small sitting-room. Bemused, I sat quietly, waiting to see what they intended to do until they all went into prayer mode, which once again made me feel safer. The ladies sang a few hymns in wavering soprano tones, while the men's baritones enriched the room.

The assistant took my hand and placed it into that of the priest. He explained to me that they were going to pray over me and for me and that I must not be frightened if they began to speak in 'tongues'. Puzzled, I wondered what he was on about. He assured me that if that happened it would be Jesus talking through them. Well, I admit I felt very cynical and, while grateful that those kind people wanted to help me, thought that whatever they were up to was probably a complete waste of everybody's time.

The two men began to pray over me while the ladies clasped their hands together in tight hopefulness. Suddenly, the men began to talk nonsense. They were totally unintelligible, gabbling in scribbles and I thought, "Ah, this must be the tongues." Their voices rose in crescendos, booming throughout the small room. Not how I imagined Jesus would converse and never imagined that he was going to turn up personally for the goodness of my soul and sanity.

Suddenly, and most surprisingly, I felt something rising inside me from my chest to the base of my throat. I felt as if I were going to be sick and my mouth opened and I could feel the 'something' was fighting to stay inside me. I could feel 'It' being drawn up and the feeling of 'Its' panic to stay. It was an extraordinary and most unpleasant experience. My throat was constricting and I thought I was about to vomit embarrassingly over the men but, as I retched, only a rush of air hurtled out. It seemed like I had been rid of some kind of invisible force. Immediately, I was overcome with an enormous feeling of relief and I began to sob (totally against my will) and sank onto the floor weeping. My little boy, who had been watching, rushed over and flung his arms around me.

"Hallelujah!" boomed the men, "It's worked! It's worked!"

"Hallelujah, the Lord be praised," echoed the women.

What's worked? I wondered in confusion, as the men helped me to my feet and sat me down in a chair, my little lad still clutching me, my arms tight around him.

"It doesn't always work, you know," the priest said to me. "But thank you, God, thank you, Jesus, this time it did."

Well, I did not know what they were talking about but I did know I felt a lot better. I was confused about what I thought I had felt rushing from me but put it down to imagination. I did not discuss it. I did not ask them what they had been doing. I was feeling dazed. I was offered a cup of tea and everyone was smiling. I was totally bemused but thankful and, after farewells, left with the feeling that a big load had been lifted from my mind. From that day onwards, I felt so much better.

About ten years later, I read an article in a magazine and could not believe my eyes. It was about the experience of a woman who had gone through a similar thing to me. She had been prayed over in tongues, had the feeling of 'an entity' inside her that did not want to leave, then she had vomited an invisible 'thing' out as air. She was writing about an exorcism. Good Lord! Very belatedly, I realised I had been exorcised! If I had known those well-meaning people were going to perform an exorcism on me I would never have gone! Yes, I must have been some kind of fool not to realise what was going on – they probably did not spell it out in case I decided against it.

I came across another small item in a paper not so very long ago. I must admit, my blood ran rather cold when it referred to a blind man who had 'masqueraded as a priest' – though my guess is that he was ordained into the Spiritualist Church, which probably would not be recognised by 'orthodox' religions – who, accompanied by his male assistant, had journeyed around the country performing exorcisms on people who had been 'possessed'.

The piece mentioned that quite often the exorcism worked, at other times it did not, and sometimes it went very wrong. On one occasion, the 'priest' had performed an exorcism upon a woman, which did not go to plan. Halfway through the ceremony, she ran screaming hysterically from the room. On her return home, totally out of character, she brutally attacked her husband with a carving knife and killed him. There, but for the grace of God, nearly went I. The description fitted the two men and their ceremony to a tee, especially their statement "It doesn't always work". It must have been the same people but, in my case, it did work, thank goodness.

Clearly, I had been possessed by an entity of some sort that had slipped in when I was dying. Perhaps it was the spirit of the woman I had psychically heard who had killed her baby and was in purgatory with it forever screaming. I do not suppose I will ever know – but I do know, that despite all, I shall be always be grateful for those kind, well meaning people who led me to that exorcism, as well as the synchronicity (a 'random' set of chance events that cross the horizon of credibility and imply that hidden rules may be at work) which led me to being freed, as well as 'chancing' across those two articles which explained what had happened to me.

★ ★ ★

Psychometry: *The occult power of divining the properties of things by mere contact.*

Spiritualism: *The condition of being spiritual; the philosophical doctrine that nothing is real but soul and spirit; the doctrine that spirit has a real existence apart from matter; the interpretation of a varied series of abnormal phenomena as for the most part caused by spiritual beings acting upon specially sensitive persons or mediums.*

Spiritualist: *Someone who has a regard only to spiritual things (sometimes with someone who holds the doctrine of spiritualism or spiritism.*

Exorcize: *To call forth or drive away (a spirit); to deliver from the influence of an evil spirit; to command by some holy name.*

Exorcism: *The act of exorcizing or expelling evil spirits by certain ceremonies; a formula for exorcizing.*

Exorcist: *A person who exorcizes or pretends to expel evil spirits by command.*

Mediums: *In spiritualism, the person through whom spirits are said to communicate with the material world;a person of supernormal sensibility.*

Psychic or psychical: *That which is of the mind or psyche; a spiritual medium.*

Metaphysics: *The branch of philosophy which investigates the first principles of nature and thought; ontology or the science of being; loosely and vaguely applied to anything abstruse, abstract, philosophical, subtle, transcendental, occult, supernatural or magical.*

★ ★ ★

After having met the kindly spiritualists, I have to say I did not feel so alone or so crazy as I had before. They certainly did not think I was mad, so while I could not apply logic to the frightening supernatural things that had happened to me, at least I had been told that such things did happen – not just to me but to other people as well. I declined their offers to join the Spiritualist Church circle – messages from the dead really did not interest me – and I certainly did not want to encourage more spooky occurrences – they were much too scary for me. Unfortunately, however, they continued and stepped up a bit in 'attitude'!

THE DREAMS CONTINUE WITH A VENGEANCE

June 8ᵗʰ 1968: a boat capsizes

The next dream involved my daughter. I dreamt I was on a *tin* boat and she was in the hold. I knew that there was danger and that I had to get her out. I fought my way down into the hold to save her. The dream then switched to a beach where people were sitting enjoying the sun. I could see a lot of little girls drowning – some already dead, their hair floating in the waves. Some survived but most did not. I was racing up and down the beach trying to get people to help save the children, but it was as if I were invisible, and they carried on eating their sandwiches, not noticing the disaster which was happening in front of them. I felt distraught and did not know how to help.

The following day there were no reports on the television, nothing on the radio or in the papers. But I knew that the dream had some significance as it had been so vivid and was 'one of *those* dreams'.

I was due to help supervise the children on a school trip by train. Because of the dream I thought it was a warning of some kind and we should not go. Maybe the 'tin boat' represented a train? I anguished over the situation until my husband got really annoyed with me. Convinced by him that I was being neurotic, I took my daughter and worried the whole day that disaster would overtake us – acting like a demented mother hen, keeping children away from train doors and looking everywhere for danger. We arrived home safely after much secret anguish on my part and I realised that I was, indeed, becoming a neurotic.

Validation

My blood ran cold when I read the newspaper on the morning of June 30ᵗʰ 1969. A new aluminium boat had sunk on its maiden voyage. A party of schoolgirls from a local convent had been given the opportunity of a trip on this vessel's maiden voyage. It was an innovatively designed flat-bottomed oyster boat called The Red Bank that had flipped over, only 150 yards off-shore with the majority of the girls trapped in the hold. Only a few survived.

I was devastated. My dream *had* been valid. It *had* been a school trip. How close to *tin* could aluminium be? The only difference was that my daughter and myself were not on the boat – though, somehow in 'spirit', I had been an observer on it.

If I had not been mad before that dream, I nearly went crazy then. I could no longer apply the telepathy notion because of the three-week intermittence, nor could I arrive at any logical conclusion. Thoughts went round and round in my head until I wondered if everything went round in a circle and I was merely remembering something that had happened in another cycle of time – perhaps my very existence was a memory and I had been long gone. I could not even grasp clearly what I was trying to formulate in my mind and culmi-nated with the decision that maybe it was not necessary for me to understand the reasons for the dream, but to acknowledge to myself that somehow fore-knowledge of events was possible.

Funnily enough, after that conclusion, the disaster dreams eased off and I had less frightening – though still presentient – ones instead.

During all this time, I had been keeping a dream diary, as I needed to be sure I was not deluding myself. I kept a notepad by my bed and jotted down anything I dreamt as soon as I awoke. Because I wondered if I were supposed to give warning to someone – I was not quite sure whom – I needed to have as much detail as possible, but there was never enough. I had the clues to identify the dreams – 'between Devon and Cornwall', 'the tin boat', and so on – but it was never enough. I needed more information to pinpoint 'who' and 'where' and be able to avert the disasters. I felt I must be on some kind of mission. I felt very lonely, too.

An empty pram

I had another dream where I saw some friends pushing a large but empty pram. I wondered why they looked so proud, as there was no baby inside it. The pram then changed into an aeroplane and the father flew off, piloting it himself.

When I next saw my friend, I asked her if she was pregnant – I hesitated to ask because the 'empty pram' would seem to deny that she was. She told me that she had thought she was and was thrilled about it but it was a false alarm. She also told me that her husband's best friend was learning to pilot an aero-plane.

A tumbling wall

I had a dream about another friend, where I saw him knocking down some walls at his house. I was very afraid that he would get hurt if the whole lot fell on top of him.

In reality, when I saw him I warned him about my dream, but it was too late. The previous night he had come home inebriated and had driven into a wall, which fell down on top of his car!

★ ★ ★

When I was first trying to establish my sanity and that what was happening to me was paranormal not madness, I tried to find books on the subjects that were affecting me. There must have been lots available but I never managed to find any at all. However, I did eventually come across a very interesting one about dreams in which it explained about scientific experiments on dreamers in laboratory conditions. I was interested to learn that without REM (rapid eye movement) dreams people cannot function. It is a necessary part of our survival and depredation brings about disorientation and malfunction of the body. Torturers have found it an effective method of intimidation. The book also explained how you could control your own dreams – which is what I decided to do. Maybe this way I could discover the relevant clues or links, so far missing in my dreams, to divert catastrophes or at least get a fuller picture of the forewarning that could be helpful in some way. When I had the next vivid dream, I was able to think consciously while the dream was taking place and waited for the moment to take control. It was extremely difficult – almost impossible – imagine watching a television film and 'willing' the scenes to alter to your own story line – an impossibility, which is how it feels in a dream.

An abduction?

I dreamt that a green Jaguar car stopped and the driver leaned over to open the passenger door and a girl got in. As the usual observer, I felt alarmed, believing she was being abducted even though she had entered the car quite willingly. Whilst I was dreaming, I was determined to find out the location. Trying to control a dream is very difficult – but I knew I wanted to see a signpost. I managed to look around until I saw the bottom of one. With *enormous* difficulty, I directed my gaze to the top of the sign but, disappointingly, the wording made no sense. The next obvious clue would be to view the car number plate and memorise it. I managed with difficulty to bring my perceptions back to the car and to view the plate. This time I had no problem reading and memorising the number. I woke up, repeating it over and over in my head. Remembering it so clearly, I did not think it necessary to record the number immediately. This was a huge mistake because I had forgotten it by the time I sleepily reached for my dream diary. After so much effort I had failed.

There was soon a newspaper report to verify the validity of my dream – a suspected abduction of a young woman by a man in a green Jaguar car in *Switzerland*. No wonder the words on the signpost did not make sense to me, as I had been expecting an English location. Had the control of my dream been better, my intervention would not have been necessary, for it transpired that the girl was all right, had known the man and was not hurt in any way.

I did not like trying to control the disaster dreams, having the eerie feeling I should not be doing it – my sleeping mind was grappling with forces in an alien otherworld, and while 'they' were able to manipulate me, it did not sit easy with me to attempt my own manipulations. Despite the efforts involved trying to control dreams, I still never received enough 'evidence' to present to the police or to the people involved. I eventually came to the conclusion that I was not supposed to avert any disasters. I had no real evidence to present as the vital clue was always omitted from the dreams, but I wondered why the dreams kept coming and for what purpose.

A burglar?

I dreamt I was asleep in my parents' home. In the dream, I was awakened by something and sat up in bed feeling frightened. I saw a man looking in the window. He had strange ginger hair. Convinced the man was dangerous, I got out of bed and rushed around making sure all the windows and doors were firmly locked. Everything was safe except the back door and, as I hurried to lock it, the door opened before I could reach it. I was engulfed in waves of fright as the man stepped in. The family dog rushed towards the man, but instead of attacking him she flopped onto the floor, belly up, at the same time wagging her tail furiously. As she did this, I laughed in relief, as I realised that with the dog's acceptance of him, the man must be all right. As he patted the dog, he laughed with me.

On awakening, I was worried. Although the dream had a happy ending, it was still one of 'those' dreams, so I thought I had better warn my parents in case a man did try to get into the house and frighten my mother. At least they could be on their guard. I did not see my father but told my mother to keep the back door locked, just in case. When I saw my father the next day and voiced my concern about the dream, he told me not to worry, as it was nothing to do with their house. As a journalist, he often liaised with the police for stories and, in this instance, was aware they had been searching for a man with a ginger toupee – the strange ginger hair in my dream – as they believed he was connected with a crime though, in fact, his innocence was proved.

A DIFFERENT KIND OF DREAM

21st October 1968: a deserted airfield

I had another very vivid dream, which puzzled me for a long time. I dreamt I was on a deserted airfield with a man. He was very pleasant and I liked him very much, although I was not sexually attracted to him. We were imprisoned in a deserted airfield and were both absolutely terrified believing we had been left to die. The airfield in my dream looked nothing like an airfield – more like a tennis court, with high wire netting all around us with no means of escape – but I just *knew* what it was meant to represent. Our fear was immense (dream fear always seems far worse than reality) but we did, eventually, find a way out. A door appeared, as if by magic, and we passed through it with relief. The dream switched and we walked through a gap between some buildings. I looked through an open door into the room and noticed it was a pottery. Curious, I entered, viewing everything with great interest because pottery was a craft I had never learned but something I would like to attempt. The man drew my attention to the potters' wheel and it felt warm, as if someone had just stopped using it. I looked very closely at all the tools, the wheel, the kiln, spending quite a while investigating thoroughly. The building was still and deserted. I had been so engrossed in my scrutiny of the pottery room that I had temporarily forgotten my companion, so when I looked round and realised he was not there, I hurried out to catch up with him. He was nowhere in sight, so I followed a long corridor that led me into a large and lofty church. Although it was gloomy inside, I could see how beautiful it was, with high vaulted ceilings with many fine and delicate carvings on all the struts and beams. As I had in the pottery, I took a long look around me, walking up the aisle, looking along the pews, viewing the statues and brasses on the tombs, finding myself fascinated by all the beauty in there. I stayed exploring for a long time until I decided it was time to move on. After I had left the gloom of the church, I stepped out into bright sunshine where, to my surprise, stood a blind Indian beggar. The dream changed again and I saw a strange dog with long claws. Then I woke up.

As usual, I recorded everything in my dream diary while it was still fresh in my mind. It had been extraordinarily vivid, and very long and detailed, so I knew that it was 'one of those' but was curious about the content. Apart from the terrible fear of death when I had been in the deserted airfield, it was not the same kind as the 'disaster' dreams – there being no crime, accident or 'storyline' apart from the vast detail in the pottery and the church and the long time I spent sightseeing. I checked newspapers and TV reports to see if I could find anything that compared with the dream, but nothing did.

Weeks, months then years passed by, but I never found anything that remotely linked to the dream. I found this unusual because this was the first time I had not been able to verify facts or prove a dream's validity.

However, nine years later the riddle of the dream was solved, so I am now fast-forwarding to show how it tied up with reality with more than one astonishing development.

1977: the mystery solved

A friend asked if I had met the pottery teacher who had recently moved near to me. I had not, but was interested to learn that he held evening classes in pottery that she thoroughly recommended. Given his telephone number, I phoned him without delay, introducing myself and asking if he had room for me in his class. He had and suggested that instead of taking two cars, I went in his.

I really enjoyed his company, loved his classes and became very friendly with him and his family. I never discussed my dreams with him. Over the years I had found it more prudent to keep quiet about my psychic experiences – it only encouraged disbelief and lost me friends.

One evening when we were driving towards our destination, the pottery teacher mentioned that when he had been a child in India, he and his friends used to poke sticks at dead beggars who were often washed up on the shore. I think we had been talking about the book 'Lord of the Flies' and he was illustrating how tough children could be. I asked him what he was doing in India and he told me that his father had been in the church there. My dream suddenly flooded back to me. I had the potter, I had the church and I had the beggar. I also had the strange dog – our own, whose name was Pansy Potter and whose claws needed clipping. All I needed to link the dream was a deserted airfield but I was hesitant to probe, though the question hung aloft, waiting to be asked.

I decided to question the potter at the end-of-term Christmas drinks do. Emboldened after a couple of Martinis, I chose a lull in the conversation. Turning towards my tutor, I asked, "Does a deserted airfield mean anything to you?"

I was alarmed as the colour drained from his face – it was clear that he was in shock. "Oh, don't Val. I don't want to talk about it!" He looked so terrible that all the others were staring in astonishment. I had not expected such a response and felt ashamed for causing him such distress. In order for him to recover his equilibrium, I managed to turn the conversation until everyone was chatting happily again. Eventually, he turned to me and said, "Val, I was imprisoned during the war in a deserted airfield with my family when I was a child, and we were all left to die in the heat. We didn't know what was to become of us. It was terrifying and I have never been so frightened!"

I was so taken aback by this revelation that, unfortunately, I did not take in the rest of his explanation – I was in shock myself.

I was trying to come to terms with the fact that I had dreamt about something that had happened to a man, _when he was a child_ about 30 _years previously._ I would have been a small child myself when it happened. _When I had the dream, I had never met the man_ and did not meet him until _nine years afterwards!_ Somehow, I had experienced his abject terror at being imprisoned in the airfield. How very, very curious.

If I had been baffled by all the other dreams I had received, then this one was the most puzzling. How and why should I have been given this information in such a manner?

★ ★ ★

The story does not end there. Some years later, when I was writing an article for SHE magazine about precognitive dreams, I wanted to include the airfield dream but did not know how to term it, because it clearly was not foresight or precognition. I was tired, my head ached and I needed a break. I walked down to the village for some fresh air and found myself in the second-hand bookstore, deciding on a romantic novel to unblock my mind. It was not until I had paid and was half way home that I realised I had a second book in my hand that I did not remember choosing.

Once home, I flicked through the mystery book to find it opened at a page where reference was made to 'retrocognitive' dreams – dreams of events unknown to the dreamer that had happened in the past – which explained to me how the airfield dream should be termed for my magazine article.

How astonishing that I had in my hands a book I had not realised that I had picked up and purchased and to find it opened at a page containing the very descriptive word I needed.

Even more astonishing is the fact that, after I had finished the article, I could not find that book again. Though I did not realise it at the time, it had been metaphysically presented to me and then whisked back through the ether to its proper home. Curiouser and curiouser, as Alice said.

★ ★ ★

The potter could not deny that I had somehow tapped into a terrifying incident in his past – or tapped into a memory of the incident. Not believing in the paranormal, he felt it might have something to do with a glitch in time. He lent me a book called 'An Experiment with Time' by J.W. Dunne, which gave me my first indication that other people had such dreams of awareness before the events. Dunne had such dreams himself and had endeavoured to give a scientific explanation for them – his theory

60

being that time is not just a fourth dimension added to the three dimensions of space, but is an infinite series of dimensions. The book was a struggle for my intellect and, I have to say, too difficult for me to comprehend, but it was nevertheless a great help knowing that I was not the only person to dream ahead of time. Later on, I came across another book on a similar theme, 'Memories, Dreams, Reflections' by Carl Jung – who also had precognitive dreams – so while I still did not understand how or why I had them, I was now aware that so did both an eminent professor and a well-revered psychologist, and therefore felt in exalted company.

ODDS AND SUNDRIES

The first manned spacecraft

When the first manned spacecraft went up into space, the public were worried whether the spaceman inside would survive when it returned to splash down in the ocean. I had a dream where I saw the spacecraft come down and, as it hit the water, I saw what looked like oil seeping down the sides. It looked 'wrong' somehow. I was worried that the operation would not be successful.

When the event took place in actuality, we sat glued to the television. It was exactly as I had dreamt, but what I had perceived as oil seepage were burn marks, which were apparently expected. All was well.

A sad new mother

I had another dream regarding a friend of mine who was expecting a baby. In the dream, I saw her in hospital, but she looked so sad. I thought perhaps that the baby had died.

When I heard that she had safely delivered the baby and returned home, I rang her with congratulations and mentioned I was so pleased everything was all right because I had seen her looking sad in my dream. She then told me my dream had been correct because there had been something badly wrong with the baby's foot but, after a successful operation, he was fine with no further problems.

The use of an American telephone

Another dream found me in the middle of a crowd and something happened – a murder, I think – and it was necessary for me to phone the police. I found a telephone box to dial 999. I had my coins ready, but when I heard the operator answer, I could not get through because my coins would not work in the slot.

In frustration, I came out of the telephone box to hear a voice plainly say to me, "In America, you put the money in *before* you dial!"

A few nights later when I was watching an American film on the television, I noticed that when a woman phoned the police to report a murder, she put the coins in the telephone box before dialling. An insignificant dream, but interesting.

A murder site

In another dream, I had been in a house I did not know and noticed a cat eating in a disordered kitchen. As I climbed up some stairs I saw blood on the wall, then discovered an old man who had been murdered.

Some while afterwards on television's 'Police Five', the presenters were asking for information about crimes and reported an old man's murder. The camera toured the scene of the crime – the old man's house – and I recognised it as the one in my dream.

The last two dreams began many 'television preview dreams' giving me a foretaste of future programmes.

Casing the joint

I dreamt I saw two men with 'prison haircuts'. One had ginger hair. They were waiting in a parked car outside my friend's house. I thought they were burglars.

I phoned my friend telling her to watch out for the thieves and to make sure her doors and windows were locked. She did see them a few days later, recognising them from my description, waiting in a car outside her house. She phoned the police who were able to reassure her there was no threat to her. The men were actually under police surveillance. They were 'casing' the bank opposite my friend's house and the police had undercover men monitoring the two men's activities.

Altogether, I recorded around 200 precognitive dreams, but eventually wearied of writing them down – by then there was no doubt in my mind that future events could be foretold in dream form. I realised that, because I never got quite enough information, I was not meant to intervene nor was it possible for me to change the course of any events.

The dreams were often cryptic, to be solved quite easily after the event. I always wondered why the dreams did not just give me normal details, instead of 'dreaming up' such clever riddles – but maybe this was essential so I could not intervene – merely understand afterwards.

The 'disaster' dreams were unpleasant for me and quite frightening, but after I *had come to the conclusion that the reason I was getting foreknowledge of future events via dreams was because I was <u>being taught – they were lessons from another dimension</u> – the dreams dwindled away almost entirely and I then got different 'tuition' which made me realise my assumption was correct. These days, I occasionally get a dream which I recognise as 'one of those', but they lack the impact of old and seem merely a way of letting me know my dreaming clairvoyance still works and my old school masters are still around.*

I eventually deduced that if I were receiving tutoring from a non-physical source, then only shocking experiences and dreams of national disasters would have any real impact – I was forced to consider, evaluate and try to reach conclusions in a very solo, bewildering, confusing and lonely place where there were no guidelines, no references, no help. I believe now that the horrors of the hospital and the 'possession' by an entity was part and parcel of the course. It is possible that the horrors were initiations to be endured and, by coping with them the way I did, I passed the initial 'exams'.

My schooling was by no means over but, by degrees, became gentler and I grew to look forward to the lessons. However, if my assumptions about schooling were correct, I was still in kindergarten and had much more to learn, many more strange experiences to encounter. But – I am pre-empting the narrative.

I jumped forward nine years in order to 'fast forward' to the culmination of the deserted airfield dream and the recognition that it was a 'retrocognitive' dream, so I now take you back in time to 1969 to the chronological order and continuation of my story.

SHADES OF EGYPT
GYPSY MUSIC 1969

As a journalist, my father enjoyed a life that entailed meeting and interviewing interesting people, many of whom he befriended or helped in small ways whenever he could.

One old gentleman he met had spent time, as a young man, in Egypt as part of a team of archaeologists at the opening of Tutankhamen's tomb in the Valley of the Kings. Wanting a memento of his experiences, he helped himself to a twelve-inch square of raw-edged cotton cloth that he had kept throughout his life. As a token of regard to my father, the old boy presented it to him – no doubt nearing the end of his days, he wanted this relic to go to someone who would appreciate and look after it.

When my father handed me this artefact, I felt awestruck even though it looked like a piece of torn-off cotton sheeting. Knowing that what I held in my hands had been part of the treasures in a burial chamber of an Egyptian king made me speechless. My father said, "Keep it and look after it." I could not believe that I had in my possession such a treasure that to me was just as valuable as gold and precious jewels.

I took the cloth home with a feeling of awe and, after wrapping it carefully, put it in the back of my desk drawer for safekeeping.

A year or so passed and I was still regularly having vivid dreams, but they had changed direction from time to time and I learned to interpret and understand them. If I did not understand them, then I still recorded them in my dream diary.

One night, I had another vivid dream. This time, I saw an oscillating golden spiral. After gaining my attention, it changed into a rod with the spiral moving around its top. The spiral then changed into a snake moving around the rod, then the rod became the body of the living snake. The snake then joined head and tail to become a moving, golden, sideways-on figure of eight – the symbol of eternity.

I woke up with a jolt. This dream seemed important and symbolic, so I picked up my pen to record it, but the pen 'took over' and I began writing automatically. Unlike the time the baby-murdering mother had come through, this was different. The writing began, "You must worship the Sun..." and the pages filled as my pen raced. I was very excited because it was clearly ancient Egyptian philosophies that I was receiving.

Unfortunately, when my husband woke and saw what I had written, he threw the pages into the boiler to destroy them. I could not remember what I had written.

The next night, my daughter Lucinda ran crying into the bedroom because she had had a horrible dream. She said, "Mummy, I was in a place with no doors and some men with dark skin, wearing funny clothes didn't like you and wanted to kill you..." I calmed her down, tucked her back in her bed and she slept peacefully.

In the morning, I was getting Lucinda ready for primary school when she said, "Mummy, may I speak some Egyptian, please?"

I said "Of course, if you want to," trying to hurry her along, not believing, of course, that she would be able to. To my astonishment, Lucinda then began to speak in another language. My goodness, how my blood ran cold! I knew it wasn't French, Spanish, Italian or German, and while I did not know what the Egyptian language sounded like, felt sure my little girl was speaking it. It was a weird sensation.

I said, "Oh, that was interesting," but my mind was whirring. How could a five-year-old child speak in a language other than her own tongue? To my knowledge, she had not even learned about Egypt at school. There is no way that she could have known about that ancient civilization, let alone speak the language, and yet she had just done so.

I queried her about the dream she had had the night before. I asked her if she could draw for me the kind of clothes the men had worn. I drew the outline of some people to make it easier for her and asked her to draw the clothes she had seen on them.

Shivers ran down my spine as I watched her sketching the type of attire depicted on the friezes around Egyptian tombs. She drew the short skirts the men wore, and strange high hats, as well as rods in their hands. It was uncanny. I presumed then that her reference to 'a place without doors' would have been the interior of a pyramid after being sealed up.

Unfortunately, my husband burned her drawings as well, but they are something I will never forget.

After Lucinda left for school that morning, a Bulgarian guest staying in our house emerged from his room, yawning. He was in England to learn the language. His family had fled Bulgaria during an uprising and had moved to Belgium when he was young. We had really bonded with this man and his family and I had felt some kind of connection between us.

I noticed him flapping the curtains in the sitting room. He looked very pale and worried. "What on earth are you doing?" I asked him.

"Nothing" he said, *too* nonchalantly.

"Tell me," I insisted, and in the end he admitted that he had seen a '*huge beetle thing*' climbing up the curtain, but it seemed to have disappeared into thin air.

"Like a *scarab beetle?*" I asked pointedly.

"Yes," he muttered, knowing the improbability of one being there. I wondered what on earth was happening because something definitely odd and definitely Egyptian was going on in our home.

I had not mentioned anything to our Bulgarian guest about my daughter speaking Egyptian or about our strange dreams, so he was not playing a joke or being influenced by anything we had said. I realised that something weird was taking place and recalled the piece of Egyptian cloth in the back of my desk drawer and felt sure it was linked to what was happening. Perplexed, I got on with my day in a thoughtful mood.

In the afternoon when Lucinda returned from school, she helped herself to some tea then disappeared into her room to dress up. A friend had given her a ghastly yellow nylon-flocked evening dress, which Lucinda loved though it really did not suit her at all. Following her, I helped her into the dress, thinking how awful it looked. Minus her two front teeth and the reflective yellow giving her a sallow complexion, she certainly did not look like the fairy tale princess of her imagination.

Our guest called me from the sitting room, so I left Lucinda and saw that the Bulgarian man was holding out a record to show me. "I think you'll like this. It was smuggled out of Bulgaria when my family fled and it's the only recording – quite unique."

I waited with interest while he put the record on, but as soon as the music began my heart nearly stood still. *It was the unforgettable Gypsy music I had heard many years before!* I recognised it straight away and stood transfixed. What an amazing 'coincidence'! The violins played fast and furiously every bit as exhilarating as when I had heard them in my bedroom. How very exciting, but also how very strange – because this was the only recording available, it proved without doubt that I could not possibly have heard it before, except in a clairaudient manner.

The music had not been playing for long when Lucinda came into the room in the ghastly evening dress and began to dance. I watched my little girl – normally with little co-ordination – change. She seemed to grow in stature, becoming graceful and exotically beautiful as she clapped her hands and stamped her feet to the rhythm. She swirled and clicked fingers in the perfect choreography of a difficult dance routine while the ugly dress now looked magnificent. I just stood and stared in amazement – it was too unreal to comprehend! I glanced at our guest to see that he was equally astonished.

My five-year-old daughter had somehow shape-shifted into a Gypsy dancer performing some kind of intricate flamenco. How on earth could it have happened?

In reality, the music could not have lasted long but seemed to go on for ages, as did the dance, both eventually coming to a beautifully timed conclusion. As spectators, we were both lost for words after having witnessed such an amazing performance. Lucinda, who after completing her dance had returned to her gappy-toothed, normal self, stood, a little breathless, before us.

Because I really did not know what to say after my daughter's amazing transformation and incredible dance routine, I inadequately asked, "Where did you learn that dance, darling?"

"What dance, Mummy?" replied my bewildered little girl. She had no recollection of dancing at all and returned to her room, the ghastly dress trailing behind her, leaving us staring at each other in amazement.

What a combination of extraordinary events – first, I was introduced to the Gypsy music I had psychically heard so long ago, and second, my daughter had transformed into a Gypsy dancer before my eyes and those of a witness, and third, it tied up with my Romany blood and Gypsy guide.

I had chosen the names Lucinda Lee for my daughter, liking the derivative Cindy for when she was young, and also Lucy Lee when she was older. I recalled the book I had picked at random from my grandfather's library. I had discovered that one of the most famous Gypsy palmists was named Lucy Lee. Was this yet another 'coincidence'? So many things seemed to be slotting into place and making some kind of sense, but what did Gypsies and Egyptians have in common to link them together?

I delved into history books to discover that Romany Gypsies were often called 'Egyptians' as it was believed they originated from Egypt. Some travelled across Europe settling for a while in Bohemia – hence another description as 'Bohemians'. Their style of clothing became popular for outrageous and arty people who in turn became known as Bohemians. That they travelled across Bulgaria was inevitable. I could now make a connection between ancient Egyptians and Gypsies, carried in our family genes, but it still did not fully explain what had happened to us. The 'connection' I had felt between our guest and his family now made some kind of sense.

Past lives and reincarnations came into my thoughts – had both my daughter and myself lived as Egyptians as well as Gypsies in past lives? Were old friends or foes communicating?

I told my father about the dreams Lucinda and I had experienced and of Lucinda asking to speak in the Egyptian language. He looked concerned and found it very curious that the night before he had been studying the ancient Egyptian language – part of his Masonic rituals. Masons originated from ancient Egypt; they were the architects and builders of the pyramids. He felt, given my story, that the piece of cloth he had entrusted to me should be returned for him to present to a more suitable place. I agreed with him, assuming that he would give it to a museum. I was sad to return such a link with an historic dynasty, though having just discovered the story of the Curse of Tutankhamen, felt the material would be better out of our home if the spirits were annoyed about its plunder from the tomb! My father, however, decided that the material should be burned to appease the spirits. He told me that when it was burning, a malevolent face materialised in the smoke and the feeling it invoked in him was most unpleasant. The face disappeared as the last fragment of material turned to ashes.

When preparing this book, I asked my now grown-up daughter if she remembered the dream. She said that she did and also that the men in the dream had been raping me, but as a child she did not know how to describe what she saw other than 'hurting me' – that was what had upset her so much at the time – and that as a five-year-old she should have had no knowledge of, let alone witnessed, such a horrible incident. What an awful thing for a child to experience.

When my daughter told me this, I remembered being horrified at school when I learned that when Egyptian royalty died, their living slaves were entombed with them to wait on their every need in their journey to the 'other world'. The tombs were then sealed. How dreadful to be left alive in a cold dark place with no hope of rescue. No doubt there were oil lamps to light a little of the darkness, and food that would last for a while – but madness and abuse would have been born out of fear. I now have to consider that in a past life this might have happened to me. Maybe my daughter was with me in that life also and this was a memory being dredged up – though these thoughts had not occurred to me at the time of the 'Egyptian episode'. Maybe we had been entombed alive in the very place from where the old man had taken the piece of cloth.

Lord Carnarvon, who financed Howard Carter's excavation of Tutankhamen's tomb in the year 1922, allegedly died due to his part in the discovery, and there were a string of unusual deaths of people associated with the find. The press had a field day with inventive 'scoops' of 'the curse of the tomb', but there is no doubt there were potent forces that came with the cloth in our possession. Luckily for us, we got away with only disturbing dreams and strange occurrences.

★ ★ ★

Xenoglossia: *In psychical research – a person's knowledge of a language he or she has never learned.*

★ ★ ★

PART TWO

PALMISTRY
MARCH 1971

A girl friend phoned one day with the suggestion that we went to consult a palmist. Believe it or not, I did not know about palmists – I had led a very sheltered life! In many ways I am glad that I knew nothing about the paranormal because when all the strange experiences happened to me over the years, my very ignorance about such things proved they were not drawn from my subconscious or from what I had been told or had read in a book.

I was in the middle of writing and illustrating a children's book – I had not done any writing or drawing for a long time – and I really did not want to stop my creative flow but, thinking it might be interesting, drove over to pick my friend up and off we went to a dingy house in London. I was asked to wait in the dimly lit, brown hallway while my friend went in for her reading.

I had dressed myself differently and left off my wedding ring to erase any obvious clues. I thought the lady would probably be a charlatan, using observations to guide her readings and had no faith that she could tell anything about me just from looking at my hand.

When I was called into the compact room, a thin wraith of a woman sat at a small circular table covered with a lace cloth that hung to the floor. She asked me what my zodiac sign was and then preceded to give me information about my sun sign, which I thought was nothing to do with palmistry but her way of padding out the reading. Then, to my astonishment, as soon as the woman took my hand in hers and looked into my palm, she said, "You've just started writing and drawing again, haven't you?" How could she have known that? It was not the sort of stock phrase that would apply to anybody and be true.

Everything she told me was so accurate I decided she could not possibly be a fraud. I wanted to know more about palmistry and was determined to find out.

Up until now, though I had scoured shops for books that might explain all the phenomena happening to me, other than the one on dreams, I never had success. Luck was with me this time and I found some excellent books on palmistry, which I studied from cover to cover. I was totally fascinated to learn that everybody has individual palm and finger prints and that each line, as well as the shape of the hands, the length of each finger, even the length and shape of each joint, tells a story.

Each day I would study palmistry, leaving dishes piled high in the sink to the annoyance of my husband. One evening when he came home, I cried out in excitement, "Guess what I have learned today – that certain lines can show a murderer!"

Jokingly, he held out his hand, saying, "What, like this?" – and, to my dismay, there were the relevant lines on his palm! I hurriedly researched my books once more, relieved to find that many creative people had these lines, but if they were only on one hand – as on my husband's – nothing untoward to worry about. Phew! It was a line of stress and aggression that needed creativity to release the tension.

Thankfully, my husband (an artist) painted most evenings when he returned from work, thus diminishing any urge he might have felt to throttle me when frustrated by my untidiness.

I soon realised that palmistry is a science that can be learned by anybody but, unfortunately, it has been dubbed as a somewhat dubious 'occult' occupation. I think it is probably unlikely that anybody would take up palmistry unless they were interested in esoterics, so is mainly used by psychics where clairvoyance often comes into the reading – such as in my own experience with the palmist regarding 'painting and drawing again'. This would not have been shown by the lines on my hand, but picked up clairvoyantly.

Because I found palmistry so fascinating, I began to air my newfound knowledge. Friends were soon queuing up for me to read their palms, one of them even asking me if I would be the palmist for the school fete.

My first reaction was to demur– I did not think I was good enough to go public as a professional palmist.

My sense of theatrics, however, soon had its say. I began to think of ways in which I could get around my novice knowledge of palmistry. If I made a very exciting   consultation room – our touring caravan – had 'Gypsy' helpers dressed appropriately, if I were disguised in black wig and brown make-up and were to give away leaflets on sun signs and palmistry – even if I gave poor readings, the clients would have had enough entertainment to keep them happy.

I informed the school that I would do it, but that I needed plenty of time to set up our caravan in the school grounds in preparation for the big day.

With the help of friends, we swathed the inside of the caravan, transforming it into a mystical cavern. I found lots of 'props' to add authenticity – a green fishing float for a 'crystal ball', an old brass 'hubble bubble', a small cauldron, and anything that I could find that looked a bit spooky. To finish off the effect, I bought some tarot cards in a shop, which I placed next to the 'crystal ball' on my table. I was astonished at the atmosphere created.

Next, it was time to buy some bright material to make myself a stunning long-skirted Gypsy outfit and make similar outfits for my children. I borrowed a black wig, bought some dark tan make-up and was ready for action.

We attached a large tent to the side of the caravan, making a spacious waiting room in case of wet weather where we could have tables groaning with goodies to sell, such as lucky heather, pegs, beads, baubles and charms. There were two doors to the caravan, one to be used as the entrance and the other as the exit.

Friends helped me with the details and I had seven enthusiastic Gypsy helpers all waiting for the day with dark make-up and outlandish outfits ready.

As part of my plan was to supply leaflets on the various sun signs, it was necessary for me to do some research before I could compose them. I knew about my own sun sign – as most people do – but knew very little about the other signs, so this was my first study of the signs of the zodiac.

I became extremely interested in what I was doing and learned a surprising amount, determined that one day I would study astrology in more depth, but in the meantime had my work cut out typing and photocopying the individual sun sign leaflets as well as handouts on the rudiments of palmistry.

There had been a great discussion about what name I should choose. I did not want anybody to take me seriously so a frivolous name was called for. The one that amused me most was 'Madame Salami', so once that was established, my husband painted a wonderful sign in fairground style – "Madame Salami, Palmist" with a large painted hand displaying all the major lines. When the big day arrived, everything looked absolutely wonderful – but I was getting very nervous – what was I letting myself in for? I hoped I would not disappoint my clients or make a complete fool of myself.

I slapped on my dark make-up, pinned on the black wig and donned my Gypsy outfit. The children were soon togged up and looking outlandish with brown faces and hoop earrings. I adjusted their headscarves and made sure their peddlers' packs – small trays on strong ribbons around their necks – had all the beads and rings in place for selling. Everything was fine and we were all ready, so I withdrew into the caravan wondering if I would get any clients for consultation. As I looked around at the transformation I could feel that a mysterious atmosphere had been created.

When the fete was officially opened, I peeped through the door and got the fright of my life. There was a queue of both children and adults that filled the tent and snaked half way around the playing field. Gracious! How was I going to get through them all?

Before taking on the role of Madame Salami, I had felt that my expertise with palm reading was not going to be very satisfactory, so had decided to assess my clients' characters from their appearance, which would help me with a profile. However, after the first person came in for consultation, I soon realised that this ploy was not necessary – the only things I focussed on were my clients' hands.

My first customer was a little girl and I was not sure who was more nervous. I did not do a very good reading, but she was happy enough and left through the exit door with a handful of free goodies.

Despite adopting the silly name of Madame Salami, I noticed that people hung onto my every word, believing what I told them. Clearly, I had a responsibility not to tell them anything that might cause them worry. I have since heard of palmists who tell their clients alarming data – such as death at an early age. How very unkind to cause such distress. I felt that discretion should always come first.

To my surprise, I found that words were coming out of my mouth that my brain had not formulated but which related to my clients and had nothing to do with the lines on their hands. I am sure that because I had created so much atmosphere and energy in the caravan, my Gypsy spirit guide was there, actively helping me become a serious, professional clairvoyant/palmist.

Much to my astonishment, all the readings were really successful, but at one point I became rather worried when a small boy at the head of the queue looked frightened and was reluctant to come into the caravan. I asked him, "What's the matter, love?"

"Ere, Missus," he said, "I've seen all them people go inter yer place, and not one of 'em's come out!"

I had to chuckle to myself. The poor little lad must have thought I had magicked them away! I soon put his mind at rest by telling him about the second door so, happily reassured, he came in for his reading.

Next in the queue were three children in wheelchairs. I knew they would want me to give them hope for their future. In my ignorance, I wished they had not come, because I did not know what I was going to say to them.

I should have known better because they all had really good hands, and clearly my guides were helping me for I 'knew' all their dreams. I asked the first, a boy, if he wanted to be a photographer when he grew up. He gasped in amazement that I knew his secret desire and said, "Yes!" I did not want to give him false hopes, but I told him that there was absolutely no reason why he could not become a photographer and that the first step was to ask his parents to provide him with a camera.

It was the same with the girls. I guessed what their dreams were – clearly my guides were putting the words in my mouth – and gave them the same sort of encouragement, telling them never to give up on their dreams. I often wonder, as forty years have passed and they will now be adults, whether my words of encouragement helped them with their careers.

I noticed, without exception, that all the adults I saw that day seemed to have very little self-esteem. They wished they could write that book, play that piano, cook that gourmet meal or display other skills they never believed possible. All they needed was some encouragement – the potential was there in the lines of their hands and they grasped enthusiastically at my assurance that they could do it if they tried. I know I sowed a lot of good seeds on that day, which made me very happy.

The highlight of the day was when Hurricane Smith – a pop singer with his current song 'Hey Babe, what do you say' high in the charts – came to have his hand read. There is nothing like a famous personality to add to the excitement of an event.

The day was a huge success and so were my readings. I was totally exhausted by the time I had got through the long queue. As well as being able to contribute towards the school funds, I had learned how I could help people through palmistry and that I had received assistance from my guides. What a wonderful experience and what a lot I had learned.

★ ★ ★

Palmist: *Someone who tells a person's fortune from the lines on his or her palm.*
Supernatural: *Dictionary definition: above and beyond nature; not according to the laws of nature; miraculous; magical; spiritual; occult.*
Paranormal: *Dictionary definition: abnormal; psychologically not explicable by the laws of nature or reason.*

A SHORT INTERLUDE

There is absolutely no psychic content in this anecdote – I just want to name-drop. Because I really liked the dress I had made for Madame Salami's debut, I decided to wear it to a dinner party that we had been invited to by a doctor from Windsor who had purchased one of my husband's paintings. I was excited because Michael Parkinson – the famous television host – and his wife, Mary, would also be attending.

I had purchased some trendy over-the-knee 'guardsmen' boots made of shiny black plastic that were all the rage at the time. I thought I looked the bee's knees in my ensemble and hoped that Michael Parkinson would think me scintillating enough to include me as a guest in his show – well yes, I admit to being overly optimistic!

All went very well. The evening was most enjoyable and the Parkinson's proved to be a most entertaining couple. I was seated next to Michael at the table and wit, humour and wine flowed. He had many amusing tales to tell of problems with guests on his show.

There was, however, trouble rumbling beneath the table that I feared would block my chance of television fame. As I sat, the plastic boots had welded themselves together and every time I moved they reluctantly disengaged with a disgusting flatulent sound. I was mortified and though I tried hard to keep still, the inevitable kept happening. What should I do, I wondered? If I informed Parky that it was my boots making the noise, he might believe I was making an excuse. If I said nothing, he would assume I was a rude woman with uncontrollable functions. Eventually, after an umpteenth awful boot-parp, I turned to the famous man and despairingly gasped, "It's my boots!" The gallant gentleman replied that he had heard nothing but, whilst continuing to be incredibly charming, he refrained from inviting me to be a guest on his show.

To think that I might have been a television star by now if it had not been for those dreadful boots...

OUIJA BOARDS
1972

*Before writing anything about my own experiences using this method to contact spirits, my advice is **do not do it**! I have heard of people who have either committed suicide afterwards, gone mad, or become possessed.*

There are many malevolent 'low plane spirits' – not necessarily human – who stay close to earth on the lowest etheric level causing mischief. There is a kind of twilight world that lies between physical reality and the spirit realm, where the malicious dead can linger and cause harm, as well as all kinds of demonic forms keen to find a physical body to enter. When you use the Ouija board, you are showing these creatures of the dark a 'light at an open window' for them to home into.

The first time I did this was at a friend's home one evening with a few of her other friends. I had never heard of the Ouija board but my interest in the paranormal was escalating, so I was interested to see what happened. I did not know that it could be dangerous. We did not have a board but used letters of the alphabet that were arranged in a circle with the words 'Yes' and 'No' placed either side. An upturned wine glass rested in the centre onto which we all placed a finger.

"Is anybody there?" called the girl in charge. I giggled as we all looked so silly waiting for something to happen. I had hopes that my Gypsy guide would turn up and give me some kind of useful message. The girl spoke again, "Is anybody there? If so, please go to 'Yes'." This was repeated several times until the glass shifted just a little bit. I thought someone was moving it deliberately. Eventually, the glass slid to 'yes'. We had contacted a man who spelled out his name. When I asked him how old he was, the reply was 'as old as the hills', which I thought was very cryptic.

We asked lots of silly questions until the man in spirit instructed us to go upstairs to the lodger's bedroom, where we would find him dead. We were shocked as well as very frightened but, en masse, bravely climbed the stairs to fearfully open his bedroom door, expecting to find a gory corpse waiting for us.

Thankfully, there was no dead body in the room, so we clattered downstairs, took up our positions round the table again, and asked why our spirit had told us such a lie. The reply was, "Because you are all being so stupid."

I realised the point of that exercise was that we should not be so flippant. After all, if you were a spirit and called down to answer silly questions instead of getting on with better things, then it would be annoying! We were lucky that we had contacted someone who was pointing out that we should not enter into this lightly, but I still did not realise the potential danger and tried it a few more times with only silly results.

★ ★ ★

I had another friend who lived in a very old mansion that had once held court to King James. It was quite a spooky place.

One day we decided to have a try at the Ouija and set out the alphabet and the wine glass.

First of all, I got a message from a woman who had passed on – she said she had been the girl friend of a man I knew. She swore a lot at me and the messages were unpleasant.

My arm was aching, so I swopped hands, using my left hand. The glass whirred round and round and when we asked for a name, it spelled out PAN. I said, "No, come on, what is your real name?" It then spelt out SATAN. I did not believe it really was Satan but that a spirit was being mischievous. When next the glass spelled out THE DEVIL, I became rather nervous, but when I felt the most horrible feeling spreading along my arm, which I can only inadequately describe as a feeling of hatred and evil, I really did think something horrific was happening. Just as this frightening sensation reached my upper arm, I quickly withdrew my hand from the glass, as did my friend. She gasped, "Val, something terrible is going on here!" Feeling shaken, I agreed. We threw all the bits of paper into the fire, washed out the wineglass and tried to gather up our shattered nerves. My arm felt numb for quite some time and we were both sure that we had been reached by something satanic.

I wondered what would have happened if I had kept my hand on the glass? Would that feeling have eventually reached my heart? Would it have had a fatal effect? Or would I have been possessed by some malevolent being? Who knows? It was enough to stop me from trying to reach spirits with that method again.

★ ★ ★

Some time later, during the course of conversation my father mentioned to me that a master of the black arts – who called himself a black magician - had previously owned my friend's mansion. Hmmm. It was a frightening thought that we had been in touch with Pan, Satan and the Devil in the house where devil worship had once taken place. My father also mentioned that it was suspected that a ritual murder had taken place in the house and that this man had buried the body in the cellar, covering it with very thick layers of concrete. This had never been verified as the floor had not been dug up, but there is usually a basis of truth in all rumours. Although the black magician had been long-gone from the area, it seemed that whatever he had conjured up during his occupancy had remained there and we had summonsed it again. A daunting thought.

★ ★ ★

Ouija: A board with signs and letters of the alphabet on it, used with a planchette in attempts to receive messages from the dead.

TOUCHING ON THE DARK SIDE
SEPTEMBER 1972

There were two more occasions when I touched on the dark side – or, more accurately, when it touched me.

One night, I had another vivid dream. I dreamt that I was in the country, living in a house that was surrounded by woods. The countryside around me was so unusually *green*. I found myself standing on a sloping path. To my left there was a hedge between the house and myself, with ranks of stinging nettles either side of the path. To my right was a dark wood.

My hand grasped a long, unusual spear and, as I raised my arm, I could feel the weight of the spear as I balanced it. I aimed and then threw the weapon,

76

which went some way before landing. I was clearly practising. The dream was not frightening in itself but it had overtones of darkness, which I did not understand.

As usual, I recorded the dream in my dream diary, but the next day when I searched for news reports that might explain the dream, I was unsuccessful.

A few nights later I visited a girl friend. We played records and chatted over a glass of wine. Time was getting on when I noticed how strange the music sounded. My friend remarked on it herself, saying that it was a favourite record, but it sounded unusually different and there was a weird atmosphere in the room.

I also noticed that the room seemed to be filling with ghostly swirls of mist. My friend was smoking a cigarette but I did not think one cigarette could produce so much smoke, or that it would be so dense and whirling. Feeling uncomfortable, I stood up and walked over to the window. Just as I did this, I felt something 'whoosh' towards me like an arrow. I could feel an icy blast as it divided around my head. I immediately put my hands to the window to see if there were any draughts coming from it, but there were none at all. I said nothing but felt very uneasy and I could see that my friend was also nervous. "There's something very peculiar going on in here," she said, "and it's getting on my nerves!"

I agreed. As is often the case with me, when I am frightened anger overtakes me. I was fed up with feeling frightened, fed up with not understanding what was happening to me and so fed up with ghosts and ghouls. I began to shout at the entities, or whatever they were, to disappear and go back to wherever they came from. My friend did the same. We jumped around the room waving our arms and shouting in anger and derision at our unseen visitors.

I think we might have found the correct antidote, because the ghostly mist, or whatever it was, began to slide out and disappear, the music became normal again and the atmosphere changed from spooky to calm. Since that time, I understand that with entities you are supposed to remain calm and guide them towards the light, but swearing and anger did the trick that night!

When my girl friend assured me she was all right to be left on her own, I departed, but instead of going straight home decided to visit my father instead. It was well after midnight but he was still in his den. Bursting into his calm sanctuary I must have alarmed him by shouting, "I'm so fed up with things that go bump in the night!" He quietly listened to everything I had to tell him, starting with the Disembodied Voice, the music, the dreams, culminating with the dream about the green place where I had been throwing spears.

"I could take you to that place tomorrow," he told me. "What you have described is where a black magician lived who is a fanatic about Zulu spears, constantly practising throwing them."

As is often the case in my dreams, I see things through the perception and body of somebody else and, clearly in that dream, I had been in the body and mind of the magician, seeing through his eyes.

My father admitted that he was worried about the dream, telling me that he had been an influence in getting the man deported from the country because of his activities. It was apparent to him that the man was not able to get psychically through my father's 'defences' – but he had been able to get through mine, in turn affecting my father. I did not like the sound of that! What would the sinister man's next trick be? Clearly, the 'whoosh' of an 'arrow' that divided around my head earlier on had been the whoosh of a Zulu spear. At least its blow had been deflected and had not caused me any problem – but what else could the man do? How strong were my own defences?

To my surprise, my father then told me that it was small wonder I was prone to clairvoyance because many of my family – on both parents' sides – were seers and psychics of some kind. This came as a shock because I had not been aware of this. I complained that I wished I had known this earlier because it would have saved me from believing I was going mad. Dad's explanation was that he chose not to tell me as it might have unnecessarily influenced me and it was better that any clairvoyance came to me naturally.

I told my father about the amulet which my silversmith had nearly finished, sketching the design for him to see. My father amazed me by telling me that it was almost the same as one of the ancient Masonic symbols. He also mentioned that he had been wondering why, night after night, his Masonic crystal glasses in his drinks cabinet had been shattering, one by one. Was this some kind of spiritual warning?

As I left to go home, my father asked me to visit him again the following evening to meet his friend Harry who was a Rosicrucian – a member of the Rosy Cross Order – who might be able to give me some useful advice and help, as he was quite knowledgeable about the paranormal.

★ ★ ★

After my father introduced me to Harry the next evening, the three of us went into my parents' sitting room, joined by the family dog. Harry asked me a few questions, then handed me a sacred book. Pointing to a passage, he asked me to read it out loud. I wondered why I was supposed to do this but did as I was told. As I began to read, I became aware of an insidious and frightening *Cold* advancing into the room. I could feel icy tendrils gripping around my ankles. I began to feel very frightened as the room got colder and colder until it was intense. Our dog, who had at first been curled up quite happily on the sofa, was now whimpering in fear, her hackles raised.

My voice faltered because I knew that the terrible Cold was something evil, or had brought with it something evil, and I was its target. I was trembling and very frightened, but, in the same way as on the previous evening, anger overtook my fear. I had had enough of these ghastly experiences and felt it was time to put my foot down once and for all, so with an air of decision, I disdainfully ignored the Cold, put the book aside for a moment and turned to my father saying, "Please switch the electric fire on. Let's get some heat in this room and get rid of this stupid cold." I was determined not to be frightened any more and to ignore the presence that was stalking me. I noticed the electric fire did nothing to dent the icy cold and as I resumed reading the passage I faltered and made mistakes, but as I drew strength from within, my voice grew more confident until the words rang through the room.

This was *real* and I was in the middle of something appalling, but I was not going to let it get the better of me. I then felt the cold slinking sulkily away from me until the room temperature was back to normal.

I had been the target of some metaphysical force, but I had won the battle by refusing to give in to it. I realised then that occult forces cannot do anything physical to you, the only weapon the dark side has is *Fear* and fear can be overcome.

So I had learned another lesson and, although it had been quite appalling, I felt strengthened by it.

Both my father and Harry told me afterwards that they had been absolutely terrified when they realised that something awful was materialising. Harry–who was quite a magician and told me that, as an exercise of mind over matter, he could set fire to a dead tree just by thought alone – confided that he had never been so frightened. Something else to be learned – grown men being scared – so it was not just me being afraid of the unknown. They both reassured me that I had dealt with the situation famously.

I do not remember now what the book was that I read aloud from, or why I was asked to read from it, but it was obviously of some significance – good against evil – and it certainly produced results.

★ ★ ★

DREAM PSYCHOLOGY

I wish I were a better writer, capable of setting down the terror I have been through up until now, but all I can say is, think of the worst nightmares you have ever had, then treble the fear.

Since childhood, I had recurring nightmares of a bull chasing me through a field. I would run as fast as I could with the frightening creature pounding after me, its head lowered with huge horns ready to gore and hot breath billowing out of its nose. Sometimes my legs would just not move as the creature thundered after me, at other times I could not get over the gate or through a fence, but I always woke up, hot and sweating with fear, before the creature actually reached me.

Not long after the episode of The Icy Cold as described previously, I had the bull dream again.

The maddened bull was chasing me across a field and I was running for my life, as usual. This time I felt so angry because I was running away from the blasted animal yet again. I had had enough and was not going to run any more. I stopped and turned round to face the bull as it thudded towards me, its nostrils wide and snorting. The creature's horns were lowered for attack, its hoofs kicking up clouds of dust as it accelerated heavily towards me. I was so terrified because I really thought I was facing death, but was determined not to give in to my fear any more. The damned thing could go ahead and kill me.

The bull was nearly upon me – I could feel its hot breath on my face and my heart thumped with fear as I waited for the creature's horns to plunge into my stomach. Much to my surprise, it skidded to a halt, just missing me by an inch. It then turned away from me, looking foolish, and wandered off through the daisies, whereupon it lowered its head and began to graze at the grasses, as docile as could be. If I had wanted to, I could have put my arms around him and kissed his nose, but as the creature was my nightmare, I refrained and left him grazing in the sunshine. How extraordinary – my nightmare terror had transformed into an innocuous bovine cutie and I awoke with all the joys of a vanquishing hero.

I realised there was a clear message to me in that dream: if I face up to my fears, they are never as dreadful as I think they are going to be, and since that realisation I have proved this over and over to myself in real life. I had come a long way from the shy and retiring girl I used to be.

I also realised how important dreams are. They hold cryptic clues and messages to help us in our daily lives. It is up to us to solve the riddles they present and use the answers to our advantage. It could be argued that dreams come from our subconscious – but what exactly is that? I am inclined to believe that the 'sub-conscious' is our link from guides and helpers and that when we heed those 'intuitions' we are on the right track.

★ ★ ★

OLD NICK AGAIN
APRIL 8TH 1973

I dreamt that I was an office girl, walking along a corridor and about to enter an office on the left. Another secretary passing by grabbed my arm and told me, "Don't go in, the Devil is behind that door!" I took no notice, determined to enter and flung open the door.

There, sitting behind a neat and tidy desk, was 'the Devil', wearing a smart grey suit, a white shirt and ordinary tie, with his hair neatly combed back and in place. He appeared to be the epitome of the perfect businessman. His hands were clasped on the top of a desk that was totally devoid of clutter. Filing cabinets were behind him and office surfaces all round the room, but there were no office papers to be seen. Everything was completely tidy and neat.

The Devil leaned across the desk to shake my left hand but I knew that the 'left path' was the evil one, so proffered him my right hand, saying I was not scared of him and had done no wrong. Unruffled, he smiled. Business was running so smoothly that it virtually ran itself. His office was evidence of this – so devoid of any apparent work to do, it was indicative of 'wheels well oiled'. People like myself who were not corrupt and who would like to see the world without problems, did not worry him at all. He smiled at me politely and dismissed me from his mind.

When I woke, I thought what a strange, analogous dream it had been. 'Evil Incorporated Worldwide' is doing very nicely without any input from 'himself'. His employees efficiently run his various umbrella companies dealing with War, Corruption, Terrorism, Discord, Famine, Disease and everything else negative. He was now merely a figurehead.

This was my second brush with 'the Devil'. I had previously been told that while there is no actual 'Devil' as such, because of my religious upbringing that is how I would perceive evil. It was strange that my perceptions had seen the Devil as an ordinary businessman, and how astute and true my dream was. There was no need for 'the Devil' to work any more – he had planted the seeds that were being effectively nurtured by his human minions.

★ ★ ★

A ROMANY CARAVAN AND A WEDDING
MAY 1973

I did not go out to work after my children were born, believing it was more important to be there for them. However, I found a way of earning some money by making tissue paper flowers at home – this being the time of 'flower power'. My husband and I used to take his paintings on Sundays and hang them on the railings in London's Bayswater Road, children in tow, but as we stood on the pavement waiting for rich customers to buy a painting, I found I was attracting the unwanted attention of gentlemen who believed *I* was for sale! Making the flowers was originally a ploy to establish the reason I lingered on the pavement but proved a turning point for my creative abilities. I had discovered an enjoyable way of earning, doing something I was good at, unlike my doubtful office abilities. I soon branched out and also sold my flowers from a stall at the local market.

I bought a knitting machine with some of my profits and created long rainbow scarves and Greek bags. I also made rag dolls, cuddly toys, hobbyhorses and candles.

One night, I had a rather obscure dream, which on awakening, I scribbled down in my diary. I recalled it had something to do with the weights and measures inspectors. I also had a vague recollection of two Gypsy caravans located in what I felt was the village of Brasted. A woman in the dream was selling the caravans, but had told me, "They are expensive." One of the caravans was in a bad condition, the other looked sound and was painted in what looked like black and red, but I could not see clearly. The dream changed and I noticed same odd-looking oven-ready turkeys. They were so small, much smaller than spring chickens and looked blue in their plucked form. The dream changed again and a lady was dishing up fish and chips and, for some reason, I knew that my husband and I lived in separate homes.

Nothing in the dream made much sense, but despite the vagueness and my lack of recall, I knew it was 'one of those', so jotted down what I could remember.

It was market day, so as usual I left early in the morning to set up the stall. This was always hard work, heaving huge sheets of polythene over the top of the iron struts of the stall, tying it down firmly so it did not blow away and making sure the stall was rain proof. In cold weather, fingers and toes became frozen despite many layers of clothing.

I had finished displaying my goods on the stall and began to put descriptive price tags on them. I had just finished writing 'Long Woollen Scarves' on a label, when a memory of the dream came back to me.

I only remembered the words 'weights and measures', which brought to mind the Trade Description Act. I realised my scarves were not woollen, but acrylic, so I had caused a misrepresentation in my description of them. I quickly changed the label and made sure that everything else on my stall was correctly described.

I had only just finished when two men came to my stall and thoroughly scrutinised everything on it, reading all the labels and asking me a lot of questions. They told me they were Customs and Excise men, checking that goods complied with the Trade Description Act. If I had not remembered the dream and acted on it, I could have been in trouble and would probably have been heavily fined.

This was the first time that one of my dreams had actually applied to myself and also the first time that I had been able to take action to avoid a consequence.

After the men had departed, a neighbouring trader told me that in all the thirty-four years he had been trading, he had never seen any representatives of the Customs and Excise department. Clearly, this was a one-off occasion and that I had been singled out was unusual. When I told the trader I had the dream that made me change the labels, he told me that he had dreamt the previous night that an outsider was going to win the Derby. Its name was Red Rum and the horse's extraordinary win is now legendary. I told him to bet on it, as I was sure it would win. He must have made a fortune!

Later on that day, the father of one of my daughter's school friends came and chatted to me, thanking me for helping his son the previous day after I had taken him to hospital with a leg injury. The man was the postman for Brasted so, remembering about the Gypsy caravans in my dream, I asked him if he knew of any in his village. I was disappointed when he told me there were none. Bearing in mind my Romany ancestry, if I could have been granted one wish in the world at that time, it would have been to own a Gypsy caravan.

He mentioned that he sold pigeons and if I wanted to try some, I could have a couple free of charge. When he gave them to me I was surprised to see that they looked exactly like the 'turkeys' in my dream. They were small and they had a blue look about them. As two incidences in my dream had come true, I then reasoned that there was the likelihood that I would be lucky enough to soon find the Gypsy caravans – I asked the postman to keep a look out for me.

I have mentioned that precognitive dreams are very vivid. They are so vivid that I remember most of them to this day, forty-odd years later, even though I might forget what I did yesterday or ate for breakfast today. The dreams make such an impression on me that they are unforgettable.

During the course of writing this book, I discovered the dream diary gathering dust in the attic. I was surprised that I still had it after several house moves, and while I remembered my precognitive dreams, it was interesting to thumb through the dream diary to discover one or two I had forgotten – the caravan dream being one of them. My heart beat with astonishment because it now made sense. It had been a foresight of something that was to happen years later in 1984.

To complete the astonishing finale to the Gypsy caravan story, I will now fast-forward to show how the contents of that dream came to fruition, making sense at last. The reason that the dream was vague was because I had foreseen many years into the future and the 'memory' was therefore understandably hazy.

* * *

1984: eleven years later

The years had gone by, my husband and I had separated and lived in different houses in Norfolk. My children were grown up and they both had their own homes.

I was still recovering from the debilitating effects of the marriage breakdown and had reluctantly agreed to a pub meal with an acquaintance whose wife had just left him. I felt sorry for the man and had only agreed to the date out of compassion. I was not really in the mood for small talk and am ashamed to admit that my thoughts were drifting. I suddenly interrupted the conversation and heard myself say, "What I most want in the world is a Gypsy caravan." Astonished that I had uttered such a statement out of the blue, I *instinctively knew* that he would reply, "And I know where there is one!" – which is exactly what happened.

Who had put those words into my mouth? How did I know exactly what my acquaintance would say? With excitement, I queried the location – which was just along the road at a village called Brancaster *(in the original dream I had felt the caravans were in the village of Brasted. The words are not so dissimilar),* behind an antique shop. I could hardly wait to have a look as I still cherished the dream to own a Gypsy caravan, little believing that I ever would.

There was a full moon, so after leaving the pub we walked up a small lane at the back of an antique shop where I could see the silhouettes of <u>two</u> caravans. My heart thumped with excitement.

The yard was closed for the night, so I viewed the vans from the lane. The moonlight diffused all colours but one of them looked as if it were painted black and red, the other seemed to have peeling paint and looked in a bad state of repair *(exactly as I had written in my dream diary, though I had forgotten all about that dream at this time).* I could barely contain my excitement.

Awed at having made such an exciting discovery in such an unusual manner, I knew my spirit guides must have orchestrated the manoeuvres! I resolved to be on the doorstep first thing in the morning.

The following day I arrived just as the shop was opening and the owner took me into the yard to show me the caravans. One was almost beyond repair *(as recorded in my journal)*, but the other was beautiful. It was not black and red as it had seemed in the moonlight *(and in my dream)*, but was painted burgundy and green, and had lots of carvings of little birds carrying cherries in their beaks all around the sides. There were carved bunches of grapes adorning the woodwork, a utensil box underneath and a hayrack on the back for storing horse fodder. The interior was delightful, with a fitted bed, seats, chest of drawers, seating – all painted on a background of burgundy with swirly showman designs in white. I was beside myself with joy.

I asked the lady the price. "Oh, it's a lot of money, dear," she replied *(as she had in the dream)*. My heart sank when she told me the amount but, quite honestly, even at a lower sum, I did not know how I could buy it. I did not have any money of my own – my husband, despite our differences, was still supporting me until I found a job. I could see no means of being able to get the caravan. But my heart was set on it. I pleaded with the lady not to sell it to anybody else until I could raise the money.

As I drove home, I wondered how I could find the cash to fulfil my dream. I searched for my building society book that had a small amount in it to keep the account open. I wondered if it had gained any interest over the years and I was pleased to find that it had. Not enough to buy the caravan, but then a miracle happened. A cheque arrived in the post – a small insurance policy I had taken out years before had matured. I almost had enough. I returned to the antique shop and bargained with the owner who agreed to lower her price to the amount I had available. I was now the excited possessor of an authentic Gypsy Burton caravan, or 'vardo' in the Romany language. My wish had at long last come true!

By this time, I owned a horse named Tiffany, a sturdy Welsh cob, that I knew would be capable of pulling the load and I did not think it would take her long to learn. I daydreamed of travelling the open road; of Tiffany's hoofs clip-clopping as she ambled along. I could park at the sides of the road and earn some money with my paper flowers as well as by reading palms – Madame Salami had paved the way for that.

As things turned out, reality was different, but in my mind's eye, my horse Tiffany and I travelled every highway and byway and had many adventures. Unfortunately, poor Tiffany dropped down dead of a twisted gut – a horrible death – before I had even tried her in the traces.

After the trauma of Tiffany's death, I had wonderful dreams of us together on the open road, she pulling the caravan, me walking beside her with my hand tucked into her head collar. The sun shone, the sky was blue, the birds sang, the grasses and wild flowers grew high beside the road and we had the countryside to ourselves. Together we chatted for hours on end. I would wake up euphoric but could never remember what we had spoken about. The dreams were very vivid, so I am quite sure that she had visited me in the night and fuelled my fantasy, giving me the gift of virtual reality as well as a talking horse.

Because I had forgotten all about my original caravan dream so many years before, I did not make the obvious connections when I purchased my vardo, and the only evidence that I had dreamt about it was in my old diary, hidden away in a box in the attic.

★ ★ ★

1985

Another year went by and my life was sorting itself out. I had a new boyfriend and was in the throes of an exciting romance with him. My happiness increased when my daughter, Lucinda, told me she was going to get married. After much planning, she decided she wanted a 'Gypsy wedding', using the vardo to collect her from the church with a jazz band leading the way. Everyone was to dress in Gypsy style and the venue after the church was to be the village hall, decorated like a French Bistro with a fish and chip reception – guests were asked to queue at the local chippie next door! *(If you recall, the original hazy dream from so many years earlier showed a lady dishing up fish and chips.)*

On the big day, the wedding procession turned into a mini Mardi Gras and was just as exciting. The whole village turned out to watch and I have never seen so many smiling faces. We even had the village policeman directing traffic. It was a wonderful day, with even the aftermath from Hurricane Cindy that blew in from America – Lucinda's childhood nickname was Cindy – providing flurry and added zest to the occasion. How many girls have a personal hurricane turn up for their wedding?

It was not until a few years after the wedding that I searched for and found my dream diary. Imagine my surprise to discover the notes of the forgotten dream involving the weights and measures inspectors with the vague reference to the caravans.

My daughter had no access to my diary, nor had I told her about that particular dream, as it was so obscure at the time. Because it had been forgotten, there is no way that it had influenced the theme of the wedding or indeed my purchase of the vardo.

In retrospect, the dream was like the vague memories of something that had happened many years ago rather than something that was going to happen in the distant future. Certainly another odd phenomenon to ponder over – but how very strange was the series of coincidences.

There was something else very special that culminated with Lucinda's wedding. My paternal grandfather had presented me with a small apple tree, grown from an apple pip from an ancient Oslin tree and planted at Lucinda's birth. He had named the tree The Lucinda-Oslin. The Lucinda-Oslin never grew more than a couple of feet high, so when we moved to Norfolk – Lucinda was then aged twelve – it was easy enough to dig up the tree and take it with us. It had never blossomed but, other than being small, it seemed healthy enough. We re-planted it in a piece of garden that Lucinda tended herself, but it still did not blossom or grow much. When the house was sold, none of us had a garden large enough to replant the apple tree, so it remained where it was, but as luck had it, a friend purchased the house, so we often used to visit and watched the tree's progress. During the year of Lucinda's wedding announcement, I noticed that the little apple tree had produced, for the first time in its twenty-five years, a plethora of beautiful blossom. By the time of the wedding, its slender boughs were bent to the ground with a wonderful crop of apples. This was the only time it ever bore fruit. What a wonderful wedding gift from her long-departed great-grandfather.

The fact that the horse hired to pull the wedding vardo was named Blossom could be no more than a happy coincidence – or could it? But it certainly adds a neat ending to the very remarkable story.

★ ★ ★

MORE PRESENTIENT DREAMS
BACKTRACK TO 1982

You will recall my mention of the young man from Bulgaria who brought the recording of the gypsy music I had heard psychically so long ago. I had some interesting dreams about his family.

Young love

In one dream, I saw his mother with a young man and the love that enveloped them was very apparent. I thought it must be one of her sons whom I had not yet met.

It transpired that it was her secret young lover, her son's friend. When I eventually met them, I recognised him, and their love was tangible. They are still together today.

The search for a murderer

While touring with our caravan, we visited the family in Belgium. During our first night I dreamt that while we were asleep in the caravan, the father came out in the night with policemen and a number of other men, their torches illuminating the darkness. They demanded entrance to our caravan and searched thoroughly under beds and in all the cupboards. They would not tell me what they were looking for, but I knew that they were looking for a murderer. *(In my dreams, I do not necessarily have to see or have things explained, as the 'knowledge' is there.)*

During the whole of my week's stay, I was in a fearful state. I was convinced that my children were going to be murdered. *(In the dreams, for some reason, it is always my own children I worry about although they have never been part of the actual events.)* I made a real nuisance of myself, making sure that they were never out of my sight. I did not tell anyone why I was being so neurotic, but it was clear that they all thought I was acting like an over-protective mother.

The day before we left for home, our friend casually mentioned that there had been some excitement just before our arrival. He explained that a murderer had been on the loose in the area but had been apprehended after an extensive search by police and local volunteers. I wailed, "Why didn't you tell me?"

"Why should I?" he queried. When I told him that the reason for my neurotic behaviour was because I had dreamt that a murderer was on the rampage, he just replied, "Ahhhh." Ahhhh, indeed.

A SURPRISE VISIT

I then had a dream about a dear American friend. I dreamt that he intended to pay me a surprise visit. I was so excited and told all my friends. Knowing that it was possible to control my dreams, I decided on another experiment. I would tell myself just before I slept that I must dream the date of his arrival. It worked – I was given a date in July. I cleaned the house from top to bottom and made all my preparations to surprise *him*!

To my dismay, the date passed without the expected visit from my friend. I felt foolish because I had boasted to everybody that I was able to predict his arrival. Up until now, this was the first time any of my dreams had been inaccurate – maybe I had become too complacent about my powers of prophecy.

A month or two passed, then an airmail letter plopped on the mat. I recognised the writing. I had not been complacent after all, because my American friend had written to tell me that *he had been planning a surprise visit to see me in July!* He had bought his ticket, checked his passport and arranged for his visas and was all ready to depart when something urgent had cropped up forcing him to cancel his plans at the very last moment.

So I had been correct all along, *but this was the first time I had proof that fate is not necessarily fixed.* I had received all the information about an event that was to happen in the future, but at the last moment the plans changed. The complexities of fate, fortune and the future are vast indeed.

A PRECOGNITIVE DREAM OF THE FALKLANDS

One night in 1982, I dreamt of enemy aircraft flying over our home. As I stood watching them overhead I felt so worried, as it was apparent that another war was under way. The dream changed and I was high in the sky with the air crew who, I was surprised to note, were only young boys of around fifteen or sixteen years old. They were absolutely terrified, having to fly the planes and to fight in a war. I was puzzled because they were speaking in Spanish. *(As usual when in this kind of dream situation, I was invisible to them and also, as I usually did, I could feel their fears and emotions as if they were my own.)*

On awakening, I mentioned the dream to my husband. Although he did not like what I told him about my dreams and intuitions, he had got more used to my proclamations. It was ludicrous to believe that the Spanish people would suddenly declare war upon England, but I still felt very worried because my dreams usually held some sort of truth, not always apparent until the dreams were verified by factual evidence.

A few days later, I read newspaper headlines announcing that the Argentineans had invaded the Falkland Islands – a British colony – and that many of the pilots were frightened young men of around sixteen years old. The language they spoke? Spanish.

ILL WILL

I would do anything to help the friends who were always contacting me for either advice or favours, but on the rare occasions I asked for assistance for myself of any kind, they were always 'too busy'. My feelings were often hurt, and when one of them did something really spiteful, I picked myself up, thinking, "Oh well, what goes around comes around," believing the universe meted out judgement accordingly. I then put the person and the incident out of my mind.

All the people who had upset me were involved in car accidents. While none of them were injured, in all cases the cars were a write-off. There is a limit to coincidences and I began to get worried. Never mind the universe – was I subconsciously willing car accidents onto hapless victims? This seemed far-fetched, but maybe I was. As is usual, another coincident occurred when I picked up Colin Wilson's heavy tome, 'The Occult', where he makes reference to exactly this kind of thing. He advised the best way to obviate such unconscious revenge tactics was to think only good thoughts of one's enemies. It is not easy to do this when people are unkind, but it must work for, to date, there have been no more car accidents!

I had been made aware of the power of the mind, so concluded that if negative thoughts can be sent out like arrows to destroy, then it must be possible to send positive thoughts for good – which is, of course, what prayer and healing is about.

A MAGICAL BABY

There was a woman living in my road who was desperate to have a baby, but had eventually come to the realisation she never would after fruitless consultations with her doctor and undergoing many hospital tests. This was well before IVF treatments were available. I felt very sad for her, so asked her round to my house and we talked about her problem over coffee.

I was suddenly overcome with the knowledge that I could magic her a baby! Maybe my knowledge of mind power prompted me when I said to her with absolute conviction, "You *will* get pregnant and your baby will arrive before October is out." I must have sounded like an oracle, but because I was totally convinced that my prediction would come true I could neither have stopped myself from saying it or believing that it would happen.

She smiled sadly and said, "No, I don't think so."

I grinned, full of positivity, and replied, "You'll see."

After she had gone I chastised myself. Maybe I should not have said what I did – it would be so cruel if I had given her even the faintest hope and was then proved to be wrong. However, I was convinced my prediction would happen and, as the weeks went by, waited to see her bloom with burgeoning pregnancy. A few months later, there was no sign that my friend was expecting. I felt the pangs of doubt, especially when she was rushed into hospital with a burst duodenal ulcer. In intensive care, she nearly died and it was touch and go for her for some time. Still very ill on her return home, she did not seem to recover and when further complications set in was taken back into hospital for observation.

I was really concerned about my prediction because the time had run out if she was to conceive in order to give birth by late October.

A week or so after my friend's second return from hospital, she arrived at my back door, looking pale and wan but with a smile on her face. Pleased to see her, I asked her in, sat her down and busied myself by making her a cup of coffee.

"I wanted you to be the first to know," she said with a glow lighting her pallor, "Against all the odds, I am pregnant, just as you predicted I'd be!"

I sat down in astonishment!

"I know, it seems so improbable, but apparently I was pregnant when the duodenal ulcer burst and nobody realised. It was a miracle that the baby wasn't killed by the operation. When I went back to the hospital for observation, it was whilst running tests that they realised I was pregnant. All the doctors and medical staff were absolutely amazed the baby had survived through it all! Isn't it incredible?"

I agreed excitedly, asking, "When is the baby due?"

"Late October, " she told me.

Ah ha...

It happened that my friend's son was born on 31st October – Halloween – which I thought very apt, especially as I was convinced I had somehow magicked the baby. Perhaps my certainty was merely foreknowledge, but I do not believe so as the feelings were different from my usual precognitions. On this occasion, it felt as if I really had organised the granting of a wish. It seems like my adage *is* true that all things are possible!

★ ★ ★

SPRING 1973
UFOS AND ALIENS

One sunny day, I was strolling down a quiet leafy lane in the countryside near to my home. I was on a hill where I could see, from between some trees, the main road below.

A most peculiar sensation came over me. It was if someone else were viewing the scene through my eyes. Looking down on the main road, the 'intruder' saw vehicles as if for the first time, as they raced along emitting petrol and oil fumes. The person, seeing through me, reacted with dismay. I felt him thinking, "Oh, it's all wrong," meaning the cars, the fumes, the way of life. And then the strange sensation left, leaving me as myself once more and wondering what had just happened and who had been viewing the scene through my eyes.

This was in the era when there was less traffic on the roads and we did not yet realise that fuel emissions are causing damage to the planet's ozone layers, as well, of course, to flora, fauna and, subsequently, mankind.

It is impossible to describe how I knew I was host to a person from far away who was able to use me to view a scene on this planet – but I just *knew*. These days I easily acknowledge this *knowing* when it comes out of the blue, but at that time I was still floundering, trying to make sense of all the strange things that kept occurring, so while I *knew*, I did not always entirely trust that intuition.

I was used to pondering deeply after each of my strange experiences and coming up with improbable theories. However, on that day I was left with the idea that *perhaps* people from a more advanced planet could 'tap into us' to view what we are doing, seeing literally through our eyes. I really believed this is what had happened. How I wished I knew all the answers!

I continued to speculate on my theories. Since childhood I had wondered why there are so many humans on this planet of differing colours and physical appearance. I could never believe it was because of evolution, weather conditions or pigmentation.

Sure I had been host to someone from another planet, my thoughts wandered on. I thought of our warring natures, wondering why we have inherited the tendency for more violence to each other in our genes than that necessary for survival. My thoughts led me to the conclusion that maybe our planet Earth had been used as a penal dumping ground for undesirables from different planets – a kind of Australia of the galaxy. This would account for the different looks and colourings of the world population. Maybe the spacemen who left the original offenders here hoped that they and their descendents would become peaceful and spiritual, carving out a good and harmonious existence on this planet – if so, not much progress then!

If galactic journeys brought the first settlers here, this indicates that superior beings were already in existence all those millennia ago, while by now their scientific endeavours must be supreme, making it child's play to view our progress. Thus, 'telepathic viewing' across the solar systems would be a simple procedure. My thoughts wandered further. I had often wondered how, from the era of primitive man, there had been such a jump in intelligence – where had all the information come for astrology, for instance, for the technology for building the pyramids? I could only assume that it had been given to early man from superior beings from elsewhere.

Pleased with my revelational, if radical, thoughts, I aired them to friends and family, only to receive derisive snorts of laughter and opinions that I was insane. I have never understood why people never *consider* possibilities outside their current understanding.

Soon after this strange experience, Erich Von Daniken's book containing controversial theories ('Chariots of the Gods') hit the bookshelves. He was convinced that many of the Bible stories gave strong indications that space men had visited our planet. He also believed that space men had taught the Egyptian people how to build the pyramids, which were lined up with planets in our solar system. His theories were very interesting, but unfortunately, with his later books, he received a lot of bad press. His enthusiasm was deemed to be far fetched and he was ridiculed for his beliefs. However, he had a large following of people keen to stretch their imagination. Von Daniken's theories were also shaking the foundation rock of Western religion. His theories intrigued me, as they made my own thoughts more feasible.

★ ★ ★

OFF WITH THE FAIRIES

I was writing a children's fairy story and suffering from writer's block – I could not think how the story should continue.

After my husband had gone to bed one night, I had a brainwave. How stupid I was – I should just pick up pen and paper and let the fairies tell their own story!

With the very real belief that this would do the trick, I curled up in a chair by the fire and, with pen poised over my note pad – this was long before writing was made easy with computers – waited to see what would happen. Soon, the ink began to flow and the story wrote itself steadily. I eagerly followed the plot as it unfolded. I had absolutely no idea of how the story would progress. As the words formed themselves so quickly on the pages, I read them as if I were reading a book – it was a strange experience. I was so impressed with the help I was being given and wished I could see who my muse was.

When the story was finished, I was really pleased and not a little overawed – the tale had written itself magically. I put my notepad down and turned off the lights to leave the room. Because of some building alterations we had done, the light switches were inappropriately positioned away from the exit so, after turning off the lights, it was necessary to walk around all the furniture as well as some stairs to find the door. Normally, this was not a problem if the hall light was on, but on this particular night the rest of the house was in darkness so I was unable to see until my eyes adjusted to the gloom. I was aware of an unnaturally intense impenetrable darkness, a kind of deep inky blue, in which I could see strange flashes, or orbs, of light that illuminated nothing. It was rather weird but I thought it must be something to do with my concentration during writing.

As I felt my way blindly around the furniture and the open-plan staircase, I was surprised that my eyes had not yet accustomed themselves to the darkness, or that the lesser gloom from the garden was not apparent through the open curtains at the windows. I found myself unexpectedly disorientated in my own room and, bizarrely, had to sit down on the carpet, totally lost.

I sat for a while, waiting for my eyes to adjust to the darkness in order to locate the door. I was puzzled why I could not see the night sky through the window, but after waiting a long time in the intense dark, far longer than should have been necessary, I spotted the glint of glass and outlines of the garden beyond the window. At last I had my bearings and was just about to stand up *when I realised that the room was gradually changing shape and stretching out into the garden!* As it did this, I got the curious sensation that *I was shrinking in size myself* – like Alice in Wonderland did after she had swallowed the contents of a bottle labelled 'Drink Me'. I truly thought magic was about to happen and quite expected a troop of fairies to come tripping through the room, so I settled down again, excitedly waiting for them.

The room had by now moved half way up the garden, and I felt as if I were about one foot high. Disappointingly, nothing extraordinary happened, except that the room had stopped shifting. I wanted to stand up and explore the new territory but did not in case it 'broke the spell'. Any moment now, I thought, as I waited for the fairies or *something* magical, but instead, to my dismay, the room slowly began to shrink back into its correct position.

I was very upset that no mythical creature visited me, no people from another world, no Fairy Queen with glittering wand – not even the smallest unicorn. It was such a huge let down that I forgot for the moment that something extraordinarily impossible had just taken place.

In retrospect, I realised I must have been in the centre of some kind of quantum physics leap. I wonder what would have happened if I had tried to walk in that supernaturally distorted room?

I spoke to Harry (the Rosicrucian who had been in the room of the Icy Cold with me) and he said it was the kind of thing that happened to him prior to astral travel. Maybe if I had attempted to rise when in the middle of that experience, I would have found my etheric body floating off into the garden while my corporeal body stayed put. Of course, I shall never know now. Perhaps I might have walked off into a parallel dimension. I think either of these options would have been possible had I made the experiment, but sadly I did not. Maybe my tutors guided me to stay seated to view the alteration of the room, purely to exercise my brain into further probabilities.

Latterly, I have found out that orbs of light show that spirits are around, so the flashing lights, or orbs, that I saw might indicate that there were 'fairies' or similar spirits in the room with me.

★ ★ ★

ANOTHER DREAM COMES TRUE
HIGH CLIFFS

As time went by, I was still having vivid dreams but they chopped and changed around, as if teaching me there are many aspects to foreknowledge. One was puzzling, having no disaster or crime involved. It was short but very real.

I dreamt of some very high cliffs, at the same time hearing the sound of torrential waters. I was concerned about flooding. I then saw water rushing along a gully. This dream puzzled me, for while it was 'one of those' there was no story attached to it.

Not long after the dream I met, for the first time, one of my husband's colleagues. He talked about the house he had recently moved into which he informed us was a renovated water mill called High Cliffs – named for the high cliffs upon which the house was perched. I recalled my dream with excitement, so asked if we could visit.

When we arrived at High Cliffs, I immediately recognised the location from my dream and I could hear the same sound of torrential water. As we rounded a corner, I could see the water as it rushed along a narrow channel, which led to the mill's wheel where it then gushed under the property with a deafening roar. This was the first time I had actually visited a place that I had dreamt about without any prior knowledge. We were shown around the property, and while we sat drinking coffee I was interested to hear that the house was haunted. My husband's friend told us that one of the cupboard doors would not remain shut. They had locked it and even on one occasion nailed it, and yet it still burst open. I wondered why I had dreamt about the place – what was going to happen there? What disaster was I suppose to avert? I asked about flooding and apparently it had been flooded in the past.

No disaster that I knew of ever happened after our visit. What was strange was the fact that we would never have been invited there unless I had asked, and I would never have asked without the dream, so why should I have dreamt such a dream? The fact was that the 'coincidence' was real – first the dream then meeting my husband's work-mate who spoke enough about his home for me to identify it from the dream – then finding the location of the dream's content was accurate in the visual and aural description of the location.

* * *

A STRANGE OCCURRENCE IN THE WOODS

I had finished writing the children's fairy story mentioned earlier and had begun to illustrate it. I had taken my sketchpad into the centre of our local wood – every inch of which I knew – and was sketching in a secret little clearing. I was enjoying the tranquillity, feeling at one with nature and knowing no other human being was likely to disturb me. I had climbed laboriously over a huge fallen tree and was leaning against the trunk of another as I drew. I was completely hidden from view, enjoying the sounds of birds singing around me, the sun on my face and the rustling of leaves in the gentle breeze, when I was aware of louder rustles coming from undergrowth near my legs. To my surprise, a fox emerged from a narrow bramble tunnel and was standing by my side. Because of the tight confines of the little glade, in effect, we were both 'cornered' with no way of quick escape. I was initially alarmed and fleetingly wondered whether this was a vixen with cubs nearby, in which case she might attack me, but realising I could do nothing, I just relaxed totally, did not move a muscle and mentally acknowledged this unexpected visitor.

The fox, after its initial shock at perceiving me, instead of fleeing in fright, nonchalantly looked up at me when – click – I felt an unexpected 'mind connection'. There is no way of explaining how it happened – I wish I could do it to order – I just felt the connection and knew what the animal was thinking. "Isn't it a lovely day?" he (for it was a male) small talked. I agreed with him. He sniffed at my knee, his nose making contact. I relished the amazing moment. I did not move at all in case I frightened him and he looked up at me again with bright eyes and a grin on his face. "You're all right," he told me in a friendly manner. He then casually shook himself right down to the tip of his scruffy looking brush, his back legs momentarily lifting with the momentum, looked up at me once more and said, "I'll be off now, then – things to do, places to go...." Taking his time, he turned round and casually pushed himself through the undergrowth. He was whistling a merry tune as he left me. Of course, he did not actually verbalise or whistle, but my mind connection with him gave me his happy mood, what he was thinking, his feelings and his acceptance of me. It was a most wonderful experience!

I had kept totally still during this interchange with the fox and, after his departure, I kept the same position because I was numb with awe – though my mind was whirring! I just could not believe that the impossible had happened. That gorgeous fox had accepted me without any fear, actually touched my knee with his nose and given me the once over; we had made mind contact and had exchanged pleasantries. What a privilege and what a magical experience.

If mind contact (telepathy) can happen between a fox and a human, clearly animals can communicate between themselves, and how crass of us to believe we are the only creatures on this planet with communication skills!

What was more astonishing about that experience was the fact that someone in those woods was keen on shooting foxes and hanging them on the branches of trees, wounded, to die an agonising death. The local fox population would therefore know that humans were not to be trusted and certainly to be avoided, so the fact that my fox had accepted me was more than a privilege.

MIND CONTACT WITH A HORSE

I did not expect to have such a wonderful meeting of minds again with an animal, yet it did happen. My children were keen to take riding lessons, so I thought I ought to have a go myself to see what I was letting them in for. When I was taken out on a hack (a ride in the countryside rather than a lesson at the stables) on a horse named Valour, it was only the second time I had sat on a horse. I did not know how to steer – in fact I knew nothing and was quite scared, sitting up so high with nothing to keep me on. The stable girl was flirting with the other two male hackers and completely forgot about me trailing behind. Because I had not got a clue how to make the horse follow the others, which normally she would have done – horses being herd animals they like to keep together – she chose to follow her own route, which was to a spot in the field where a lot of farmer's strawberry boxes were piled up, forming a wide circle that narrowed into a cul-de-sac. Valour took me along this track, but while the boxes had been stacked low at the entrance, they became higher and higher and were soon above the horse's head. The space between them that made up the track had narrowed considerably, with little room for manoeuvre. We reached a dead end in a confined space and I knew that all the whitened boxes looming about Valour's head were beginning to spook her and that any moment she would go crazy. He ears were flat to her head and panic was fast setting in. I had no idea what to do to turn her around in the small space or how to calm her. Without saying a word, I just thought in my head, "Don't worry, it's okay," and felt that 'click' again of mind connection with her, as I had with my friend the fox. She calmed down and, with that connection still in place, I telepathically asked her to turn around, then to walk back through the boxes that would not hurt her, and then catch up with the others. The mind connection was awesome and the horse did everything I asked of her, calming down so suddenly once the connection was made. My complete lack of equestrian skills did not matter. We had together sorted out a potentially dangerous situation through our minds and come through the situation together calmly as a team. Like the occasion with the fox, it was an awe-inspiring experience and one that I cannot justify with words.

* * *

A TELEPATHIC DOG

We had a pet dog called Pansy Potter. Because we lived in an unmade country road that seldom saw a car, Pansy wandered around at will and she had various friends that she visited. Despite her freedom, she still liked to be taken out on proper walks, but I seldom found the time to walk her regularly. However, sometimes I would think to myself, "Oh, I'll take Pansy out for a little walk." No matter where I was when I had made that decision, Pansy would come skidding round corners to my side, her tail beating furiously with delight, tongue lolling and eyes sparkling. Without fail, she always picked up my thoughts. It was so obvious that telepathy was at work. I never felt the 'click' of connection with her – but she was obviously able to pick up on my mind.

CATS

Rory

I had seen a beautiful silver tabby at a neighbour's house, so asked where she had obtained it. She told me that a local farmer's wife bred them, so I phoned to book a kitten from the next litter. Luckily, the cat was pregnant with an imminent birth and the farmer's wife said she would telephone me as soon as the kittens were born. The days passed by and I had a dream in which I saw a litter of poorly kittens, too ill to survive, except for one that looked strong, with strange clusters of red in her spotted grey fur. I heard the name "Rory" just before waking. I phoned the farmer's wife to ask if the kittens had been born. She apologised, saying, "Oh, I'm sorry I didn't contact you, but most of the kittens were poorly and have died." Before she could say more, I asked, "Has the survivor got tufts of red hair on its head?" She sounded quite astonished and told me that indeed it had. She had not contacted me because she did not think I would want one that was not completely silver tabby.

I told her that I would certainly have the kitten without even seeing it and that it had already been named Rory! I found out later that Rory is a name sometimes used in Scotland for a redheaded person. I wonder who had named her for me.

Rory became a much-loved member of the family though she seemed to be particularly attached to me, frequently giving me private performances of her 'witch's cat act' – humped back, fur standing up all over making her look like a cartoon cat being electrified, front legs and paws splayed with claws projected and racing around the room sideways until I was doubled up with laughter. She did this for nobody else!

I planned to let Rory have one litter of kittens before having her spayed, so we were all very excited when it was apparent she was in-kitten. Again, I dreamt the number and colours of the litter and before long five pretty babies arrived, just as my dream had predicted. Rory was an excellent mother and reared her kittens well, and in due course I found homes for all but one. We did not really want a second cat, but this remaining one had stolen our hearts. My daughter had already named her Emily and I was wavering in my resolve that she must go. Sadly, poor Rory, after having proved to be a wonderful mother and never leaving their sides until they were five weeks old, took herself off for an outing and did not come back. She had been killed by a car. Needless to say, we were all devastated, but had the consolation of keeping little Emily who was a very contrary and amusing kitten.

My daughter had always been a real chatterbox and quite often exhausted me with her questioning. Sometimes I said 'Yes' when I was not really listening. One day, a large envelope plopped onto the mat addressed to her. Curious, I asked her what it contained. "Mummy, it's the entry forms for the cat show at Olympia. You said I could enter Emily". Oh dear! My daughter had seen the cat show advertised on the TV programme, Blue Peter, and I had evidently given her the go-ahead to enter our cat. Having apparently agreed, I did not have the heart to disappoint her. Expensive procedures had to be made, with inoculations, a new cat basket, cushions and collars. Emily was a very pretty cat, though not as strangely marked as Rory. She was mostly silver but had a hint of pink in her fur. I explained to Lucinda that she must not be disappointed if her cat did not win because there would be many others far more beautiful than Emily.

"Don't worry, Mummy," my little girl told me, "I am going to *will* the judges to give her the prize!" We entered Emily into the classes for Most Unusual Cat, Blue Peter and Best Kept Cat. When the day of the show arrived, we reached Olympia to see with dismay long entrance queues winding around the building. I had never seen so many cats before in one space and my respect for felines in general rose a thousand fold – here was a species of animal that, despite the fears they must have felt and all the indignities they went through, remained calm, unruffled and dignified throughout.

Lucinda leant forward on her chair, staring with gimlet eyes at all the judges who came round, *willing* them to give her cat a prize. She was only about seven years old, so I really do not know where she got the idea to try positive thought. Much to my surprise, though not to Lucinda's, Emily won first prize in two classes and came fourth in the Blue Peter section. I am quite sure that the power of Lucinda's mind *had* influenced the judges – so here was yet another lesson for me to learn, this time via my daughter.

Because we had Emily spayed, never giving her the opportunity for children, some time later we decided to get a 'proper' silver tabby from the original source and this time we got a beautiful kitten with the most wonderfully dotted coat. I named her Ermintrude, and in time she became pregnant. I was sure she would have the most gorgeous kittens, so was rather dismayed to have a dream in which I saw her with two very ugly babies with not a hint of silver. In my dream, I said in dismay, "Oh, Ermintrude, how could you!"

A few mornings later, I went to check on her to find she had given birth and was purring with motherly pride and delight at two ugly little kittens curled in her arms. They really were the ugliest I had ever seen. I could not help myself exclaiming, "Oh Ermintrude, how could you!" and then, with amusement, recalled my dream. The kittens should have been beautiful, yet despite all odds, the dream was accurate.

The kittens were soon scampering around, much loved and making us laugh at their antics. A friend was pleased to have one, naming him Louigi – because he looked like an Italian gangster. We kept the other one and called him Sidney. Because he had an enormous nose, my husband insisted on calling him Sidney Konk and the name stuck. Yet another dream had proved prophetic.

A SIMULTANEOUS DREAM WITH ANOTHER PERSON

I had another dream with a different format, which was most unusual. In my dream, a friend drove to my house in her Mini. I watched her from my window as she got out of the car and could see that she was terribly upset. She walked along the path looking totally anguished, her shoulders hunched in despair. I opened the door and, as soon as she had stumbled in, I enclosed her in my arms, rocking her with sympathy to ease her pain. Neither of us said a word, but it was clear that in her distress she gained comfort from me.

The next day when we met, she greeted me with, "Oh, I had an amazing dream about you last night. I dreamt my husband was having an affair and I was so desperately upset I got in the car and drove to your house. When I got out of the car, I could see you at the window, and when I reached the door you just opened it, took me in your arms and rocked me. I felt so comforted." I told her I'd had the same dream and was able to show her the notes I had written when I awoke. We were both amazed that we'd had the same dream, only differing from the situation of our own perspectives. As far as I know, the husband was not having an affair!

This is the only time I have had a simultaneous dream with another person, but it does illustrate how minds can link during sleep and dreaming times and reinforces my belief that telepathic contact is possible, especially during sleep when the mind is relaxed and can 'travel' easily.

★ ★ ★

AND YET MORE DREAMS

Train tumble

One night I saw a train crossing a high arched viaduct across a river. I saw the track split and carriages slowly tumble into the river below. Some carriages hung in the air. The dream did not last long but was certainly disturbing. I felt all the accompanying terror and upset usual in such dreams. I later saw the television report of the event – which had been in India. I also read a newsletter in a national newspaper from another person who had dreamt about the event, with the same feelings of anguish that I experienced.

★ ★ ★

Not only did I receive dreams of events contained in this world, I often had dreams of such unearthly, beautiful places, which I believed came from another level altogether. The colours were indescribably exquisite and the creativity I was shown not possible on this worldly plane.

An exquisite gown

In one dream, I saw a lady dressed in the most amazing robe. I was a good dressmaker myself at the time, designing and making my own creations, so that when I looked at the gown, I knew it would be impossible for it to be created in this world. I can only inadequately describe it as being covered in little bird feathers, each tinted with incredible pastel hues that we do not have in this world. Each tiny feather was embroidered with miniscule seed pearls. I looked hard and long at the beautiful design and realised the impossibility of making such work – I knew that without doubt I was scrutinising something that came from another world, another dimension. I also knew that however clever my sleeping mind might be, it was not capable of imagining that kind of artistry.

* * *

I had many other dreams where I visited beautiful places, with colours and designs, not workable here, that were 'other worldly'. I had no indication where they might be, but feel confident that after my demise I shall visit them. Death is no threat to me – it promises so much wonder.

The Tate Gallery

Just prior to my first visit to the Tate Gallery in London, I had some interesting dreams, one of which contained huge, shiny black ants that were scurrying at random on what appeared to be human bodies on an African plain.

Another dream was very odd and lengthy and seemingly profound. It incorporated time and different dimensions in a red and sterile world. Not a place I will want to visit again. The dream took place in a house devoid of furniture, but with some toys, and a fireplace was a key feature.

The third dream was also very peculiar and I can only describe its content as space and the universe with a moving mass of shapes and designs that I could only describe to myself as a cosmic copulation of shape and light matter.

When I visited the Tate Gallery, I did not like the modern art but was intrigued by the selection of Salvador Dali paintings. To my surprise, I noticed a large canvas displayed that was the epitome of my ant dream. My dream had been virtual reality while the picture was static, but it was nevertheless what I had seen in my dream, with the black ants being the main feature. I do not remember what the artwork was titled, but when I spoke about it to a curator, he told me that it had only been put in place the day before and not displayed previously.

I then noticed another painting that I was informed could not be hung in the past as it was considered pornographic. It was the static impression of the cosmic copulation I had dreamt of in moving form.

Finally, although I did not see the actual painting, the friend with whom I had attended the gallery purchased a postcard of Rene Magritte's painting entitled 'Time Transfixed', which made me shiver inwardly. It was the perfect illustration for my lengthy dream about time and dimensions, with a toy train steaming out of the fireplace.

How strange that I should dream obvious 'realities' of three different artists' works.

* * *

A SAD PROPHESY
1974

I met a poet from Norfolk who was visiting a mutual friend. He was very keen to have his hand read but I was unable to read his palm, being totally distracted by the words SUICIDE, SUICIDE, SUICIDE that filled my mind, obliterating all other thoughts. Shocked at this reaction, I had to pretend I was too tired to concentrate, merely telling him it was clear he had great creativity and to keep writing the poetry.

Later on when I was alone with my friend, I asked if the poet had ever attempted suicide and she told me that he had. I felt marginally better, believing I had picked up something from his past, not his future. However, I worried about him and eventually wrote him a letter, but he did not reply to it.

After a while, his sister contacted me to inform me that he had died. In fact, he had committed suicide. I felt devastated, especially as it was evident that I had been given foreknowledge of his intentions. For quite a long time I felt overcome with feelings of guilt. Maybe if I had queried any suicidal tendencies with my palm reading, I could have helped him. With hindsight, I concluded that had I been meant to help him, my guides would have shown me the way.

TIME TO MOVE

We were the first occupants of our newly built home in Kent, yet it always had an unwelcoming atmosphere on any return, even after a five-minute absence, though we seemed to breath a better feel into it which lasted for a while. Sometimes in the night, I would wake up with horror, feeling that some kind of presence was trying to suffocate me. I had difficulties keeping babysitters, because they were always frightened of 'ghosts' and did not want to return. The children often used to wake up terrified and, all in all, it was not a happy place. I had come to the conclusion that it could not be the building – being new and with no history – so it must be the site that was negative and bringing unwelcome reactions. We decided to move away to the Norfolk countryside where large old houses were very inexpensive in comparison to our small home, so the search was soon on.

We viewed a wonderful vicarage with a large garden that was due to be auctioned and the guide price was well within our means. We were so excited about it and waited for the auction with keen anticipation. However, before the sale date, I had yet another of my dreams. In this, I was at the auction room and the bidding was in progress. I was sitting next to a man and queried if this was the vicarage lot. He told me the vicarage was not for me, "But," he said, "this is your house". The dream changed and I found myself in a room that I thought must be a village hall or a type of 'tin tabernacle'. I was looking from the room through church or gothic-shaped windows and could see the bare branches of trees being covered in snow as it fell. On awakening, I told my husband I did not think we would get the vicarage but that we would find a house and be in it by the time it was snowing and then explained my dream. He was still of the opinion that I was no oracle but had mental problems, so did not take much notice of me but, as it transpired, the vicarage sold at a price way above the anticipated amount and well beyond what we could afford. The high price was unusual for Norfolk property at that time. We were terribly disappointed, but soon found another wonderful house with a shop, a second house and a chapel too, which was even more exciting than the vicarage. The scope was enormous. The chapel did not have the gothic windows I had seen in my dream but, knowing that sometimes dreams came in riddles, I knew that interpretations could be flexible, so became sure that this property was 'the one'.

A slump in the property market was by now taking place and the vendors were property developers in financial trouble, keen to get a return on their investment – so keen that they were willing to *exchange* the Norfolk property for our Kentish home – which we considered to be a miraculous bargain. This would mean, however, that we would have no money at all to restore the almost derelict properties and none to live on. We were taking a risk moving to Norfolk with no job prospects on the horizon, so while the extraordinary deal was so tempting, it was too much of a risk and we very reluctantly decided not to go ahead with such a wonderful offer. I was upset as well as worried that we might have made the wrong decision, bearing in mind the man who showed me 'my' house in the dream.

Searching through the property lists in a Norfolk paper, I spied another interesting old house and phoned the agents for particulars. "Oh, you don't want to see that," said the estate agent, "it's up a rough cart track away from other houses." I interrupted his tale of gloom. It sounded like just what we were looking for! The photograph showed an enchanting house with thick local carr-stone walls, gothic windows and a large garden.

When we viewed the property, I fell in love with the house and wanted it so much, dreading that we might lose it. We were lucky this time and everything fell into place.

TELEKINESIS

I had an antique glass-fronted cabinet in which I displayed some of my treasures. I kept it locked as the door was prone to swing open, but the key was always left in the lock.

When we were due to move to Norfolk, I was getting things packed and ready and had tried in vain to unlock the cabinet, but the key revolved without purchase. In a hurry to get everything done, I left the cabinet for a while and got on with other things, every now and again trying the key. Sometimes I would press on the wood panel near the lock, take the key out and try again, unsuccessfully. I jiggled, pushed and swore. Loath to break the glass, I kept trying at different times, feeling so frustrated that the key would not unlock the door, when I had a brainwave. I would try magic! Convinced it would work, I stood back and pointed my fingers at the lock, crying theatrically, "Open sesame," and watched in awe as both cabinet doors swung lazily open!

If I had been pushing on the doors, twiddling the key, or touching the cabinet in any way, the dodgy lock could have been triggered to click open, but no, I was standing well back. I can only assume that because I was certain that magic (or positive thinking) would work, then so it did.

This reminded me that my daughter, after her success with the judges at the cat show, used to concentrate her thoughts on making the light-shade rotate in her room. She told me that she just sat and 'willed' it to move. I do not know what gave her the idea.

★ ★ ★

Telekinesis: *The production of motion at a distance by willpower or thought alone.*

PART THREE

A NEW ADVENTURE

20th February 1975

On this cold, foggy day, we moved to the county of Norfolk. Tired of the hustle and bustle of life near London, my husband and I had opted for the real countryside. Property was cheap in such inaccessible corners and I was delighted to know my new home would be surrounded by fields and I would be able to feel at one with nature, especially as the best and happiest part of my childhood had been spent on my grandfather's farm in Kent and I had always wanted to emulate that kind of lifestyle.

We arrived at our new home in the late afternoon, just as dusk was falling: my husband, myself, two children, a dog, two cats and a kitten. We all shivered as we entered the large two-hundred-year-old house that was cold and very damp, having been empty for two years. It had not been modernised either, so the few commodities were less than basic. The previous owner had allowed us to bring in our furniture prior to completion of the purchase, so I had everything in place, beds made up and flowers on the table before we arrived, which made the final move a pleasure.

As I looked out of one of the gothic windows in the living room, I noticed that snow was beginning to fall – we had arrived just in time. I watched the white flakes quickly covering the ancient pear trees outside when suddenly the penny dropped. This was the view from my dream! This *was* the right house!

Because I had thought in my dream that I had been looking through a village or church hall window, I had expected our new home to be in an old church hall or something similar, so had not connected this house with the dream at all – in fact, in my excitement over the move, I had temporarily forgotten all about the dream and what the man at the auction had told me. I realised now that I had linked our future home, in my sleeping mind, with our local corrugated tin and wooden village hall in Kent that had gothic windows – just like the one I was now looking out of in our new home. In retrospect, the dream had not needed to be more explicit. How very extraordinary. I wondered who the man at the auction was who had informed me that this would be my home. It was good to know we had chosen the house '*they*' had arranged for us.

We immediately lit a fire which did very little to warm the room, but drew moisture from the walls and we could see our breaths puff in the cold air. Lots of creepy-crawlies came out from the wainscoting to greet us, but we were all so excited at our new adventure that the inconveniences were no problem.

As there were no cooking facilities in our new home, I used a camping stove which was adequate for sausages and baked beans, and by the time night had fallen we were tucking into our feast, laughing at our pets' keen investigation of their new domain and their attempts at terminating the insect invasion. It was so quiet and peaceful, isolated at the back of beyond at the end of a long, over-grown cart track with no close neighbours. I could not have been happier.

We were all very surprised to hear the sound of footsteps outside, crunching along the gravel path. Thinking that perhaps somebody had noticed our arrival – but whom? – and had come to check things out, we went to the door and became puzzled because there was nobody there. Nor could we see signs of footsteps in the snow. We did not feel uneasy, however, believing there would be a logical reason for what we had heard.

In the morning when we went outside to explore, we realised there were no gravel paths – although on close scrutiny it was evident that the grass paths had once been gravel that had long ago been pushed down into the soil. As we walked, our footsteps made no noise. We could only assume that the mystery footsteps we had heard the previous night came from an earlier age, when the gravel had been new and scrunchy. Because of the problems at our previous house, we knew how unpleasant a haunted house could feel, but this old place only felt comforting. We deduced that our visitor had been a friendly ghost, which was a pleasant thought and made our wonderful, rambling old house even more exciting.

I enjoyed every day that passed. All the rooms had fireplaces so, once we had fires merrily blazing away, the house warmed up and soon we were cosy. The house had been divided into three cottages over the years and we were living in the end one, with only two bedrooms, one sitting room, a dreadful kitchen that was tacked on and an ancient bathroom with lukewarm water. (The other two cottages attached only had earth closets in the back garden and no sinks, only taps outside!) We had great fun knocking through walls to the other two cottages, getting the house back to what it used to be. I loved it all.

Quite a few times when I was in the house on my own, I could hear the sound of children's laughter coming from the dining room although my children were at school. When one of the locals told me that the house had once been used as a school, I understood why. Happy ghost children.

One night, I was awoken by the sound of booted feet walking across the bedroom floor. My son, then aged nine, was going through a stage of sleep walking and I was worried that he might fall down the rickety curved staircase in his sleep, so I rushed through the interconnecting bedrooms to see whether or not he was in bed.

Both children were fast asleep, as was my husband. It seemed like we had another ghost, or perhaps the same one as before, and again, I felt no fear. I got the impression that the boots had belonged to a soldier. At a later date the neighbouring farmer told me the house had been used by the military at a different time to the school, so maybe my intuition had been correct. I was pleased about our friendly visitors for never did the house have anything but a happy atmosphere.

On another occasion, I was about to open the bathroom door while the family was in the garden, so when I heard the clink of china, then water being poured into a basin in the bathroom, I thought that maybe I was hearing a ghost again. Hoping to see it, I opened the door quickly, but nobody was in sight. I immediately checked the basin and the bath but everything was completely dry.

The sound I had heard reminded me of water being poured from an old-fashioned china water jug into a matching round washbowl, like my granny had used for washing herself in days gone by. It had been set out on a marble-topped cabinet long before plumbing and bathrooms were installed. I am convinced the sound I heard was from a bygone age. I found it really comforting to know that the shades of past occupants who had lived in the house were still around, keeping an eye on us.

As we were knocking the house around, it crossed my mind that the activity might have 'woken up' our ghostly occupants and that they were probably having a look at what we were up to. I felt that they were pleased with what we were doing.

As we got to know more people in the village, we were told that it was common knowledge that our house was indeed haunted by friendly ghosts. Quite often, the children felt cats jump up on their beds and knead the blankets over their legs, but when they looked there were no cats in sight.

The house was undoubtedly haunted but we were never frightened, nor were there ever drops in the temperature – the house always felt warm and loved. Interestingly, it was very close to a ley line, so maybe that made it more attractive to those from other dimensions.

A BABY IN AMERICA
MAY 1975

I had a very dear American friend whom I had not seen for a long while, but one night, when I was asleep, we met far out in the universe. I was so delighted to see him and we talked excitedly, catching up with news, so pleased to be in each other's company. When I awoke, the reality and euphoria of our meeting was still with me but, alas, I could not recall anything of our conversation. All I could remember was that his wife was pregnant. I knew that this had not been a dream – our meeting was an actuality – whether it was our minds meeting or our non-physical bodies I do not know. I just know that this time it was not a dream.

I immediately wrote to him, asking if his wife was, in fact, expecting a baby, and in his return letter he replied that sadly, no, she was not.

Rather than feeling embarrassed that I had made a mistake, I wrote by return to tell him that if I had dreamt it, then it must be true. If it were not, I promised I would burn my pointy hat!

It was not long before I received another letter from him. After an appointment with their doctor, it was conclusive that his wife *was* pregnant. I had been the first to know, and across all those thousands of miles! The baby was born in December.

After experiencing that dream, I came to the realisation that in our sleeping states, other than receiving dreams, it is possible for our non-physical selves to meet up with living people to converse and receive knowledge and that to travel distance is no problem. I also realised that it is possible during sleep to meet with friends, relatives and even pets who had 'passed over' and that one could travel to places other than the world we currently live in – or more accurately, on.[2]

★ ★ ★

FACES IN THE MIRROR – SCRYING

During my childhood, I had sometimes seen other faces superimposed over my own when I looked in the mirror. I asked my father why I saw them and he vaguely told me he did not know and that perhaps it was best not to look at them any more, so I took the magician's advice. The last time I saw them was

---

[2] *When compiling this book, I realised that nowadays hospital scans precede the need for an oracle's prediction!*

when I was about twelve – I have no recall of any other psychic activities before that age, other than nasty hob-goblins' high-pitched mischievous voices around me when I was ill. When I tried to hear what they were saying, they stopped.

I did not see the faces again until about thirty years later when I was in my new Norfolk home. This time I was too curious to ignore them, so watched to see what happened. There were so many different faces, one after the other. I felt deliciously relaxed and fell into a trance state, my head rotating, clicking away all the stresses of the day. The faces looked back at me, changing every few seconds. Some were quite Neanderthal, then changed to fairground people, then Gypsies – both men and women. Then came the proud Native American braves. After them would be the elders of the tribes, both men and women – all with inscrutable faces.

Whenever I saw the faces in the mirror, they were always in the same sequence, but there was one Indian brave who stayed the longest. He looked like a warrior and was very compelling.

I did not know why I was seeing all these people. Were they my ancestors? Were they myself in past lives? Maybe they were my guides, or perhaps a mixture of all three? I expected some kind of message from them, but never received any.

Scrying: Mirror gazing or scrying is one of the oldest known forms of divination, which involves prolonged gazing into a mirror, a crystal, a pool of water or even fire, in order to obtain visions. The famous seer, Nostradamus, was said to have favoured this method, using ink as a medium. Alternative spelling, skrying.

★ ★ ★

THE BORROWERS

I have never been a tidy housewife. Because of my sense of creativity, I have always had attractive homes, able to make silk purses out of sows' ears, and all on a shoestring. I found it easy to make any house cosy and attractive, with a scarf thrown here, artfully arranged items there and a sense of colour and co-ordination. I think I can safely say I was the original 'house doctor' and 'changing rooms' lady! Because of my various creative hobbies, as well as my love of gardening, housework frustrated me, wasting time that could be better spent, so not only did I infuriate my husband, I also mislaid a lot of things in my efforts to scoop clutter away as I attempted to appease my spouse and bring some order to the chaos.

THE MAGICIAN'S DAUGHTER

The mislaid items always turned up in the end, but I was often left to wonder if some of the lost things had been whisked away by unseen hands and had nothing to do with my untidiness. When something mysteriously disappeared, I ceased searching, knowing that it would eventually reappear. I blithely told my family that missing items had merely been 'borrowed' and were being used by the fairies. Just for the record, I had not known about the book 'The Borrowers'.

I owned a really beautiful inexpensive ring that I adored. It had a silver oval surround with a central stone that looked as if it were made from a fairy's wing, coloured delicately with pinks, blues and purples. Because I loved it so much, I seldom wore it because I was always working at grubby jobs – gardening, candle making, tending the horse, goats, chickens and sheep, so preferred to keep the ring safe in its box in my dressing table. One day I was going somewhere nice, so had dressed myself up and decided to wear the lovely ring. I opened the box to discover it was missing. I knew that neither of my children would have taken it, it was not their kind of thing, and they confirmed they had not been near it. I assumed that it had been 'borrowed' by one of our unseen visitors.

For the next three years I checked on the box, still in its drawer in my dressing table, to see if the ring had returned, but the box was always empty. I guessed it would return eventually and, sure enough, on the fourth year when I looked, there was my beautiful ring, nestling innocently in its cotton wool as if it had been there all the time. I wondered where it had been and who had worn it during its absence.

A similar thing happened, if you recall, when the mystery book appeared in my hand at the time I was writing about my retrocognitive dream of a deserted airfield. I wonder how objects can arrive and disappear through the ether.

★ ★ ★

OF PETS

The only one who was not enchanted by our new home was Emily, Lucinda's prize-winning cat, who, with the arrival of Ermintrude's babies, was now called Auntie Em. She hated the new house and refused to come out from under an antique organ, seemingly set to stay there until the day she died. I had hoped she would get over her dislike in time. Ermintrude and Sidney Konk, however, loved their new home and had explored all the cobwebby corners with great delight. Eventually, in the warmer weather, Emily grumpily came out of her hiding place under the organ, promptly packed her bags, shot out of the door into the garden and left home.

112

I had been warned by one of the local people to put collars on our cats. She informed us that there were trigger-happy gamekeepers around who shot any ferals, but if they saw a cat with a collar, would hopefully realise it was a pet and hold their fire. All our cats, therefore, wore posh collars. We were devastated that Emily had gone and mourned her loss, but thought she could survive in the fields around us and, by wearing her collar, be safe from the gamekeeper's gun.

Six months later, she was outside on the kitchen windowsill, meowing to be let in. As I delightedly opened the window, she came in chirruping her greetings and rubbing her face against mine – but with her came a terrible odour. I noticed that the collar was still around her neck, but one of her front legs had somehow got looped through it. The collar had chafed through to the bone and the flesh had putrefied. It seemed that Emily had come home for some first aid. She stayed home while the wound healed. I decided to keep the collar off in case she left home again and got into the same difficulties. One evening, Em 'told me' she would be going the next day. I just knew. In the morning, she was gone. I was saddened, but pleased to realise that telepathy had been at work and she had been able to communicate with me. She had shown that she could look after herself well and would come home if necessary. I realised that Emily, a 'mere cat', had been able to consciously decide to return for help when she needed it. I had not realised that animals were capable of cognitive thought, which gave me much food for thought.

We did not see Emily for another three years – her return is related later on.

Our dog, Pansy, thrilled to have so much land to dig in, came back with a tiny baby rabbit from one of her excavations. We had no idea where the burrow was so, finding the little creature was still alive, resolved to rear it. It was still blind, so only a few days old. I wrapped it in cotton wool and put it in a grass-filled box in the airing cupboard, and took the children into town to try and find a small bottle. We ended up with just the right thing – a toy bottle with a teat small enough for the bunny, whom we named, unimaginatively, Benjamin.

Benjamin was fed two-hourly day and night and survived. He became a loved member of the family, having lovely games with the cats and the dog. I had not realised that rabbits like to play too and was surprised at how high he could jump when he wanted to. When he was old enough to go outside, we made a nice pen for him from which he eventually burrowed out to freedom. I worried that he might not make it in the outside world and even beseeched the gamekeeper and other men that roamed the tracks with guns to call out 'Is that you Benjamin?" before they shot a rabbit. They just looked at me as if I were mad, of course. I think we all learned a lot from that little rabbit.

Another call from the wild came when somebody asked us to look after a kestrel that had been found very poorly. We had to get permission from the Birds of Prey Trust, and were given information about how to look after it and where to get its food – which consisted of dead chicks!

We got bags of culled fluffy yellow chicks from chicken breeders who did not want the cockerels. We put them in containers in the freezer. As my son had agreed to take over the rearing of the kestrel, he was in charge, but every now and again I would pick up a bowl only to find a chick defrosting in it. It was most offputting!

Leigh taught the kestrel to fly to the lure – a morsel of chick on his gauntlet. He did really well with the bird and when he went down to the village, it would sit on the handlebars of his bike. Eventually, it flew off into the wild too, so another good job done and a lot learned from our point of view.

THE MAFIA KING

Meanwhile, Sidney Konk had reached puberty. He was a handsomely marked feline but his nose was more pronounced than ever. He spent his days sitting on the porch of the dog kennel, and we wove stories around him – as we did with all our animals, their varying personalities making it easy to dream-up human-like occupations.

We realised that Sidney was, like his brother Louigi, a Mafia member. To begin with, he acquired – in our fantasy – a white hat with a black band and wore it slanted across one eye. He sent his mother off to earn money for his cigarettes and growing wardrobe – she seemed quite happy to oblige, meeting many a tabby ploughman in quiet corners of the garden. Soon, Konk (as we now called him) had the complete outfit – a black and white pinstriped suit, black shirt, white kipper tie and two-toned black and white brogues. When not paring his claws, he would lean against the kennel, practicing dexterity with his flick knife. He was getting very objectionable, fighting with the other cats – by now Ermintrude had produced more kittens and the friendly cats from the farm next door had decided our house was cosier than their barn. We decided that we must have poor Konk neutered because he was not a nice fellow.

The effect on his personality was instantaneous. Whilst anaesthetised he must have 'seen the light', for once he was home again he was a changed personality. We wove a fantasy story about him, deciding that he had been converted. We decided that he must have cast aside his Mafia connections and joined the Salvation Army in the village, and that he had donated his Mafia suit to a charity shop. We elaborated further, that he practiced the drums for hours on end and was soon playing in their band at every charitable occasion and, when off duty, he spent hours polishing his new boots and Salvation Army buttons. Konk was totally transformed.

Over time, our imagination went overboard and his story was told to anybody who would listen. One local lady asked us, "Did you name him after Konk Doddman who used to be the drummer in the village Salvation Army Band?"

What kind of coincidence is that? We had no idea of the drummer's name – apparently he was nicknamed 'Konk' because of his nose, the same as our cat.

One day, we were at the pub with friends, telling them about Konk and his Mafia suit. Going into full descriptive detail, we explained about the striped suit, the kipper tie, the black shirt, the hat, etc. when suddenly into the pub walked a young man wearing the identical outfit!

We could not believe what we were seeing. It was unusual enough to see a man dressed like that in a country pub off the beaten track that normally catered for the local farm workers, but just when we were telling our story? After the man had left, we allowed our giggles to surface and wondered whether he had got his suit from the same charity shop where Konk had donated his!

What were the odds of a fellow turning up dressed like that, or even the real Salvation Army drummer being nicknamed Konk? Far more than a thousand to one.

★ ★ ★

THE MATERNITY WARD

One of Ermintrude's later offspring, called Petal, was heavily pregnant and my son, Leigh, decided to make a maternity ward for her. He taped a number of cardboard boxes together, cutting out lots of flaps operated by string so that the 'windows' could be used as vantage points. It was an elaborate structure, taking him quite some time to make. The cat sat by his side, watching keenly as he worked. When the contraption was eventually completed, using a thick felt pen, he inked the words Petal's Kitten Producing Factory. He had put such a lot of work into this structure and I did not want him to be disappointed if the cat did not use it, so gently told him not to be upset if she did not want to go inside. However, no sooner was the full stop in place, the lad said "In you go, Petal." The cat immediately squeezed through the 'door', purring loudly. I had no idea the birth was imminent, but after she had a good look around her maternity ward she made herself comfortable and proceeded forthwith to produce her kittens. Thanks to this ingenious invention, we were able to view the birth through the various windows that opened with the strings.

I was struck by the realisation that Petal knew telepathically that my son was constructing her a nice place to birth her babies. I seemed to be learning a lot about animals in this lovely home of ours.

Leigh grew up proving to have amazing powers with animals, becoming a horse and dog 'whisperer', though it was not so much whispering that did the trick, but telepathic communication.

★ ★ ★

A DOG CHOSEN FOR ME

We already had a dog, but a friend in the village was keen to find homes for a litter of pups that her collie had just given birth to. As I had so much room and so many animals, I thought another one would not make much difference, so earmarked one of the pups as my own and asked her to keep it for me until they were ready to leave their mum. That night, in my sleep, a voice clearly told me to "Take the puppy with the most white. She will be devoted to you."

In the morning, I returned to the owner of the pups and told her I had changed my mind. There was one puppy that was mostly white with a few black markings, so I said I would have her instead. When she was old enough to come to us, I named her Daisy.

My husband was annoyed that I had brought home another dog and warned me that if the 'thing' made a peep that night it would have to go back. I woke in the night to hear the puppy whimpering in the darkness downstairs, frightened to be in a strange place away from her mother and siblings, so I crept downstairs and slept on the sofa cuddling her in my arms. She never made another sound at night after that and she was, indeed, devoted to me like the man in my dream had told me. She followed me everywhere, was overcome with joy if I singled her out for special treatment, and when I went out, she would sit in the drive waiting for me until I returned.

During these intervening years, I was enjoying life in our lovely old home. The garden was large and we had lots of animals. While I still had occasional precognitive dreams, they were mainly about women in the village who I foretold were pregnant, or dreams about the kittens' colours before they were born. I no longer had disaster dreams at all. It seemed that my lessons about dreams were over and I was learning about animals instead.

My husband, unable to find work in the area, had gone back to London during the week, returning only at the weekends, so I learned to be quite independent for the first time in my life – wives of my era were expected to obey their husbands and do as they were told – but I now enjoyed running the house on my own, knocking down walls when I felt like it, opening up old fire-places, splitting logs with an axe, gathering kindling from the wood, collecting eggs from the hen-run and digging up vegetables from the garden and running my life without orders and interference to my plans. In other words, making my own decisions. As far as my marriage was concerned, I have to say it was the beginning of the slippery slope to my complete independence.

★ ★ ★

ANECDOTES OF POULTRY
AND OTHER PETS

The following anecdotes about pets and poultry are not all paranormal, but I wanted to include them because of my realisation that birds and animals are grossly underestimated. Through my observations, I realised that they are just as sentient as we are and we should not disregard their rights and feelings. In retrospect, I realise that part of my spiritual tuition was to observe animals and recognise their paramount importance in the balance of things, so these insights are as important to my story as the supernatural experiences.

Our neighbouring farmer friend, when realising that I wanted some chickens, presented me with a black hen and her newly hatched chicks. I was absolutely delighted and we all felt obligated to name them Henny Penny, Chicken Licken and, of course, Cocky Locky. This small family soon multiplied and it became clear that we could not keep more than one cockerel, for once they reached maturity, there were horrible fights for the position of Guv'nor. I found a kind home for Cocky Locky and kept a beautiful tawny cockerel for the hens. We named him Gregory Peck and his magnificent tail plumes glinted in the sunshine with purple and green hues. The ruffles around his neck were blue-black and tawny and he was absolutely wonderful to behold. He thought so too, as he greeted the dawn with doodles under our window, while his harem busied themselves amongst the flowerbeds, clucking and cooing under his watchful eyes.

Strange guinea fowl from a neighbouring farmer would sit on our boundary wall. They had grey feathers dotted with white speckles and elongated humped bodies that looked rather like dowagers' bustles. Their calls were squawkish and harsh, but I liked to see them preening disdainfully at the edge of their territory.

My farmer friend said he would wring the neck of a third and brutish cockerel causing havoc in the hen house. He fought, pillaged and raped and had to go, but I wished I had not named him because it now seemed like we were about to commit a murder, but as I wanted to be as self-sufficient as possible, he was designated for the table and would be healthy meat that we had reared ourselves.

The deed was done outside the hen run, very neatly and efficiently, and I was left with the handsome corpse hung ignominiously on an apple branch, its feet tied with baling twine, waiting for me to begin plucking. With firmness in my breast, I plucked tentatively at the plumage, not liking the feel of his still-warm body, nor wanting to wrench out his beautiful feathers. However, I was bold and tended to my gory task.

Used as I was to the tender cluckings and murmurings of my little brood, I was soon aware of how horribly quiet the hen roost had become. Turning my head to view them, I realised that they were in shock. They were hunched and wretched after having witnessed the killing of one of their own, albeit a bully, and I had the insensitivity to dangle the corpse in front of them while plucking out his feathers! I had not realised that poultry had feelings or understood slaughter!

I removed the body and took it elsewhere to finish plucking and remove its insides. I did not enjoy the task, nor did any of us want to eat it. I thrust it to the back of the fridge and eventually made a curry from the corpse. My children were decidedly pale as I placed their meal in front of them. Even my husband looked miserable. I looked at the heap on my plate and thought, 'I knew you.' Pictures in my mind showed him crowing high on the wall at the back of the garden, flapping his wings in the sun. We all pushed our meal around on our plates. None of us ate it – it was too much like cannibalism – the dogs had no such sensitivities and licked their lips clean afterwards while we had baked beans on toast instead. So much for self-sufficiency!

After realising the emotions in the hen run, I watched them more closely as they wandered around the garden and soon noticed that they had a clear daily routine, with various resting places at set times. There were favoured branches to roost on at around noon, after which, if the weather was dry, it would be time for a communal dust bath. This consisted of scratching a shallow pit in dry earth and nestling down into it, flinging dust backwards into their feathers, then having a good shake around. This cleaned them up and presumably got rid of any mites.

Gentle clucks would accompany their perambulations, but quite often either Burlington Bertie or Gregory Peck, the two new contesters to the throne, would stretch their necks and crow. The cockerels had favourite wives and if they found a large juicy worm, they would call their spouse over with a special proud crow and the favoured lady would rush to collect the gift. The cock would watch as his beloved swallowed the worm, flapping his wings proudly then stand on tippy-toes to crow once more. It was clear that they were fond of each other. It was also clear that there was a 'pecking order', where all bullied the weakest hen.

I discovered that the tawny cockerels were gentlemen and I did not need to despatch either of them. They each had their own harem and did not deem it necessary to fight to the kill or to squabble for territories. It was, strangely, only white cockerels, after reaching maturity that caused problems.

One day I found Gregory Peck in the broody hens' run with his head hung low, his demeanour dejected, his wings drooping – he had clearly been vanquished by one of the white bully-boys and had gone to hide his shame. Whitey had taken Gregory's place and was busy raping his wives and their screeches were horrible to hear. Dissent ruled that afternoon and none but the white cock was happy.

I scooped Gregory up in my arms and took him with me to the flower garden and sat him beside me as I soaked up the sun on the lounger. I crooned to a now dull-coated Gregory and told him that he must go back and regain his wives and his position. After a little while, he seemed to understand me and his dejection left him. He began to strut around looking handsome and his feathers shone once more. He crowed a few times and decided to go back and sort out the usurper and, in next to no time, he was soon ruler of his harem again. Sid, the farmer, despatched the white rapist the next day and peace reigned once more in the hen run. Maybe Gregory Peck would have sorted out his problem without me having a gentle word with him, but I am quite sure that telepathically he picked up my advice. The change from abject misery to confidence was profound.

★ ★ ★

When a hen became broody, the other hens would lay eggs for her and she would sit until they hatched. Sometimes, more than one hen was broody, so we would end up with a lot of darling fluffy chicks. Mostly, the hens sat until all the eggs hatched, but as they had been laid at different times, some would be abandoned. On one occasion, three broody hens were crouched over clusters of eggs in the 'brooding bay'. They turned the eggs regularly with their beaks but would not move from the nests, knowing the embryos would die from lack of warmth if they did. However, one of the eggs cracked open and little Abigail emerged, cheeping. All three hens immediately claimed motherhood and abandoned the other eggs. Thereafter, Abigail had three mothers accompanying her across the lawns, each peck-peck-pecking the ground in front of them to show her how to look for her own food, each finding tasty worms and other delicacies for their spoiled charge. Abigail was so loved and cherished by the three hens, each vying to be the best mother ever!

Sometimes the shell of a 'ready' embryo was too tough for the chick to peck its way out. The puzzled mother abandoned such an egg, getting on with rearing the other chicks. If I noticed such a one, I would take the egg indoors to carefully peel away the shell and put the damp cold chick into a warm oven to warm up. The chicks looked quite horrible until their downy feathers dried out. This was a worrying procedure, as I did not want to cook the poor little creatures, but it was wonderful when they revived, got fluffed up, on their feet and cheeping – true 'oven ready' chicks! I would then take the newly revived chick to the hen run to slip it under the mother's bustle when she was not looking so that it was soon integrated into the clutch.

I was surprised to notice how proud the cockerels were when the chicks were hatched. In fact, all the poultry were interested in new births. They would rush over to view the babies, the cocks crowing with delight, flapping their wings, chests stuck out, then proceed to peck the ground in front of their children, to show them how to fend for themselves. The mother hens – who had already been training the chicks – would watch indulgently while the fathers tried their bit of domesticity and then, after the initial excitement was over, go back to teaching their children in a far more peaceful manner.

It was the same when an egg was laid. After the initial 'ouch' of an egg being laid and the consequent squawk of achievement, all the members of the hen roost would cluck in celebration. Leigh, chief minder of the hen run, would call out to me, "There's another egg done!"

One mother, a black hen of diminutive proportions, successfully raised a large brood and perambulated around the garden with her chicks whistling and peeping as they followed her. Every now and again she would nestle down on her haunches spreading her wings so that all the chicks could run underneath her and warm up – essential for them to stay alive – little heads would poke up from her feathers where they were resting all over her body, a lovely sight to behold. While the chicks were little she could easily accommodate her charges, but as they got larger she had a job to cover them all. By the time they had reached the 'punk' stage – scraggy necks, big boots and daft hairdos – it was not necessary for them to be kept warm, but they just loved their mum and her comfort.

One night, a furious storm blew up with terrible thunder, lightening and lashing rain, the gales bending trees over. Alarmed, I rushed outside to make sure the animals were safe. I searched for the little black hen and burst into tears when I saw her. She was battling the storm bravely with her wings spread out encompassing her teenage yobs and looking like a safe black umbrella. I managed to scoop them all up and got them into safety, wondering at the tenacity of that little mother protecting her large brood of almost grown children.

* * *

Our dog, Sambolina, was a lean-waisted lurcher, with slender legs and pointy paws, a mistress of guile and innocent surprise when caught with a pheasant feather stuck to her lip, and always as shiny as a freshly-dropped conker. I was amazed when my son told me she could count. He had found that when he asked her how many fingers he was holding out to her, she would bark the appropriate number. Without fail, when asked a number, she was always correct with her counting.

One day when I was sunbathing, hidden amongst the wild garden's cow parsley, I noticed Sam 'dancing' on the lawn with a plimsoll. As she pirouetted and twirled, she tossed the shoe into the air and caught it, all choreographed into a graceful ballet dance. Intrigued, I watched her dancing for some time, but as I moved to see her better, I knelt on a twig and she realised I was there. Thereafter, she acted like a dog playing with a shoe and the magic dance was done. The secret life of a dog? A dog that can dance ballet? Hmmm.

Because she poached the local lord's pheasants, the police had warned us that if she were caught again, she would be shot. At great expense, we erected a six-foot high fence to contain her, only to watch her sail effortlessly over it as soon as the last nail was hammered in. We realised we would have to find her another home before the gamekeeper's gun got her and luckily found someone willing to have her. We were heartbroken when she went.

Unfortunately, after a couple of weeks, the new owner was not happy with Sambolina, so I drove over to collect her. I barely recognised her, she seemed so dispirited and, instead of shining, her coat was dull. As soon as she recognised me, she was so happy her coat returned to its normal glossy shine in moments.

We had to find her another owner, knowing that we could not contain this cunning little rogue at home for long and that she could become gamekeeper target practice.

My husband knew an astrologer in Sussex who was willing to take her on. I had not met the lady and as I was driving towards Sam's new home, made a vow that if Sambolina did not take to her, I would bring the dog back home again. Luckily, it was love at first sight for both of them and Sambolina trotted indoors behind her new owner with never a backward glance for me, to live happily with her for a good few years. I have to say that her wayward ways did not improve and that a few Sussex sheep were traumatised. No doubt she found them far more entertaining than mere pheasants. Unfortunately, she went too far and was eventually shot for sheep killing.

So, my lesson learned from that little dog? That a dog can dance gracefully, away from human eyes. That when unhappy, a dog's coat will go dull but can immediately shine with happiness. That a dog will behave impeccably in the house but, if allowed to roam, will revert to their basic nature as a hunter and killer and, having once made a kill, will continue to do so. That some dogs can count. And lie!

★ ★ ★

EMILY RETURNS

Three years had passed by since our cat Emily disappeared, when the children told me that they thought they had seen her in a sheep field along the track nearby. I was friendly with the shepherd and had asked him to keep his eyes open for the cat, although I thought it unlikely it was Emily after all that time. I thought by now that the gamekeeper would have shot her. On my daughter's birthday (how could timing be better orchestrated?), the old shepherd came rushing to our door – "I've found your cat's home in my field – I'll take you to it!" Armed with a cat basket, a bottle of milk and a cat bowl, we excitedly trekked along the cart track to the sheep field. In front of a pile of wood sat a wild cat, hissing at us with its ears laid back – we were not sure at first whether it was Emily or not. I called out, "Emily?" and her ears pricked up. I then banged the bowl gently on the milk jug and Emily – for it was her – came rushing towards us. She had recognised us after all that time! Three years is a long time out of a cat's life and I was surprised she remembered us. What a wonderful birthday present for my daughter.

Emily did not demur as I put her into the basket. Her purrs nearly choked her as we took her home, and this time she was pleased to stay. The house, by now, must have taken on the homely smells she recognised instead of the alien smells of a dank and ancient house and it was clear that she now felt at home. Unfortunately, however, she was not well and needed veterinary treatment. She lived happily enough with us for another year and then, sadly, was run over.

It was wonderful to have a happy Emily back home with us. I think she had wanted to return home because she was ill and knew we could make her better, but because there were a lot more cats both at our home and in the barn next door, about twenty in all, they had made their territories and would not let her through. She had camped-out on the edge of the territory in the sheep field hoping to see us again, and so she did. That the reunion came on my daughter's birthday, I am sure, was no 'coincidence'.

★ ★ ★

ANOTHER NEAR-DEATH EXPERIENCE

I discovered that there were a lot of tetanus deaths in Norfolk. As I was always gardening and dealing with animals, I thought it would be prudent to have a tetanus jab, as I did not want to die in agony with 'lock jaw' – as it used to be known.

I had the jab, not even wondering whether there might be some after-effects, so became very alarmed when I had a lot of strange symptoms that evening. My hands began to hurt and the fingers curled inwards, and my jaw began to feel stiff and my tongue felt weird. I could not eat or drink, it was that bad. After phoning the hospital, I was told that some people were affected by such jabs but given no advice or assurances that the symptoms would pass.

It got worse during the night and I believed I was actually dying of lockjaw, so crept downstairs so my husband did not wake to find me cold and dead beside him in the morning. I lay on a satin-covered couch waiting for the grim reaper, with the fresh night air wafting cool breezes on my fevered brow, and thought of all the things I had intended to do with my life. What time I had wasted! Those books I had intended to write – all those things I planned to do 'one day'. I was so annoyed with myself, realising how I had allowed precious time to slip by without productive use. I do not recall being frightened – I had already had one brush with death which had been so cosy and inviting – but it was the lost opportunities to put my talents to use that upset me so much.

Kitty Purr, one of the farmer's cats who preferred our house to the barn, jumped softly through the window and carefully laid a dead mouse on my breast. Oh no, I thought despairingly to myself, even Purr realises I am dying and, sweet puss, has brought me a parting gift. She settled down on my chest, determined to keep vigil until the life was taken from me. I lay in the moonlit room, a dead mouse and a purring cat upon my person until dawn was announced with loud crowing outside the window from our cockerel, Gregory Peck. I was relieved to realise that my symptoms had disappeared and I was still alive.

Maybe I had been theatrical believing my mortal coil was at an end – and I really had – but a very clear lesson had been learned. From that day on, I made sure that I made the most of my talents and packed as much into each day as possible. I no longer assumed that I had all the time in the world to do the things I wanted to do. It is surprising what a lot can be done in a day and the feeling of fulfilment is heady.

★ ★ ★

THE HEALING OF DORIAN GREY

Although I already had a lot of cats – and received so much love and fun from them all – a friend was keen to find homes for some of her farm kittens, so I said I would have one. I chose a little black one – we named him Dudley – and put him into the basket to transport him, but before I could close the lid, a small grey kitty climbed in with a very determined manner and began to purr loudly. He clearly indicated his intention to come home with me, so I thought, Oh well, one more won't make any difference and, being a great believer in animals choosing you, rather than the other way round, took him home as well. I named him Dorian Grey.

Dorian must have been incubating cat flu and diarrhoea before coming to us because within a day he was very ill and in no time became a bag of skin and bones. I called in the vet who told me that the kitten should be put down, but I did not want that, for despite being so ill, little Dorian had not stopped purring and I thought that while he so clearly wanted to live, then he should be given the chance.

I phoned a friend, Carol, who was a psychic and spiritual healer, to ask her to come and perform a miracle on Dorian. She told me she was not going to because her guide was saying that I must do the healing myself. I was very annoyed because I was not a healer, and this little kitten was desperately ill and dying. This was no time to mess around. Carol was very firm and told me that I must do it. Still annoyed, but with resignation, I asked her what I was supposed to do.

Carol told me, "Say a prayer to whoever is important to you – it doesn't matter whether it is God, Jesus, Buddha – whoever you want. Ask your healing guide to help you. He will be there and my healing guide will be with you as well. Then lay your hands on the kitten. The rest will be done for you."

I asked Carol what happened when she did healing. She told me that first she placed her hands on the patient, then, when her hands became hot, she would know that healing energy was coming through.

After our telephone conversation ended, I was full of doubts and still annoyed that Carol would not come over. However, I had my instructions and, quite frankly, anything was worth trying. I brought the skeletal kitten into the kitchen and gently placed him on the floor where, weak though he was, he purred like fury. Looking at the ceiling and feeling very silly, I spoke politely. "Excuse me God and Jesus and my healing guide, but my kitten is very ill." I pointed at the kitten. "Please will you make him better?" I thought what a fool I must look, talking to the ceiling, and hoped nobody would look through the window.

To my dismay, I immediately felt myself go into a trance and my hands, of their own volition, started a downward descent towards the kitten. I was quite frightened because I was not in control and did not like the feeling. I tried to pull my hands away without success. They continued their downward journey and I had to bend over a little.

I then noticed a golden glow all round the kitten's body, shining brightly and pulsating with energy. It was tight to his body, about a quarter of an inch in depth. Although I was scared at what was happening, I thought that the golden glow must be his aura and a good indication of a strong spark of life force.

My hands stopped moving before I touched the kitten and came to rest on the golden glow. I tried to force my hands further but could not budge them. Instead of feeling my hands go hot, like Carol had explained, I could feel them going icy cold. Oh no, I thought, I've got the Devil instead! I should never have called the kitten Dorian Grey! I panicked and tried to pull my hands away, but it was impossible. Then reason intervened. I had called on God and my healing guide, and Carol's healing guide had arranged the healing session, so no demons would be involved. I calmed down and became interested in what was happening.

After a little while, I came out of the trance and was in control of my hands again. The little kitten was still purring happily and, as I picked him up to cuddle him, I felt sure he would recover – and of course he did. I no longer wanted Oscar Wilde's choice of name for someone who had dealings with the Devil, so the kitten's name was changed to Sparky because he so gamely clung on to his last spark of life. Sparky grew into a contrary, intelligent, humorous cat, living to a ripe old age – and if Rory had been my first 'familiar', then Sparky became the second!

Despite this amazing experience, I had no expectations of becoming a healer, nor did I wish to be one. I thought that this was just a 'one off' and part of what seemed to be another experience of the paranormal from my guides.

Little did I know then, however, that my guides intended that I would become a healer in later years, and that they would orchestrate an introduction to Reiki, Seichem and Spiritual Healing in an amazing manner.

* * *

A GOAT NAMED LELA

Our friendly farmer presented us with a hermaphrodite kid as he had no use for it. It was so cute and gave us hours of fun with its antics. We named it Lela. However, as it reached maturity, I realised that its lack of sexual gender was giving it psychological problems. For instance, my son used a sack of straw hanging from a tree for target practice with his bow and arrows, which unfortunately, the goat fell in love with. I noticed the confused creature trying to mount the sack like a billy but, having no luck with its amorous intentions, turned round to proffer itself as a female goat would. I was concerned about this, for the goat's personality had changed from that of a carefree kid into a depressed goat.

I wondered if I should call in the vet and have the poor creature put down, but was loath to take that step.

One night was particularly cold with a very heavy frost. The ground was iron hard and, when I went out to feed the animals in the morning, to my dismay I found that Lela the goat, instead of being curled up in the warmth of her pen, was lying outside almost frozen to death. I ran to find blankets, rolled her onto one and dragged her inside her pen. I covered her with more blankets and filled hot water bottles to warm her up. I did not think she would survive but I had to try. I sat in the straw with her head in my lap and she seemed to gain comfort from my crooning. I tempted her with branches of ivy but she was too ill to care. To my astonishment, all my cats and the farm cats from the barn next door congregated in the shed with me. They seemed to understand what I was trying to do and carefully climbed on top and around the goat, lending their warmth. I knew that they were not doing this to get warm themselves because the goat was freezing cold. As all the animals were friends with each other, I knew that they were offering her what they could. She seemed to gain comfort from us all being with her, took a last shuddering breath and then died.

There had been absolutely no need for that goat to lie down all night in the freezing cold yard. I felt sure that she had decided to end her life.

After this sad death, the farmer gave us Lela's mother, who was so old that she was no use to him either, but he thought we might like her "to keep the stingers down". She was very cantankerous to begin with, enjoying wrapping her tethering chain round our ankles then yanking us to the ground – but once she was used to us, she settled down beautifully, becoming part of the family and, indeed, did an excellent job of keeping the weeds at bay.

My lesson learned here – an unhappy animal is capable of causing its own death.

★ ★ ★

LAMBS' TAILS

A girl friend took me to a sheep farm one chilly March morning and introduced me to the farmer's wife. In the corner of the kitchen, by a warm Aga stove, was a tiny lamb. Of course, I oohed and ahhed and wanted to cuddle the baby. The farmer's wife did not share my enthusiasm. She told us that she was fed up with nurturing the dying runts – they took up so much of her precious time and were a damned nuisance.

"I'll take him off your hands, then," I chirped without thought.

"Done" said the woman, "that will be twenty pounds, then." I gulped nervously. Twenty pounds was a lot of money at that time and had I gone to the butchers I could have certainly bought a full sized sheep for that amount.

The farmer had stomped into the kitchen in his muddy boots and was informed of the sale.

"Well, we'd better take his bollocks off, then," he gruffly announced, "and his tail."

Alarmed, I was worried for my new baby and began to demur.

"You won't want a full grown ram rampaging around your garden looking for crumpet," he said, "and if you don't have his tail orf, he'll get fly-blown and grow maggots."

Believing that tails had been designed for a reason, I refused to let him take that off, but agreed to the masculine parts when he convinced me that it was not painful. He slipped a rubber band tightly around the lamb's male bits and said, "They'll drop off in time."

A large carton was produced and the little woolly chap was shoved inside. They gave me a bottle and teat and told me that babies' formula from the chemist would do the trick. We drove off home and I wondered what my husband would say to my latest acquisition. As it happened, he was enchanted.

We named our latest addition Lambert Ramshackle and made him a little pen with a large fire screen by the boiler where he could keep nice and warm. Our old house had pamment* tiled floors and the comings and goings of cats, dogs and chickens seemed right in it, so a small lamb seemed perfectly acceptable, too. On the first sunny day, I put a little jumper on Lambert and took him outside. Sid, our farmer friend, had given us some straw bales to make a cosy wind-free enclosure for the lamb. Soon, Lambert was frolicking amongst the daisies and attempting the succulent grasses. His little tail flicked with excitement and we soon learned that pleasure was demonstrated by this appendage – I was glad I had let him keep it. He never did get maggots.

Lambert did not realise he was a sheep and was not quite sure whether he was a chicken or a dog as he grew up. When we fed the chickens, he joined the rush for the corn as it was strewn and one day I looked out to see that his fleece was emerald green. On close inspection, I discovered that he had his own 'back lawn' – corn had caught in his coat and the warmth of his body and the damp had made ideal growing conditions. It took me ages to pick it all out!

Lambert roamed freely around the premises, and if he seemed to be missing, we knew where to find him – tucked up on my son's bed!

We had some new neighbours who started a vegetable garden and Lambert found out that cabbages were very tasty. Time to make him a pen. My husband fenced off an area for him. However, he was used to running around where he wanted, so did not take kindly to having an enclosure. When we put him in and closed the gate, he stamped and sulked and made a right to-do, so we took him out and decided that as he was used to being tethered, we would carry on doing that and the pen would do for the old goat, Jenny, instead.

As soon as Lambert saw the goat in 'his pen' he was furious. Suddenly, the pen seemed very desirable, so he stamped his hoofs in anger with his lips turned down and quivering. The old goat, Jenny, did not mind at all where she went, so as she was led out, Lambert bounced into *his* new pen perfectly contented.

Every year for the village carnival, we joined forces with the farming family next door and made up carnival floats. One year, the farmer had made a little house for the float. It had windows with check curtains and a painted front door. After the carnival, it was offered for Lambert's house. It was just the right size but he refused to go in it. He viewed it from all angles, then head-butted it until it was knocked over, with the windows and door pointing upwards. Satisfied with his improvements he thereafter jumped in and out of one of the windows, seeming to prefer this to the door, and viewed his domain from its confines while he ruminated at set hours during the day.

The old shepherd, in whose field Emily had taken up temporary quarters, advised me on the rearing of Lambert from a tiny lamb, and he liked to visit us often. He sheared Lambert the first year. I had hoped to learn how to do it, but when I watched the process, decided I might harm him, so made arrangements for Lambert to go to the local shearing sheds. I would bundle him in the back of my old estate car – he loved travelling – and, once arrived, off he would trot to the 'baa-baas'. All the other unwilling sheep would have to be dragged in on their sides and Lambert looked down on them as fools. He had no fear of the shearer. However, it was clear he felt very silly without his fine fleece and, once home, would hide behind the trees in the paddock because the dogs used to laugh at him. Yes I know it sounds silly, but they did. So, he hid until his fleece began to grow through, and only when he felt handsome again would he show himself.

Unfortunately for the old shepherd, his wife decided it was time to move out of their farmhouse into a small bungalow, which was sensible, but when his sheep were sold and his car gone, the old shepherd became very confused, only finding comfort in visiting us to see Lambert and our sheepdogs. His mind wandered and he thought his bed was in the hedge, but I would steer him towards his new home, telling him not to worry about his bed in the hedge – we would find it another day. Old age and confusion reigned. I had grown very fond of the old boy. Unfortunately, I could see that he had become disorientated very quickly with nothing to live for, and he did not last long. I was very sad when he died.

We had three sheepdogs – the devoted dog, Daisy, and her two offspring, one named Heartsease, the other Edwin. Leigh, my son, had taught Edwin how to climb ladders, and also to like wearing hats. He wore a sailor's hat, then climbed in the hammock. When he wore an army hat, he jumped in the Landrover, and when he wore a Salvation Army hat, he sat by my son's side when he was practicing the tuba. The dog was gorgeous and a real softie.

Not long after the shepherd's death, Edwin escaped from the garden, never to be seen again, presumably falling prey to the horrible gamekeeper's gun. Then, soon after my husband and I returned from a weekend away, Lambert dropped down dead in the excitement of seeing us come home. I was so miserable. When I looked at his body, so freshly dead, I did not recognise him. I *knew* in that instant that he was now gone from his body to another place and was with Edwin and the old shepherd and they were all fine together. The body on the ground had just been a vehicle for him and I was not to mourn. I had not had that experience when Lela had died. The knacker-man had collected her as we thought her corpse could be put to use as glue. We had loved her when she was alive, but while feeling sad at her death, had to be practical and not allow sentiments to prevail. With the icy ground, we could never have dug a hole for her anyway.

However, sentiment prevailed with Lambert and I did not have the excuse of icy ground. However, I knew I could not dig a hole large enough for my dead friend. My husband, having to leave for London and his work, left me with the corpse. I placed a blanket over the body and wondered what to do next. I was still distraught and thought I would be able to think more clearly if I washed my hair. That did the trick and I remembered the quarry at the end of the cart track. They had a JCB. With newly washed hair and eyes red from crying, I approached the owner and presented him with my sob story. He said he would send a JCB at the end of the day. I was so grateful.

I returned home to find the blanket had risen considerably in height. The gases in Lambert's four stomachs were accumulating. During the day I became alarmed as I had visions of him taking off like a barrage balloon, but thankfully this did not happen. Lambert's funeral took place in the evening. Believing that

Lambert might rise out of his grave if his stomach was not popped, I gave instructions to the hero of the JCB to 'do something about it'. He was very white-faced when he had finished. Poor Lambert. He had given us so much pleasure during his years with us, but I knew that he was with Edwin and the Shepherd and perfectly all right.

* Pamment – alternative spelling pammant – tiles are clay baked Norfolk floor tiles, about eight inches square and found in houses over a hundred years old. They were placed directly onto dirt floors, but in our house, when we dug some up, we found layers of different kinds of sand on top of the pounded earth. The floors never felt damp and we saw no reason to change them. The tiles polished up a treat and on some of ours were the paw-prints of small cats that had walked across them before the clay had dried out.

Writing the above explanation reminded me of the time we dug up some of the pamments. My son, Leigh, had discovered that he was a dab hand at water divining. He made himself some rods out of cut up coat hangers, bending the ends of the wire as handles. He found that he could look for metal as well as water and we would test him in the garden by blindfolding him, then putting out bowls of water or nails and off he would go. If he were thinking 'water' then he would find the water, and the same with the metal.

The famed golden torc from Iron Age Icini settlements at Snettisham was found a field away from us, so I wondered if there was any treasure in our garden, or even under the floor tiles. I set Leigh the task of finding treasure, and maybe even some doubloons, indoors. His rods went berserk over a certain part of the flooring, so I said he could take up one of the pamment tiles. That was when we found out how beautifully they had been laid.

Of course, an eight-inch hole was not large enough, so I gave him the nod to take up a few more. He found a couple of nails, but the rods were still going crazy, so he dug on. I was very excited for a while but as I was reading some torrid romance at the time, soon forgot about the slaving boy. When I eventually looked up, there was a huge pile of earth on the sitting room floor and only my son's nether regions protruding from a large hole. Three waggy-tailed dogs, a parcel of cats and an interested chicken were all peering down into the pit. I had to laugh! I also felt that we really could not dig up any more of the floor, so whether or not buried treasure was there, we never did find out. I took a photo of Leigh and the hole so that he could show his teacher. My son was so fed up with tutors and friends not believing the things he did at home, so this was proof that he was telling the truth in his school diary!

Leigh did dig up a few interesting finds by his divining method, which we lined up over the fireplace to take to the museum for identification. When we eventually realised that they had disappeared, the cleaning lady admitted she had thrown them in the dustbin, believing they were rubbish. The bins had been emptied and our treasure trove taken away and buried once again for a future generation to unearth!

MY FIRST SÉANCE

A few months later, I was invited to attend a séance. The elderly medium had apparently spent most of her latter life trying to manifest a golden trumpet from thin air – her ambition before she died. Remembering my 'travelling' ring as well as the book that materialised for me, I thought that there was a possibility that her wish could come true. I had never wanted to attend a séance before, being too frightened by my other experiences, but thought it was time my education was furthered, so sallied forth, keen to see what happened, though my logical mind doubted I would witness the trumpet appearing out of thin air.

As the old lady went into a trance, she began to speak in a deep growling voice – "Her guide is coming through," said one of the guests, excitedly. I was not expecting any messages but one came through, nevertheless, and it was from the old shepherd. I was very surprised. He thanked me for being so kind to him when he was in a confused state and wanted me to know that he was better now. I became tearful, but before I could control my tears in order to ask him if he had my pets with him, he had gone. I was aware that it had not been necessary for me to ask him, though, because I knew they were all together. The trumpet, by the way, did not appear.

MORE CAT TALES

Of the many cats and kittens we had at the family home, sometimes there would be one who was not liked by the others. The first was a kitten we named Betty Boop. She was black and white and very pristine. Her mother did not like her, nor did her siblings and, despite her prettiness, nor did we. Don't ask me why. We found good owners for her who came back to us a few months later to ask us to look after her while they went on holiday. They had spoilt her a lot, indulging her in every way. When she returned for her 'holiday' with us, the others really put her through the mill by dragging her pristine person through mud, dust and cinders until she was filthy. Poor little thing. I had to segregate her until her owners came home.

Another time, one of the kittens we had named Blossom was also not liked by the other cats. They did not hurt him but ignored him completely and would not let him play with them or join in any fun. He looked so lonely and sat on the porch of the dog kennel looking miserable and I felt really sorry for him. He was a very pretty cat, but always had smudges of dirt on his coat.

Luckily, we found somebody who wanted him, telling us they would return the following day to collect him. It was clear to me that the other cats had picked up telepathically that his chance of a new home had finally come. They all collected around him, washing him all over until he gleamed, and they seemed to be giving him advice on what not to do to spoil his chances in his new home. Although they had excluded him from their circle, they certainly made sure that he was well groomed and ready for his owner.

★ ★ ★

Not all of our cats wanted to stay with us and went 'walkabout'. We had a gorgeous longhaired black cat called Hannibal who decided to go and live in the local graveyard. We did not realise where he was for some time but, once discovered, we brought him home. After a day or so with us he would return to his chosen abode. After relentless collections and returns, we gave up. We realised he wanted to be 'in the church' and let him stay there with, perhaps, inappropriate jokes about "Let us spray". Strangely enough, however, he always turned up on Christmas Eve to wish us a Happy Christmas. You cannot force a cat to live with you if he decides otherwise – but how did he know it was the Christmas celebrations?

At Christmas time, the Salvation Army band always paid us a visit. They clambered out of the farmer's van and assembled on the lawn, large tubas, tambourines, trumpets, drums and all. In the dark of the night it was a moving sight to see them illuminated by the lights from our house. All our animals wandered round from wherever they had been to listen to the music and carols. A horse, a goat, a sheep, umpteen cats and dogs watching quietly while the rousing sounds of 'Once in Royal David's City' resonated through the trees. This was an isolated spot at the end of a cart track and to me it seemed like our own nativity scene, with the animals knowing all about the birth of Jesus being celebrated. Maybe that was what prompted Hannibal's Christmas Eve visits!

★ ★ ★

BITS AND BOBS

There has been a lot of controversy in the UK regarding fox hunting, which has now been banned by an act of Parliament.

My feelings about this is that in the natural order of things, the fox would hunt and kill for its own meals and be hunted itself by larger prey – wolves and bears – and is well equipped to evade pursuers.

Due to human intervention, there is no larger prey left to kill off the surplus foxes, so fox hunting became the norm to cull them, while enjoyment was had by the riders, the horses and the hounds. Even the fox had his own fun evading its pursuers.

Taken by a friend to see a hunt (on foot), I observed the wily fox, totally unconcerned, trotting off in a different direction to the hounds. An old boy I spoke to told me that it was common knowledge that the fox, using his own secret route, always ended up by 'seeking sanctuary' in the local church and waited in the crypt, totally unfazed by all the commotion going on in his woods, until it was all over, when he would trot back home again.

During a hunt, if a fox was caught, the hounds killed it in seconds. I understand that usually it is only the old or diseased foxes that do not escape and maybe it is a better end for them than starving to death or wasting away from an illness. I have seen my own dogs catch a rabbit, kill and rip it in two in the wink of an eye. The creature would not have known what had happened. I am told that it is the same with the dogs catching a fox. It is certainly not a pleasant thought – a fox being ripped to pieces – but it would have happened before the time of man.

I made a friend of the fox in the wood and know that in an ideal world I would not want to see any animal killed, especially foxes, but I know that in this world, man is keen to rid the land of them and I would far rather have one of my fox friends ripped to death by dogs in a second, than be slowly and agonisingly poisoned or gassed and, even worse, die slowly and painfully from gun-shot wounds. Even a well-aimed bullet would be more agonising than instant death by a pack of dogs. The fox hunting has not been banned to save the foxes – they are now being despatched by crueller methods. We have created an unbalanced world where natural flora and fauna are becoming extinct due to man's intervention. With man's over-population of the planet and subsequent destruction of untold ecological niches, there will be more elimination than just our friendly foxes. Mankind is causing its own demise.

Living in my own wonderful backwater with so many pets, I was becoming so attuned to them and noticed so much about them. I was very interested, watching how my dogs made mind contact. When we took them for a walk, I noticed that one would glance at the other with a brief flick of the ears, the other one would reciprocate with another flick and they would be off in a flash to hunt a rabbit. However they did it, they were in accord with each other and knew what the other was thinking.

The cats interacted in friendship with each other (including the farmer's felines) as they did with us. We had a heavy outside door that had a self-closing hinge. The farmer's cat, Kitty Purr, was adept at opening this door with her paw and was able to time the closing of the door, just managing to nip in before it closed on her tail. She worked out a routine whereby she kept the door open with her stomach, so that the other cats could get in. When they were all indoors, she would make the final break herself. She even did this when she was heavily pregnant but never came to any harm.

Lots of kittens were born in my house and the farmer's barn. The mother cats took care of each other's kittens, allowing time off for sunbathing or mouse hunting, and would attack, en masse, any dog that came to investigate too closely. They were a real sharing, caring, interactive community in which we and our other pets were included.

Sparky must have been watching the mother cats suckling their young and felt deprived. His close shave with death as a small kitten had made him quite a character and I was never surprised at anything he did.

I noticed that he was becoming very friendly with Daisy, the devoted dog. He began to curl up with her in a chair purring loudly while kneading her front. On closer inspection, I realised he was suckling on one of her teats. Daisy looked rather embarrassed about it but I told her that if she did not mind, then nor did I. This unlikely liaison went on for a few days and, on further investigation, I noticed that Sparky had white foam around his mouth. Daisy had produced milk for him!

I had kept in touch with my clairvoyant friend, Carol, who had guided me with Sparky's healing, and one day she phoned, inviting me to her home that evening telling me that her Indian guide wanted to introduce himself. I was intrigued and looked forward to a manifestation of Carol's guide. When I arrived at the house and we settled ourselves down in readiness, nothing happened at all. No manifestations, no messages – nothing. Things do not always go the way you want them to! We decided to 'give up' and have a cup of coffee instead. Suddenly, however, I saw Carol's face change into a Native American – in the same manner I had seen the Spiritualist lady's face change so many years ago in the church hall. Once I had registered what was happening, another face appeared, then another, and another, and yet another. Different images flashed across Carol's face with the speed of lightening. Geography has always been a poor subject for me, but as I saw the different people superimposed over Carol's face, I also knew where they came from –

'He's from Peru,' 'he's from Ecuador' – and so on. There must have been about 100 different faces and nationalities that I saw and it was quite, quite amazing. It would have been enough to see the preponderance of guides, but it was even more astonishing to be given their countries of origin. Carol's grin spread from ear to ear as I told her what I was seeing. She was thrilled that her guide had given me such irrefutable proof of spirit guides – it was almost like a movie show, and what a privilege for me to have all those amazing people show themselves to me.

After that evening, I was prone to see other people's guides superimposed over friends' faces, but as they found it very disconcerting, I had to stop myself.

Unfortunately, the slippery slope of our marriage had proved too difficult to maintain. My husband purchased himself another house and told me that I could stay in our home while he could afford to run it. I was very grateful for this generosity. I knew that I should find work to help finances and kept an eye on the employment pages of the local newspaper for secretarial work, as well as au pair work abroad. I had no success with either. My children had by now left home and, while I could easily have become a hermit at the end of my cart track, I thought I ought to be doing something worthwhile.

PART FOUR

MY FORTE AT FORTY
1979

When I reached the age of forty, although separated from my husband, I still lived in the family home with all our animals. I felt I should do something to mark this milestone. One of the things I had not yet mastered was horse riding, although I had had the few lessons in Kent when my children were little – when I made mind contact with the horse named Valour. I had not had much fun at those stables. One of the other horses I had learned on had been a huge beast that wanted to chop my knees off on tree trunks then throw me off. I had evaded all his vile attempts, but had got complacent in the stable training-barn, where I was practicing with lots of small children to lean back in the saddle, ride back to front and other exercises. The brute managed to almost dislocate my knee on a wooden support. How I wanted to cry – it hurt so much. Not wanting to ride him again, I was given another nag with only one eye, who stopped to eat grass all the time, pulling my arms from their sockets and taking no notice of my entreaties to 'walk on'. I also remembered how my thighs had bled, trying to keep my balance in the saddle.

I reasoned that not all horses would be like those at the school and it was time I learned to overcome my fears, and now was as good a time as any to have another try.

As riding lessons are expensive, I came to the conclusion that it would be cheaper in the long run to have my own horse. I had plenty of room for one in the garden. Everyone thought I was completely bonkers, and perhaps I was, but I had made up my mind. I had already seen a pretty horse that I liked – a sturdy dappled grey cob with a black mane and tail, and short enough for any fall off her back to be kind to my bones. She had recently foaled and the owner, a friend of mine, wanted to sell her. Her name was Tiffany.

I arranged for a garden outhouse to be turned into a stable, had some fencing put up around it, made a paddock in the garden, bought books about horses, invested in buckets, hay and feed and, when all was ready, Tiffany arrived. She was fractious and missed her foal and, in retrospect, it was bad timing for me to have her then. The first night she splintered the stable door, clearly not impressed with her new home. However, I had to cope, so in the morning I boldly clipped on her leading rein and set off in front of her to lead her to her paddock. I wondered if she would trample me to death but, thankfully, she did not.

As the days went by, I realised that Tiffany was not enjoying my unmasterly approaches with her. She would not let me groom her, lashed out with her hoofs and bit me and, although she never hurt much, I believed she soon would. I was really worried at my ineptitude. I had believed that once we had 'made friends' the going would be easy, but so far this had not proved true. She needed me to be the master, but I did not know how.

One sunny morning, as I attempted to groom her once more in her yard, she bit me yet again. I wondered what I should do to stop her bad behaviour, so made a quick decision to bite her back! As I nipped her neck, she looked round at me in astonishment and bit me once more. I had not realised that horses can look astonished – but she did! Her bite was not too painful, but hard enough to show her annoyance with me. I sunk my teeth again into her neck – the same degree as her bite – loving the wonderful horsy odour. Turning to stare at me with yet another astonished gaze, she bit me for the third time just to see what I would do and I returned bite for bite.

Tiffany then heaved a huge sigh of relief and settled into a relaxed posture – I had won the battle of wits and will and she let me finish grooming her. I was now in charge – and was now the boss! Much later on when I related my story to a friend, I was told I had chosen the right position to bite her – stallions bite mares on the neck when mating, so my choice was one that instinctively gave Tiffany a feeling that I was the dominant one.

Now emboldened, I began to groom her inside her small stable. Still feeling nervous of her, I hoped she would not press me against the wall. As soon as I formulated the thought, she did exactly that, seeming to have read my mind. I had to crawl under her belly to get out, which was very nerve-wracking. Had she wanted to, she could have kicked merry hell out of me – but she waited calmly for me to extricate myself.

I was feeling very encouraged by my progress, but had not yet combed her tail. I had been astonished at the range of her kicks, so did not trust her enough to stand behind her to tackle the tail. I reasoned the best way to do this was with the gate between us. She stood near the gate and looked blankly at me when told to back up. After the episode in the stable, I felt sure that she was a mind reader. I reasoned that she must have seen the picture in my mind when I thought of her pressing me against the wall, so this time, I made a picture in my head of her backing up to the gate and me combing her tail over it. She looked at me, heaved a sigh as if to complain, "Oh, if I must," then backed up to the gate. It had worked – she was definitely telepathic! I hooked her lovely long tail over the five-barred gate, and combed her feathery fronds to perfection.

Soon after this second breakthrough, I decided to do another experiment with telepathy – which I have to mention was totally different to the 'mind contact' I had with the horse, Valour, and the fox. Tiffany was clearly reading *my* mind, while I could only guess at her thoughts.

My bedroom overlooked Tiffany's paddock, where some old pear trees grew. I stood at the open window, watching her below and made a picture in my mind of her walking a figure of eight around the pear trees. She looked up at the window and saw me, heaved another weary sigh as if to say, "Do I have to? Oh, all right then," and plodded dutifully around the pear trees in a figure of eight, looked up again at me as if to say, "Satisfied?" Her mission accomplished, she carried on grazing. There was no doubt about it, telepathy worked!

Grooming her was an easy pleasure now she no longer kicked or bit and we enjoyed a mutual trust. However, she began to tread on my feet – something she had not done before. I made the mistake of pulling my foot out from under her hoof – ouch! It was so very painful! The next time she did it, I tried leaning against her shoulder to push her away and she lifted her foot. This happened too many times to be coincidental and I realised she was doing this on purpose – maybe joking with me. This made me laugh and, when I saw her lips quivering, realised my horse had a sense of humour and was laughing with me!

Whenever she tried any tricks on me after that I knew it was in fun and it always made me giggle, then she would toss her mane and snort and then 'laugh', realising I had rumbled her and soon we had another kind of rapport. Who was teaching whom, I wondered?

When I groomed her long winter coat in the spring, it came out in tufts, which floated to the ground. I noticed that the birds nesting under the roof pantiles flew down to pick it up and take it back to their nests.

I whispered gently into Tiffany's ear, "If you look closely and keep still, you'll see the little birdies come down and use your hair to line their nests." I did not expect her to understand my words but my guess is that while we talk we are making pictures in our mind all the time. The message got through, for she watched with keen interest as the birds boldly helped themselves by her hoofs and made their way back up to the roof carrying their booty to disappear under the eaves.

There was a small field next to Tiffany's paddock and every morning the farmer opened the barn doors to let out his small herd of cows and their calves to graze in the sunshine. Tiffany always looked out for them, craning her neck in keen interest, but as soon as they came thundering along to greet her, she turned away and pretended not to notice them. As she had eaten all the grass in her paddock, only stinging nettles were left in the hedgerow and she pretended to eat them in a supercilious way as if to say, "Oh, you poor dears have only got grass, I've got these delicious stingers." This always made me laugh.

Every day I took Tiffany down to her field in the village where we would pass a handsome piebald named Mr Chips. It was obvious to me that Tiffany really fancied Mr Chips because she craned her neck in order to see him as we neared his field, but when he galloped over to say 'Hallo', she turned her head away and pretended not to notice him.

Mr Chips had been castrated so I did not fear that he would jump over the fence with amorous intentions, but one day I was alarmed when Tiffany took the matter into her own hoofs. She made a beeline in Mr Chips' direction. No shyness now! To my horror, she turned round and backed up to him. He got excited (despite his lack of gender) and tried to mount her over the fence, with me in the saddle! Wanton hussy! It was not easy for me to diffuse that situation, but I was out of the saddle quicker than I had thought possible!

One day, about three years after she had been with me, we rode past a field in which her young foal grazed contentedly. She had not seen him during that time and I was interested to see whether they would recognise each other after such a long duration. It was obvious that they did as soon as they saw each other. Tiffany rushed over to the fence to see her foal. There was such a joyful reunion, while Tiffany nuzzled her foal's neck over the fence with lots of mutual nickering of affection. It was plain that they certainly had not forgotten each other. Why do we assume that animals have no memory or affection for each other?

Tiffany and our old goat had struck up a good friendship and they liked to sleep in the same stable. I had made a barrier out of a spare door to safeguard the arthritic old goat, as she was rather wobbly of leg. The chickens liked to roost on it and their gentle clucking was very soothing and a warm ambience reigned.

My farmer friend informed me that the reason why the cavalries of old kept goats as mascots was because it had been discovered that, for some reason, goats had a calming effect on horses, and so one was always kept in the stables to stop the horses from spooking. Certainly, Tiffany and the old goat obviously enjoyed each other's company.

The stable was very small, only just large enough for Tiffany to lie down with the goat in the corner. I would often go and sit with them in the hay after my day's work was done, joined by the dogs, sheep, chickens and cats, and enjoy their gentle company.

One day, I noticed that there was a clutch of eggs in the centre of the stable floor that I had missed. I was amazed that Tiffany had avoided treading on them. I removed them but later, when a mother hen brought in her tiny chicks to scratch around in Tiffany's straw, I was concerned that they would be crushed by Tiffany's hoofs. To my complete astonishment, I noticed Tiffany gently wave her back hooves around to disperse the chicks and only place them down when what seemed like radar had told her they were out of harm's way. This gentleness with her feet made me more aware that when she trod on mine it was no accident!

Tiffany's tenderness was displayed on another occasion. My animals always liked to be near me, so when I talked to Tiffs as I leaned on her gate, the cats would often climb up and sit on the top of it to join in the conversation. One evening, one of the tiny kittens scrambled up. Tiffany seemed very interested in the kitty and began to gently lick its coat, and then – while I held my breath – took the little tail between her huge teeth and very, very carefully nibbled from base to tip to remove any bits of dirt. Astonishing.

I wish horse owners did not cut the tails of their mounts. It might look all very neat and tidy after grooming, but they are designed long for a purpose! I noticed that Tiffany's tail could reach every inch of her body and rid her of irritating flies – she could even flick them away from her eyes. If you own a horse, think twice before reaching for the scissors.

I mentioned previously the cattle that used to gallop over to say hallo to Tiffany in the morning. I learned a lot from them, too. There were about four or five cows in the field next door, who had cosy straw-filled stalls to sleep in overnight. The farmer preferred to get 'the real thing' transported in for his ladies rather than artificial insemination, so one day, a huge lorry drew up and down came the gangplank. All the cows were most interested to see a handsome black bull with short little legs appear and give them the once over with an appreciative look. They batted their long eyelashes coquettishly. The bull was a real gentleman because he never ravished his ladies in sight of any of us, but we could see that very quickly a loving relationship had blossomed between him and his harem. He would graze contentedly amongst the daisies while the cows kept near to him, every now and again coming over to lick his ear and rub his neck with theirs. It was a cosy, loving, domestic scene. The sun shone down on them, the birds sang in the hedge around the field, the sky was blue and I realised that cattle are no different to us, given the opportunity to set up domestic bliss.

The time came when Sir's lorry came to pick him up. The girls were distraught and so was he. They all bellowed in anguish and long after the lorry had departed with their prince, the cows lamented his loss.

In time, they all produced the prettiest little calves that frolicked in the field close to their mothers, but I do not think for one moment that they ever forgot their man.

I could not help but realise that if any of that small herd was sent off to the meat market it could be termed 'Happy Meat'. Those animals had had a pleasurable life, they ate good food, they grazed in the elements, had the sun on their backs and the fresh gentle breezes in their lungs. If they were slaughtered, not so nice, but at least they had a good life and the humans that consumed their meat would benefit from it. I do not think anyone can benefit from 'Unhappy Meat' from cattle or other animals and fowl that are kept in cramped 'factory' conditions.

I do hope that the day will soon dawn when legislation insists that all farm animals benefit from a free and contented life.

DAFT DILLY

One of our cats was called Daft Dilly. She could not co-ordinate, was cross-eyed and not very bright due to her mother being kicked prior to the birth. Dilly was a loving little cat, spending most of her days purring loudly as well as tripping me up constantly as her chosen place at all times was between my feet. She attempted to catch butterflies and stalk birds but was totally unsuccessful.

She was so dippy that we had to watch her when she was near the fire, as on a few occasions her tail had caught alight, to her complete oblivion.

We once had a poorly hen that seemed to be dying. Hoping to revive it, I brought it indoors, put it in a box with a stick for a perch. Dilly and the hen became bosom pals. Neither creature could groom itself because of lack of coordination, but they worked out a system whereby Dilly washed the hen with her tongue, while the hen pecked through Dilly's coat – each propping the other up and both feeling needed and nurtured.

Lucinda did not approve of all these animals in the house. She had a friend coming and demanded that the chicken was taken out of the kitchen, as it was 'disgusting'. She was right of course – the place must have been teeming with bacteria, but my opinion was that our immune systems needed germs! However, I put the chicken in the garage but unfortunately it then took a turn for the worse.

I realised the poor thing was dying, so had a word with it so it would not be frightened. I was standing in the garage doorway saying, "Don't worry, dear. You will soon be going to heaven, where lots of lovely angels will welcome you at some pretty pearly gates. They have wings, just like you, so you will feel at home. All your aches and pains will go and Chicken Licken will be there too...." I carried on, elaborating on my theme and getting somewhat carried away with my narration.

You know that feeling you sometimes get when someone is watching you? I turned around to see the postman leaning on his bike behind me. I felt such a fool. He had been there the whole time. He must have thought I was as daft as a coot.

I think Dilly missed her friend when she died. When the little cat was about three years old, she became very ill and I thought that she probably needed to be put down. I looked at the sweet little cat purring at my feet, trying in vain to pounce on a butterfly, and wished with all my heart that she could catch one, or even better, a bird before she died. I walked around to the front of the house, Daft Dilly in-between my feet as usual, when I heard a loud 'thwack!' A bird had hit a window and lay on the ground with its neck broken. Dilly ran over in a flash and ate the bird with great relish, beak, claws and all. She was so happy and believed that she had stalked and caught her own prey. I'm quite certain my wish had been granted and that this had been no coincidence.

Poor Dilly had to be put down a week later with liver failure – which was very sad as she was the cutest of cats – but at least Daft Dilly had got her bird before her demise.

GHOST ANIMAL ANECDOTE

Apart from the ghost cats that my children had felt on their beds when we first moved to Norfolk, here is another anecdote to show that animals sometimes like to stay around the home they loved on this world.

When I lived with my parents, we had a small crossbred Old English sheep-dog. Years and various pets later – the last being a Staffordshire bull terrier – my parents moved to live near me in Norfolk. The child at my parents' old house kept telling her mum that she often saw a small shaggy sheepdog playing in the back garden. The little girl believed that the dog had belonged to my parents. She was told not to be so fanciful, and that if she had seen a ghost dog, it would have been a staffy. The child was so insistent that her father phoned to check with my dad who was able to verify that they had once owned the dog described by the child.

SYNCHRONICITY

A good example of synchronicity is the anecdote I mentioned earlier about our cat, Sydney Konk, in his Mafia suit, and the young man who walked into the pub when we were recounting the story to our friends.

Here is another example showing how synchronicity works. The farm cat, Kitty Purr, and our cat, Basil, were inseparable. Kitty Purr was a sensual puss with come-hither eyes, who kept herself well washed, and Basil (who never did) was a ginger tom of disreputable appearance. All our animals had wonderful personalities and we wove stories about their occupations. Basil's persona seemed to be that of a scrap metal merchant/used car salesman who wore either a greasy flat cap or old trilby hat, loud check jacket, baggy trousers held up by braces and a waistcoat stained with a multitude of past meals. He always had a cigarette dangling from his mouth, drank whiskey and drove a dented, untaxed lorry that listed to one side and had bald tyres. For high days and holidays, he drove a Jaguar that had seen better days, filled with rubbish with old peeling parking tickets stuck on the windscreen. A multitude of letters, bills, invoices and fines were shoved along the dashboard after the glove compartment had become full. The rest tumbled over the floor. He always seemed to forget his wallet so Kitty Purr had to pay for any dinner dates he took her on. We cast him as an utter, but loveable, rogue. Kitty Purr was his 'secretary' and wore tarty clothing; short tight skirts, high heels, dangly earrings and had a strong Norfolk accent. Our story about the pair grew and we fantasized with all sorts of scenarios.

It was with surprise, therefore, when a new comedy sit-com hit the television screens. Bill Maynard (more famously known as Greengrass in 'Heartbeat') was cast as a second-hand car dealer who drove a Jag filled with bills and tickets and whose secretary was just like our Kitty Purr's character. Their clothing, personalities and story lines were almost identical to the ones we had fabricated in our story.

The adage that there is no such thing as a new idea is true.

Another occasion when a similar synchronicity took place was when I had designed a family of large rotund rats made out of colourful felt. I had written a story about them, which I was illustrating with photographs – my rats were pictured in various scenarios.

A friend, the late Maurice Dodd (who dreamt up 'The Perishers' in The Daily Mirror) asked me, after seeing my rats, if I was doing a new television series with them – he had been in some studios and seen 'The Wombles' being filmed as a pilot prior to their release. I had no inkling about the Wombles, but my designs and ideas were so similar that it was useless for me to take my ideas any further.

THE NATIVE AMERICAN BRAVE
1982

I had been busy in the garden. I have always loved to dig, to plant, to feel my hands in the soil, to watch my plants grow, feeling as I do so at one with nature. I would dig all day, pulling out the weeds, splitting plants where necessary and re-positioning them, enjoying the fresh air and birdsong, my animals around me, watching as I laboured. On this particular occasion, I had climbed into bed with an aching back after a good day's hard work with a feeling of satisfaction.

I had just sunk into the cosy confines of my bed when I noticed a Native American brave standing in front of me. His arms were folded across a bare-chest while his handsome face remained impassive. Even though I had never seen a manifestation before, I felt no sense of astonishment as his gaze bore into mine. "You write book," he said quite sternly, then he began to fade. Quickly, before he disappeared, I cried, "What about?" "As a child," was his cryptic reply and he vanished from view.

I grabbed my notepad and pen and wrote down what had happened, wondering what exactly he had meant by the words 'as a child'. Did he mean that I should write about my life as a child? How would that interest anybody? Or did he mean that I should write as a child, clear and simply – but about what? It didn't make any sense to me, though it was clear I should begin writing a book as soon as possible. I decided to 'sleep on it' as things are usually clearer in the morning.

As it happened, I still could not decide what it was the Indian brave had wanted me to write about, but needed to tell someone about seeing him. I phoned my clairvoyant friend, Carol, but as I began to relate my experience, I realised that while it had seemed perfectly natural at the time, I had only seen the Indian brave from the waist up and he had appeared no larger than a picture post card. "Oh," I said, in disappointment, "I must have imagined him, then." "No, you definitely saw him," replied Carol, "I usually see my guides small like that – there is no point for them to go to the effort of materialising large, when little does the trick!" Well, that made sense.

I puzzled over what I was supposed to write about. I recalled that his features remained enigmatic after I had questioned this. He had said, "As a child," then disappeared. I wondered if he meant I was acting like a child in questioning him, for his message had just been "You write book." Having delivered that statement, he had begun to fade when I interrupted him with my query. Therefore, it became apparent to me that I should be able to figure out by myself what my book should contain. I reasoned that he would hardly go to all the trouble of manifesting to order a torrid romance, but would surely require something spiritual, meaningful and helpful to those who read it.

I thought of all the strange experiences I had had over the years. Did he want me to write about those? But who would be interested? Anyway, I did not think I'd had enough to fill a book.

I sat down with a note pad and began to list the dreams, the precognitions, the voices et al., and felt really surprised as the list grew longer and longer. My excitement grew – maybe I *could* write an interesting book – the sort I would like to have discovered at the onset of my psychic experiences, which would have made me realise that I was completely normal instead of going through the agonies of wondering whether madness had set in – to know that these experiences *can* and *do* happen, are perfectly natural and that precognisance and premonitions have always been part and parcel of our lives since the dawn of time. Maybe, I thought, most people have similar experiences to me during their lifetime, but blanket them in convenient forgetfulness after having passed them off as mere coincidence. I realised that this was why my Native American brave materialised to instruct me, so that readers of my book can learn from what I have written, to look for the hints from their own guides, to follow their own intuitions, which will lead them to a more fulfilling and wonderful route through life.

I now had a quest to fulfil, which was quite daunting.

As I explained in the foreword, the book did take a long while to fruition. I had my daily life to maintain with all its trials and tribulations. I began many drafts and discarded them. I was used to writing short pieces for magazines but a book was very different.

However, I was sure that there are time differences between the physical and non-physical world and that I would complete the work at the right time. Since my first instruction, I received many more amazing paranormal experiences that I was able to add to my story, making it twice as interesting, so I did not feel guilty that it was not completed sooner.

★ ★ ★

UNIDENTIFIED FLYING OBJECTS

Norfolk skies are incredible. Because the land is fairly flat (though it does have some delightful undulations) the vast skies stretch as far as the eye can see and host some amazing sunsets. Far away from the orange glare of street lighting that obscures the night skies in towns and suburban areas, with fresher air and less pollution, the huge night blanket is a wonder to behold. The universe stretches into infinity before your very eyes, with a million trillion stars twinkling brightly in the clear atmosphere. Shooting stars can often be seen, especially on frosty nights, and reports of UFOs are not uncommon.

One dark night, around nine o'clock, I was driving towards the seaside town of Hunstanton with my teenage daughter and her boyfriend to collect my son, Leigh, from Sea Scouts.

As we drove along the road in the middle of open countryside, we could see a very bright light above. "Oh look, a spacecraft!" I jokingly commented. Winding down the window, I yelled out to the sky, "We'll take you to our leader!" and flashed my headlights to draw attention. The two teenagers, used to my ways and enthusiasms, wound down their windows and shouted greetings as well. We did not think it was a spacecraft at all, more probably a light from a low aircraft or a helicopter – we were just having fun.

To our immense surprise, the bright light then shot off at an unimaginable speed. One minute it was there, the next instant it was far up in the skies, a tiny pinprick of light that made a triangle across the heavens. One instant it was at the apex, the next instant far across the sky to the second point and then in the next wink of an eye, it completed its triangle, all without visible movement. It executed this manoeuvre a couple more times, then flashed its lights as if to make sure of our attention. It was as if it were proving it could not possibly be an aircraft – surely no secret aircraft could travel such distances in a blink of an eye. It seemed as if those in control of 'the craft' were making a statement.

Next, in less than an instant, the bright light returned to hover in front of my car. Luckily for us, there was no other traffic, as I drove erratically, watching the pulsating light above us, instead of concentrating on the road. The light then moved ahead of us and I followed it, egged on by my two exuberant passengers.

The light led us to an empty and isolated car park at the top of Hunstanton's cliff. By now, we were very excited, feeling like the Three Wise Men following the Star. The light was huge by now and slowly descending. I stopped the car and turned off the engine and watched with bated breath. *Because the night was so dark, and the light emitting so much brightness, we could not see the shape of the craft, but we were sure that it was a spacecraft that was landing before our very eyes and we were probably going to meet some aliens!* No noise came from the descending craft – the only sound came from our uneven breathing.

For the first time, doubt crept into my mind as the craft was almost at ground level.

I recalled the reports of abductions by extra-terrestrials, where people claimed to have been whisked away and forced to undertake painful operations. Others had returned hours or days later, miles from the original location, disorientated and unable to remember what had happened to them. I also remembered reports from people who had suffered radiation burns. Then, there had been witnesses of UFO near-sightings who recounted that their cars had stopped and would not start again, while hours had been lost that they could not account for. There were no reports of anything pleasant.

Should I be putting my young passengers at risk – and what would happen to my son if we were whisked off to another planet and nobody collected him from Sea Scouts? Reluctantly, I decided I should not stay to see what happened.

Excitement was waning fast and fear taking over – how much more frightening it must have been in biblical times when 'chariots' came down from the sky – so I turned the engine key. To my horror, the car refused to start and I recalled those reports again. But I persisted and the engine coughed into life after a few frantic attempts and off we zoomed, away from danger – or what could have been the most exciting moment of our lives!

If I had been on my own, without the responsibilities of motherhood, then maybe I would have stayed to see what happened. I do regret not braving it out.

We were not the only people to have seen a spacecraft that night and also during the following week. There were reports of similar sightings as well as daylight views of cigar shaped UFOs. There were enough reports to reinforce what we had seen and to know that we had not been hallucinating.

Although I was not aware of it at the time – nor indeed for many years later – there had already been reports of UFOs seen in Rendlesham Forest, Norfolk, in December 1980 – officially described as 'unexplained lights'; there were also radiation traces but such reports were denied or covered up until recent times.

My father's job as a journalist and hobby as an aviator gave him access to unauthorised information, including an interesting conversation with a Norfolk wing commander who admitted, unofficially, that many UFO sightings had, indeed, been made by pilots of aircraft. The wing commander also told my father that officially he would deny that statement! I wonder why the MOD deems it necessary to deny the existence of sightings of unidentified flying objects.

After that first experience, I was eager to have another UFO encounter. One night when driving alone to a friend's house, I saw a similar bright light in the sky. This time I vowed I would wait to see what happened if it made a descent. Wanting to make a good impression for our space visitors, I rummaged in my handbag for a lipstick then chased the light along the winding country lanes, erratically applying my pale pink lip-gloss.

My bizarre thought was to look my best if I were going to meet little green men. I flashed my headlights as I had before, but this time, to my disappointment, the light disappeared as suddenly as it had appeared, so I never had the opportunity to act as the Norfolk ambassador for our planet Earth. I'd had my chance on Hunstanton Cliff and had blown it. No second chance.

WAS GOD A SPACEMAN?

I had hired a stand at The Festival of Mind, Body and Spirit in London to sell the candles I made. During the five-day duration, I spent my breaks visiting other interesting exhibitors, almost overlooking one stand. A man sat at a table under a homemade banner with the painted wording, "WAS GOD A SPACE-MAN?"

My interest quickened and I approached the man – who was French – at the table. Even with my own radical theories about spacemen, I thought he was probably a crank but was still keen to find out what he had to say. I asked him about his spacemen and he said the best way for me to comprehend the story was for me to read the book he was selling with the far-fetched title 'Space aliens took me to their planet – a true story'. On realising I was an exhibitor at the festival, the Frenchman kindly lent me the book, which I later purchased because it was so fascinating.

The book was written by Claude Vorilon, a Frenchman who had duel professions, first as a racing car driver and secondly as a racing journalist. His story began one day when he felt the urge to drive to a remote mountainous region in France to do some jogging. It was foggy and through the gloom of the mist he saw a bright light, which began to descend very close to him. *As I read on, I recalled my own similar experience on Hunstanton cliff.* To his surprise, and fear too, he realised he was seeing a spacecraft as it landed. Transfixed, he watched as a door opened and a little man alighted and walked towards him.

I read on: after greeting each other, the spaceman invited Claude into the craft, informing him that he had been chosen by them – the Elohim – because he had the ability to write down their story and that he had been brought there that day by telepathic means. He said their story had been told by word of mouth in ancient times and then subsequently written down in a book now called the Bible. When the Bible was translated from ancient Hebrew, an error had occurred in the translation of the word 'Elohim' which, being in the plural, meant '*those* who came from the sky'. It had been wrongly translated to the singular as '*he* who came from the sky' and later referred to as God and made into a Deity.

To many people, this might seem quite shocking and shake the very core of their belief system, but to me it rang true, relating in some ways to my own theories.

Some parts of the book were very far-fetched, but I did not dismiss what I read, as I had long ago realised that the improbable could happen. I was certainly interested to read that, according to the author, the aliens contacted us by telepathy. So my theory about a spaceman seeing through my eyes when walking down the lane may not have been as crazy as it seemed!

Perhaps the disembodied voice that stopped me being killed in the car crash when I was eighteen – page one – was not the heavenly stereotype with wings, but a little green man, busy keeping observation from a far-off planet through some kind of advanced telepathy.

Claude Vorilon claimed that he had, on one occasion, been taken to the Elohims' planet, where the colours had no comparison to those on earth. *My interest quickened when I read this, for many of my dreams had taken me to places where the colours were so indescribably vibrant and clear. I could not help but wonder if, like my precognitive dreams, I had been given a small insight into another planet's existence.*

The object of the spaceman's visit was, according to the book, to inform us how we were created. His explanation was that we were not a result of random evolution or of a supernatural 'God' but a deliberate creation using DNA by a scientifically advanced people who made human beings literally in their image. They chose our planet because it was the nearest in atmosphere to their own. Because there were teams of scientists who worked in different locations, each team came up with slight differences in colour and appearance. The alien informed Claude that this is all described in Genesis, but because the men who translated it all those years ago could not possibly comprehend our present day technology, they termed what they translated as being in 'miraculous' form.

The spaceman went on to say that as we have now reached the stage where we would soon be embarking on the scientific experiments of cloning human beings, then we should be ready to accept the updated version of how we came to be on this planet. He mentioned that it was possible to reproduce anything using samples of DNA taken from bones, hair or skin.

The meeting with the spaceman in which Claude Vorilon was told to write down all the information and have it printed in book form was in 1973. If any cloning experiments were taking place at that time, it was not something the general public knew about, so the book's contents seemed extremely far-fetched.

Reading through the book, it seemed like a science fiction novel. A few years later, however, I noticed a small item in a newspaper which stated that some scientists had managed to grow cultures using DNA samples from a piece of skin – borrowed from a museum – from a quagga – an extinct creature, half zebra, half ass, with the possibility of eventually reproducing the animal when their techniques had progressed. Was this the first attempt at cloning?

Since then, Dolly, the cloned sheep has been created in Britain, and many other experiments are taking place causing huge controversy.

Note: on December 26th 2002, it was reported that, allegedly, a cloned baby had been born through a company called Clonaid, an offshoot of Claude Vorilon's following.

The Frenchman on the festival stand, pleased with my interest in the book, told me that a movement had been founded (The Raelian Movement), members of which would all be meeting in August for a Course of Awakening at a camp site in Montpelier, France, and suggested that I should join them. He told me that there would be many young men who would be interested in me and that nudity and free love, while not compulsory, was encouraged and sensual meditation was practiced each day. Hmmm. I thought this all sounded rather dodgy and had no intention of making a journey to France! This sounded like a strange cult to me, who might rid me of my virtue, my money and my mind!

However, for some reason, I noted down the address of the movement and when the festival ended and I returned home, my mind was full of conflicting thoughts.

If I could only see Claude Vorilon to gauge what he was like. Perhaps I could judge from his appearance whether he was crazy, plausible or even saintly – in which case, perhaps, I might decide to pay a visit to France. If he were a convincing con man it would be impossible to tell if he were bona fide, of course. I could not get the man's story out of my mind and thought about it constantly.

Not long after my return home from the exhibition, I collected a newspaper from the newsagents one Saturday morning. It was not until I got back into my car that I realised I had also bought a copy of the TV Times – not a magazine I normally purchased – and was annoyed with myself. Wondering whether to return it to the shop, a page fell open and I noticed a distinctive photograph in it. It was Claude Vorilon! There was a short piece about him and his claims, with the information that a programme was being broadcast that very evening! How extraordinary. Although by now I should have been accustomed to these coincidences, they still never fail to astound me. It seemed my wish to see Claude Vorilon was being granted.

Although my husband and I were separated at this time, he still came home at weekends – we lived at opposite ends of the house and our relationship was very prickly. However, he was interested when I told him 'Rael' was on the television in the evening, because I had already told him all about the book, so he watched the programme with me, which turned out to be very amusing, about eccentric people and their outrageous claims.

When Claude Vorilon was interviewed, he remained very composed and dignified despite the ridicule meted out to him. His English was not very good which made it difficult for him to elucidate his alleged experiences and the presenter had a field day asking him what the planet was like that he was taken to by the little green men. However, I was struck by something Claude said about colours on the planet, especially those of the sea, which he said we could not even begin to imagine here. I felt I knew what he was talking about because of the colours I saw in my dreams – I could not even begin to describe them to myself.

It seemed so auspicious that my wish to see Claude Vorilon had been granted, even if not in the flesh, but I was no more able to assess whether his story was true. I had no flash of intuition, no *knowing*, but deduced that the 'coincidence' of picking up the TV Times meant I should pursue this path whether I was apprehensive of it or not.

After the program had concluded, I felt a really strong urge visit Holkham beach, a short distance along the Norfolk coast from us. I was surprised that I wanted my husband to go with me and equally surprised that he agreed to take me. We journeyed in the uncomfortable silence of estranged spouses along the winding coast road. Once parked, we walked through the pinewood that accesses the beach. The tide was a long way out, the sea's edge hidden behind a distant sand bar. Once we had climbed over this, the calm sea was in full view, its waves lapping gently on the sand, sighing gently with its ebb and flow. Beautiful colours shimmered and danced across the waters – colours totally out of this world – pastel hues so luminescent and otherworldly – colours I could not identify because I had never seen them before. I looked at the sky, at the clouds, but it was overcast, no sun was shining, no blue sky was evident. There was nothing that might have reflected on the water to give such a stunning effect.

My husband, an artist, exclaimed, "Look at those colours – I've never seen anything like them in my life!"

Three things struck me: one was the 'coincidence' of finding myself with the TV Times, alerting me to the programme showing Claude Vorilon. The second was the urge to visit this particular beach and to take my nearly-ex-husband with me – as a witness to what we would see – the third was Claude's mention of the indescribable colours of the sea on the planet he had visited and now we were viewing colours just as indescribable.

If I had gone to the beach on my own, I do not think I would have believed my own eyes, but with my husband there, even in our acrimonious state at the time, he was able to confirm that he too witnessed the out-of-this-world colours shimmering on the sea's surface.

After these extraordinary coincidences had happened, I felt even more compelled to take the trip to France and no sensible argument with myself could dissuade me.

There were only three English members of the Raelian organisation at that time, one of whom, coincidentally, had also written a book on the Bible story very similar to Claude's – David Medina's, 'Elohim's Nursery', published by Regency Press. I contacted the English representative who arranged to meet me at the campsite. I booked my place on the course and purchased a coach ticket to Montpelier before I could change my mind.

I was terrified of what might await me, but reassured myself that if I reached the campsite and found I did not like it, I could leave and go home. If I did not go, I would never know what I had missed and it just might prove fruitful in my quest for understanding. All the 'coincidences' along the way, which had led me this far, reassured me to a certain extent, but the fear of the unknown did not lessen, despite my maxims to face them squarely.

I packed a rucksack with a small tent, a billycan and a small stove and a few items of clothing, and set off, full of total fear as to what I was letting myself into. Sheltered during my childhood and then marriage, I had never travelled anywhere on my own in England, yet alone abroad.

Reinforced by my dream about the bull (by facing my fears they were never as bad as I thought they might be) I did not back out of the trip. The coach drove me out of Norfolk down to London, but it was not until I was milling with young back-packers at Victoria Station in London, boarding the coach to France, that I was stirred with excitement. I realised I was having my very own adventure and began to enjoy myself. Despite the fact that I was now aged forty-five, I felt 'grown up' for the first time and was pleased with my progress.

Still fearful of the nudity and possible orgies I had to face, I arrived at the camp to find all my fears swept away in an instant. So many kind, beautiful people, some clothed in pretty garments, some nude and totally natural. I was put at my ease immediately, and before long I heard a familiar voice "Valaree – I thought I recognised you!" It was the fellow from the festival, so from then on I no longer felt nervous.

I had been hoping to glean more information about the aliens (or The Elohim, as they were referred to), but it seemed that the book held all the information and the course was to enable us to become more aware of our own potential and to learn to make the most of our lives. The sensual meditation, which I had been nervous about, turned out to be totally harmless. We merely learned to appreciate life through our senses – touch, vision, smell, hearing, taste as well as the extra sense, telepathy.

We were told to imagine ourselves as having been programmed like a computer by our parents and teachers, who in turn taught us by rote, and that it was time to de-program. I had a wonderful week, learned a lot about myself, though I was no nearer to deciding whether Rael – as Claude Vorilon now called himself – was an impostor or not.

For three years I made contact with the Raelians at the Course of Awakening in France and Switzerland, made a lot of wonderful friends and my life was changed, though I still kept an open mind on the claims of Rael.

I even found myself speaking of this story on the local Norfolk Radio, where phone-ins were used for listener participation. There were many who angrily rang to admonish that what we were talking about was the work of the Devil and that we should be avoided at all costs.

More spectacular synchronicity happened during the radio show, concerning one of the other speakers who was giving a talk on an entirely different subject. He interjected at one point when I mentioned the Hebrew word 'Elohim' (those who came from the sky) being wrongly translated from the plural to the singular. This gentleman 'coincidentally' was a professor of ancient Hebrew and confirmed this translation mistake had indeed been made and never rectified – which does rock the foundation of the now established Church. How does this kind of coincidence come about? That a professor of ancient Hebrew was on the same radio programme and confirmed the mistake – it is almost unbelievable.

Claude Vorilon, the man who claims to have met the Elohim, now calls himself 'Rael'- Hebrew for 'messenger'. His organisation, named The Raelian Movement, now has many thousands of members in different countries. Rael's aim is to inform people without trying to convince and raise enough money to build an embassy on ground where the Elohim in their spacecraft can land without fear.

When I first read the book and later met Rael, his claims seemed improbable, but in the twenty-nine years since he began to pass on his messages, they are now far more believable, especially as cloning is now a very real procedure.

Because my life took a very different turn, I no longer took part in any of the Movement's activities. I could not decide whether Rael was telling the truth about meeting the spacemen and, of course, I will never know. Maybe if I had waited to encounter the occupants of the spacecraft that was descending on Hunstanton cliffs, I would have had the same experiences as Rael.

Whether or not Rael's claims are true, from what I observed at the courses, I could see that he has helped many thousands of people to make the most of their potential and enjoy their lives to the full. I certainly gained a lot from the courses I attended, which, in turn, changed my life for the better as well as confirming that some of my far-flung beliefs were a possibility.

'REVOLUTION'
1985

Excitement stirred the Norfolk town of King's Lynn to magnified proportions when the news was announced that Goldcrest Films were using the town as the location for a film called 'Revolution', starring Donald Sutherland – my hero – Al Pacino and Nastassja Kinski. Also included were Sid Owen –'Rickie' from

Eastenders, then aged about nine – who was cast as Al Pacino's son, Joan Plowright, Annie Lennox, Robbie Coltrane, William Marlowe and many more.

Even greater excitement rustled the lives of ordinary folk when it was discovered that a multitude of extras were needed and that casting was to take place. I heard they were looking for a couple of 'whores' and thought it would be fun to apply. When I filled in my application form, I mentioned that I 'played a good tart'. This paid off because I got the job. It pays to be bold!

'Revolution' was a film featuring mediaeval New York, and King's Lynn was transformed overnight.

Nell – my co-whore – and I proved to be an excellent team. The director called us 'the old trouts', making sure we were at the front of the sets. Heady stuff. The 'gentry', dressed in all their finery, kept well away from us, warning young 'soldiers', wet behind the ears, to ignore us or we would get them into trouble. Clearly we looked the part! We had a ball. Nell and I had to shout out coquettish remarks to Al Pacino – contact with the great star. He was a quiet man, keeping out of the limelight, seldom speaking to anyone, but he always greeted me on set with a courteous 'Good morning'.

I soon became a prima donna, if only in my own eyes. As I rolled up late, as usual, one morning, a group of extras yelled at me "Val – quick – they are looking for you and want you in the office! Whoops, I thought to myself with sinking heart, I'm going to get the sack! I pushed my way through the thronging crowd of extras to meet my fate. It was not bad news that awaited me, however, but good. An American television news team were waiting for me in the office, and as I was introduced to them I wondered why they had called me in. It was soon explained that they had asked for the actress with the best personality to follow and film throughout the day for their news programme. The casting people had suggested me. While very flattered, I guessed that the film people probably did not want the television crew interfering with the film's progress by trailing after one of the real stars – but as I was only an extra out of the thousands on set, I was really excited to be chosen. The television interviewer quizzed me on my role. I wanted to come over as amusing and a bit saucy without causing offence to staid American matrons and felt I managed a professional performance.

At the end of the day, after the American television crew had trailed my every move, I was bedraggled and soaked from torrential 'rain'. Asked how I felt, I replied, "I've enjoyed every moment!"

I wished very much that I could see the finished result of my interview on camera to see if I had performed as professionally for them as I had hoped, but knew that it was designated for America's Coast to Coast programme, and not for Britain. Stupidly, I did not think to ask if they would send me a copy.

While filming, I was also running a bed and breakfast service from my home, and a few weeks later an American couple booked in for the weekend. I lived near Sandringham, ideally situated for their sightseeing.

When the Americans arrived, I greeted them at the door in my neat B&B attire.

The husband looked at me quizzically and said, "Gee, I know you! Where have I seen you before? No, don't tell me." He thought for a while, then a smile lit his face, "Gee, you're a whore, aren't you? I saw you on Coast to Coast Television!"

While most women would have despaired at such a greeting, I grinned with delight. Fame at last!

The American informed me that the programme had shown me being interviewed, sandwiched between Donald Sutherland and Al Pacino.

I asked my guest if I had given a professional performance and also if I had been as amusing as I had hoped and he enthused for hours! He told me that I had been wonderful, that I was clearly a 'renaissance woman' and that I ought to be interviewed on the Johnny Carson show.

Although I had previously wished I had seen the programme, meeting the American was in many ways even better, for I had been enthusiastically recognised by someone from over the ocean who had given me a far better prognosis of my performance than had it been my own critical evaluation. It was certainly a very good example of synchronicity.

This whole episode totally satisfied my latent aspirations for a star's life, quelling vague feelings harboured within in me that I could have been an actress had I tried that route.

★ ★ ★

MULE SAFARI FOR TWO
(A CAMEO)

Earlier on in this book, I told of my journey to France to visit the Raelian group. One of the new friends I had made invited me to Switzerland to participate in a mule safari across the Alps. I wanted to include this anecdote in the book to illustrate that if you face your fears in life there are many rewards to reap that you might never even have dreamt were possible.

★ ★ ★

SWITZERLAND

The fresh October morning dawned for our mule safari. At six a.m., we set off in a fine mist that hid the mountain peaks from view. Ghostly-looking cows with neck bells that tolled hauntingly waited by sheds to be milked, with tendrils of fog swirling around their legs, while nearby muck heaps steamed, filtering stray beams from the rising sun.

When we reached the stables, our mules were waiting for us, saddled and pannier-bagged. Used by the military – who were stationed in hidden mountain caves – for manoeuvres, these sturdy beasts earned extra money for their owners from people wanting a private excursion across the mountain regions.

I had never seen a mountain at close quarters. The distant ranges were so beautiful, with their shadowy peaks dipped with every purple hue, melting into the sky. I imagined our trip would take us to grassy slopes similar to those in the film 'The Sound of Music' with the Von Trapp family. And so it did.

As we began our ascent, we travelled steep paths beside creosoted log houses with red geraniums tumbling down the black walls. These houses were on stilts to deter rats, and under them logs were neatly piled in readiness for winter fires. We travelled through pine forests, the resinous aroma a delight to my senses. Deep blankets of fallen pine needles deadened the clink of the mules' hoofs.

Very soon, when I looked down, the villages had assumed doll's house proportions, while the sun, once risen over the mountains, brought warmth to the day and I was almost euphoric with the beauty all around me.

As we ascended higher, my mule – whose name was Rosie, despite being male – stopped. I thought he was just being stubborn, so gave him a kick with my heels to get him moving. He was most put out, bucked angrily and threw me off on to rocks, turned around and started for home. Luckily, I was not badly hurt and managed to catch, mollify and remount him. I pretended my bruises did not hurt as we set off again. I quickly realised that the poor burdened creature had merely stopped for a breather. It must have been hard, hot work toiling up the slopes and I learned that if I let him pause for breath when he needed it, he soon carried on quite happily without a prompt from me.

At lunchtime, we stopped on a grassy plateau dotted with alpine flowers and gurgling mountain rills. The two mules were shackled on an overhead wire that we rigged up, and Rosie lay down to rest. I sat beside the mule stroking his ears, breathing in his lovely aroma.

We ate our picnic with relish, enjoying the panoramic views around us. I wandered across the meadow to stretch my legs, overcome with the beauty around me. An abundance of black and red crickets were chirping loudly, the rill waters splashed over small stones, birds sang, leaves rustled, distant bells tolled melodiously and the hills truly seemed alive with 'The Sound of Music'. I hummed the Julie Andrews song as I surveyed the beauty around me.

In the distance I could see the sun-bleached walls of a cluster of wooden houses where people had stared and dogs had barked as we passed by. One boy had been playing a huge tuba as he leaned against the warm wall – a scene I have never forgotten. What a blissful expedition!

My friend asked, "Can you walk?"

I replied I could – after all, I walked from my house to the car and from the car to the shops without a problem. I did not really understand his question until he mentioned that there were two alternative routes we could take. One would involve some walking but was the prettiest. Without realising what would be in store for me, I opted for the prettier route with walking.

We journeyed on, going ever higher. By now, despite the sun, the air was getting thinner and colder and there were pockets of snow by shadowy boulders. I admired the distant view, thinking that this experience was worth far, far more to me than gold bangles and other material riches.

Many millennia ago, fissures cleaved the mountainside leaving it cut deeply into a sheer precipice at this spot, with only a narrow ledge just wide enough for the mules to traverse. The view was breathtaking and, as I peered down, I noticed, thousands of feet below, a white-laced river dashing over rocks, looking like a mere ribbon of water as it hurtled to its destination.

My senses had been so overloaded with all the beauty around me that I realised, too late, that I was sat on an unpredictable mule whose tiny black hoofs were knocking shale and small rocks off the edge of a dangerous precipice with only sheer rock rising up close on one side of me and a dangerous drop to oblivion too close on the other. There was no room to turn round to return to safety. Suddenly, I was terrified. Suddenly, I wanted to be at home. This was far too risky!

I began to panic until I realised that I must not because, if the little mule sensed my fear, he might throw me off again and this time there would be no happy ending!

Taking big breaths to calm myself, I decided it would be better not to look down at the chasm but to have trust in my mule instead, whose footing seemed very sure – even though he insisted on treading along the edge of the precipice!

I turned my face to the rock wall that flanked us so I could not see the danger around me, and was disconcerted to notice that so did Rosie. Remembering how my own horse, Tiffany, could read my mind, I deduced that perhaps Rosie, reading mine, thought ignoring the drop to death was a better option. A large angry wasp buzzed along from nowhere, adding further worry in case it stung Rosie and caused him to throw me over the edge, but after a while of anxiety, it noisily buzzed away.

My friend, riding ahead, turned around on his mule to grin at me. I vowed I would kill him when we got to safety – he had not told me were going to face *danger*, for goodness sake!

After passing along the ledge of the precipice to eventual safety, I dismounted with shaking legs, then walked back to view the scene I had just traversed. If I had realised what the trip entailed, I would never have come – but I had dealt with it and felt really pleased with myself.

More hazards were to come. I was told that we could no longer ride our mules, as the going was too dangerous. How could it be more dangerous than what we had just been through? Pointing to a narrow, zigzagging goat track that led down the perpendicular mountainside, my friend set off, pulling his reluctant mule behind him. I had no other course but to follow, and found Rosie protesting as I pulled on his reins. I reasoned that if the mule did not want to go, then that route must be really unsafe! The route was so narrow, so steep, so dangerous, that my feet were agonisingly pointed downwards at impossible angles. A shepherd tending his flock looked shocked to see where we were going and put his finger to his head indicating that we were crazy. I think we probably were.

Rosie picked his way carefully. I knew that if he lost his footing behind me, he would push me off the mountainside to certain death, but as we journeyed carefully down, I noticed that this mule and I developed a rhythm and were acting as one. We would both stop simultaneously to rest a moment, catch our breath in the thin air and find better footing, and I felt very linked to this seemingly bilingual creature that understood 'Whoa' and 'Steady boy' and 'Oh my God!'

It took an age to make the hair-raising descent to the bottom where there rushed a wide, fast-running but shallow river. I was so hot from my exertions that the snowmelt waters rushing from the high peaks felt blissful. As we waded across on foot, I delighted in drinking the icy waters from my cupped hands. The mules siphoned the water through their soft lips while cooling their hooves. I thought this was the end of the dangerous footwork and was ready to remount – but no, we had other mountains to climb and cross, and still on foot. I was horrified at the thought. With little strength left, I wondered how I could cope.

I felt so hot, so exhausted and my feet were killing me in borrowed boots. I felt I could not possibly go any further but knew that I had to – there was no going back. Amazingly, I discovered hidden strengths and endurances that I was unaware I possessed. Exhausted, I coped with the difficulties by giving myself goals – a sheep trough spied high up the slope with clear water rushing in and out of it, where, once it was reached, I planned to plunge my arms and head to cool down; or a miniscule ribbon of a river miles below, where I resolved to take off my boots and dangle my throbbing feet in the cooling water – such focussed concentration was necessary to survive. I developed a rhythm, which kept me going. In my head I hummed 'Onward Christian Soldiers' to keep the pace and, oh, what utter bliss when those goals were met!

Despite the gruelling experience, I was aware of all the beauty around me. Waterfalls cheerfully threw themselves off the top of mountain crags to plunge in foaming confusion at the base – sunlight reflecting and dancing in the spume. The perfumes of the grasses and flowers were heady, the bells tolled and tinkled melodiously around the necks of goats with curled horns, perched with cloven hoofs on ridiculously small ledges as they stared at us in disbelief. The songs of crickets and birds were music in my ears and the purple, pink and blue hues of the distant mountain ranges so stunningly beautiful. My every sense was overloaded.

Everything was glorious, even my fear, my exhaustion, my aches and pains. I can truly say *that day*, containing such beauty and rigorous feats, was the most exciting and wonderful day of my life and I now know and understand why adventurers adventure!

The beauty I experienced was spiritual and the discovery of my own strengths and endurances remarkable, and while, initially, I could have cheerfully throttled my friend for putting me through such a gruelling danger, I am so glad he did, otherwise I would never have had such a memorable and wonderful experience that will stay in my mind for ever.

Had I not decided to take the initial journey to France to meet the Raelians, my life would certainly never have been so enriched as it is now. I had followed my intuitions and taken heed of the 'coincidences' that eventually led me to the mule safari, where fate rewarded me with a plethora of amazing realities where I was as one with nature and my steed, the memories of which I will carry to my dying day. That day was a spiritual experience and, maybe, a reward for facing my initial fears when deciding whether or not to visit the Raelian Course of Awakening.

So, who would reward me in this way, I wonder? Little green men or spirit guides – or are they part of an amalgamation?

★ ★ ★

'Beguiled by Magic' – The Magician and his daughter, two year old Valerie.
Photo: Gordon Anckorn.

'Madame Salami' reading the palm of Hurricaine Smith, pop star.

'Just the gypsy in our souls' – Orphan Annie and Val having fun. Photo: Sarah Hunt.

'Off to the chip shop' – Lucinda, Nick and Heartsease. Photo: Courtesy of The Lynn News.

'Following the wedding vardo' - Val flanked by partner Kent (in shades) and son Leigh.
Photo: Gordon Anckorn.

'Trade's a bit slow' – Val in foreground a film extra. Photo: Gordon Anckorn.

'Waiting for some action' on set of 'Revolution' in King's Lynn. Debbie, Val and Nell. Photo: Courtest of Lynn News.

'Val and trusty steed Tiffany, trying to apply a little horse sense to the art of riding'.
Photo: Courtesy of Lynn News.

"Did you hear the one about…" Val with Tiffany and Kitty Purr.
Photo: Gordon Anckorn.

'Valerie and her dog Peter when they lived at Green Street Green' – Photo: Gordon Anckorn.

"What, no parachute?" an excited Val waiting in cockpit of Tiger Moth for her first flight.
Photo: Gordon Anckorn

PART FIVE

ANOTHER MOVE
SEPTEMBER 1985

Because of the parting of the ways between my husband and myself, the beautiful family home had to be sold, which was quite heartbreaking. I moved into a small semi-detached house and got on with the difficult task of trying to earn my own living, which up to now had not been a necessity – I had been married in the era of stay-at-home mums. I thought that my life would be fraught with dismal jobs and small earnings. I had not realised that I would not be able to get a job! It seemed at the age of forty-five I was over the hill and unemployable. I managed to get a few low paid temporary jobs to tide me over, but at that time my life looked bleak. My ex was very gallant and helped me out financially until I was able to cope on my own.

A DREAM OF DEATH

October 1986

One of our friends, who had died in his thirties, was a jeweller named Peter Green. I was always surprised when I received messages from him from time to time if I visited a medium. In one reading, his message was, "This will make you laugh, Val, I'm looking after the children now." It didn't make me laugh because I thought he would make a wonderful carer – he was just a big handsome kid himself when he was alive. When one of my friends lost her small child, she found it comforting when I told her that my friend was probably looking after him. When mediums saw Peter, they described him holding out a ring – his work – for identification.

December 1986

I had a dream about Peter Green, but he did not feature in it for long. Another man appeared, came towards me and took me into his arms. This was not a

161

lovers' embrace, but one of comfort in the midst of grief and death – it was almost spiritual.

When I awoke, I was disturbed at the indication of death, wondering if it was a premonition of my own demise, and that the man who had embraced me was God greeting me at the Pearly Gates! So often my dreams had to be interpreted from scant information and this dream held no clues at all. I thought that maybe it was a warning for me to be careful.

I told my boyfriend about the dream. He had been married previously and his wife had often had precognitive dreams, so he did not view me as crazy, which came as a welcome relief to me. The only thing I felt I could do to avoid the Grim Reaper was to drive carefully, so whenever I took out my car, I drove at an annoying snail's pace, checking keenly for possible hazards.

Christmas Eve arrived without mishap. I set off in my car to collect the turkey from a butcher's shop about five miles away. Driving carefully, I probably made more of a nuisance of myself along narrow country roads than if I had been driving at a normal speed. However, there was little traffic so when I reached a wide, straight stretch of the coast road with not a car in sight, I realised it was safe to go faster. As soon as I had put my foot on the accelerator a black and white collie hurtled out of a boat yard, straight in front of my car. I braked immediately but it was too late; with a horrible thwack of impact, the dog was hurled up on to my windscreen, its tongue lolling and blood flying. It was ghastly. My car skidded with screeching brakes right across the road, the dog still bouncing up and down on my windscreen, its body obscuring my vision. Luckily, there was no traffic in either direction. When my car eventually came to a skidding halt, I climbed out, shaking.

A man ran out from the yard. I walked unsteadily across the road to him, still in shock, and asked him in consternation, "Is it your dog?" I was so upset that I had killed the animal. For some reason he did not answer me, but by now another man was running from a road opposite. "It's my dog!" he said, and I turned to meet him in the middle of the road.

He was muttering to himself in shock, "What am I going to tell the children – and on Christmas Eve!"

I felt terrible. Without thought, we both instinctively put our arms round each other for comfort. It was so strange – there was I, with my heart going out to this stranger, hugging him silently, trying to make him feel better, and he was doing the same to me. He realised that I was as upset as him and that it was not my fault. I felt a deep feeling of spirituality pass between us. We did not talk – there was nothing to say – our embrace had said all that was necessary. The dog had been wandering around in the boat yard, had seen his owner coming across the road and had shot out to meet him, straight into the path of my car.

When I drove off, with a huge dent in the front of my car, I recalled my dream with a shock of understanding. *Peter Green.* I'd had a dog named *Peter* when I lived as a child at *Green Street Green.* (The dog I killed looked exactly like my childhood dog.) The premonition of death made sense in retrospect and had nothing to do with my own death.

This was a precognitive dream, but a cleverly encrypted one. Not only had my brain picked up a future event (which I was powerless to prevent) but it had formed the dream in a sort of pictorial code. I was not able to foretell or stop the event happening but I was certainly able to understand it afterwards. The curious embrace with the dog's owner had exactly the same feeling as it had in the dream.

★ ★ ★

ASTROLOGY

Summer 1987

The new owner of my old home was an astrologer and my delight was immense when she said she was going to give astrological lessons. Since my first interest in the zodiac when I did my stint as Madame Salami, I was so keen to learn more.

At the first class I attended, I actually felt the cogs of my brain spring into action. I had never been interested in schoolwork but this was something I really wanted to learn. Used to creative thinking, which requires no effort whatsoever on my part, it was good to feel my brain working in such an enthusiastic manner.

I had always thought I would not be able to understand the mechanics of astrology due to the mathematical calculations, but was relieved to realise that this was no longer necessary with computers able to process the necessary data. How I enjoyed those classes. I had first attended with an eager curiosity, but as the lessons progressed, the keener I became. I found it quite amazing to discover that characters and personalities are stamped by the planets' positions overhead at the moment of birth.

My astrology teacher surprised me by telling me that her brother and I were astrological twins – both sharing the same date and year of birth and born in the same location at more or less the same time. My twin, during his working life, was a well-known Fleet Street columnist – and one of the 'William Hickeys' – who first earned a living as an actor before turning to journalism. I, too, am a writer and have done a fair bit of acting, though the willing state of motherhood initially curbed my talents in those directions.

When I eventually met my 'twin' to compare notes, we discovered that the parallels in our life are quite astonishing. For instance, when I was around eighteen my father took me up for my first flight in a Tiger Moth. This is a light, two-seater aircraft, one behind the other, with no canopy, the pilot sitting at the controls behind the passenger. I have never been so exhilarated or more in awe of life as I was on my first trip away from terra firma. To be in the open air high above the earth was a magical experience and, as I leaned out to touch the clouds, I would not have been surprised to see an angel passing by. I piloted the plane a few times – the passenger seat had controls as well – to enable my dad to bend over the edge to take aerial photographs, never wondering what I would do if he fell out! Understandably, I was thrilled by the experience.

At that time of my life, my thoughts were centred on marriage and babies rather than flying lessons, but the opportunity was there had I wished to take it up. Peter Tory, my astrological twin, gained his pilot's licence as a young man, learning to do aerobatics in a 'Tiger', which he told me was not easy as they flew like old bedsteads, but that they were beautiful in their own way and wonderful for sunny summer day flying along the sand dunes. Now retired and living in the witch country of Salem in America, he owns a Piper Archer 111 and has joined 'Angel Flight', which is an organisation where pilots fly sick people from remote areas to hospitals.

The most stunning realisation was that both our lives had been saved by divine intervention. My life had been saved by the disembodied voice warning me of a car accident. Peter told me that he had a 'spooky' experience in Cornwall. He had climbed a cliff and got stuck under the overhanging grass at the top. He could not go up or down. He decided to grab the grass, knowing that it would not hold and he would fall to his death. At that moment, a man's arms came over and he was pulled to safety. When he had got his breath back, he looked around to thank his rescuer, but could see no one in either direction along the cliff.

Many people would probably not believe Peter's story – or mine, come to that – but as I had seen my own daughter magically lifted out of the road from almost under an oncoming car, I could accept what he told me. Peter's story gave me the affirmation that both 'improbable' rescues really did happen.

I was also amused to discover that Peter was always known as 'The Magician' within his extended family – keen on the art of illusion and sleight of hand, he kept everyone enthralled at family gatherings. This tied up with my own experiences at home.

I was astonished at the many traits and similarities Peter and I shared, and meeting my 'twin' convinced me of the validity of astrology more than anything else could have – to realise that such similar parallels in our lives were all due to the same planet configurations at the time of our birth was rather awe inspiring!

What were the odds, I had to wonder, of meeting my astrological twin in such a manner?

★ ★ ★

The nuances of astrology are a continued learning process, but the time came when I had learned enough of the rudiments to be able to read and interpret a natal chart. Invited to be the guest speaker of a ladies' club, I was asked to study a member's natal chart so that the audience could guess, from my description, the person I was portraying. Being a novice astrologer this was a huge challenge and I was understandably nervous about the task. I should not have worried as the mystery lady was soon identified – and purely from the description I had given from my interpretation of the planet positions at the woman's moment of birth!

I suspect my 'spiritual tutors' had organised the whole thing for me and this was another test or 'exam' along my journey of discovery.

★ ★ ★

A SHORT LESSON IN ASTROLOGY

So what exactly is astrology and how does it work?

An example: it is common knowledge that the moon influences the tides that ebb and flow as it circles the earth. As our bodies contain a large percentage of water, logically the moon will also pull at our bodies in a similar manner, which in turn affects how we feel. It is well known that women's moods wax and wane every month with their menstrual cycle according to the moon's pull.

We are also aware that when the moon is full, people can be strangely affected. Think of the word 'lunatic' – derived from the French word, 'lune' (moon). People with mental disorders are put on stronger medication when the moon is full. The police station is busier at full moon and people with behavioural problems need supervision and sedatives at that time. The only time I have nightmares is when the moon is full. It affects us all in different ways. Seeds sown at a New Moon grow better than those sown on a waning moon. The same applies for projects. We all *know* and accept that the moon affects us in these ways – so is it not, therefore, *logical* to assume that the other planets can also influence us?

In our galaxy there are ten near stars or planets, which affect us in various ways. The Sun, Moon, Mercury, Venus, Mars, Jupiter, Saturn, Uranus, Neptune and Pluto.

Briefly, I set out below their influences:

The Sun governs the self, our ego.
The Moon rules emotions.
Mercury gives communication skills and mental or bodily action.
Venus gives an appreciation of beauty and love.
Mars brings action, aggression, fight and passion.
Jupiter brings belief systems, sport and travel.
Saturn teaches us to learn by our mistakes.
Uranus brings us inventiveness and change.
Neptune brings nebulism.
Pluto rules our subconscious.

Depending on where the planets fall in a person's natal chart, or horoscope, it is possible to interpret how the planets' influence and give character and potential for both humans and animals. Please note the word 'potential'. Everyone is given potential, but it is up to the individual whether he uses it or not. My astrological twin and myself are a prime example. He became an aviator while I only steered a plane a couple of times. Had I wanted to pursue the potential, I, too, could have 'got my wings'.

People often want to know if biological twins are going to be the same. Yes, they can be – but there is 'individuality' that comes into play. They might have the same characteristics and potential as each other, but they also have choice. Therefore, they choose which route to take in life – to be like peas in a pod with their twin or to strike out on their own.

The planets' progress across the heavens can be mapped and their future (or past) positions referred to in an 'ephemeris' – a book of tables a bit like our mathematical ones.

If required, it is easy to check to see what the planets are doing on any given day, to see how they correspond with those on a natal chart and to speculate how it could affect the 'native' or owner of the chart in either a positive or negative manner. Unless one is clairvoyant, it is not possible to state exactly what will happen – and then it could be hit or miss – but, for example, if Saturn passing overhead was going to 'sit' on Saturn on a natal chart, then it would be sensible for the 'native' to be careful that day. Likewise, if Jupiter passing overhead were 'sitting' on Jupiter on the natal chart, then the 'native' would probably be lucky in enterprises that day.

Astrology is a very important tool in the understanding of yourself and those around you – especially children, who can be guided into what is right for them and not just what their parents dream for them. It is a science that can be learned and appreciated by anybody. Unfortunately, it has been viewed as an occult and dubious practice of 'fortune tellers'.

I really look forward to the day when the craft of astrology is no longer viewed with suspicion and outlawed by religion. Hopefully, in the future it will be taught in schools as part of a national curriculum. But first the 'shrouded mystery' has to be put aside.

During my palmistry days I was interested to discover that the craft linked with astrology and that I could guess from the feel of my clients' hands which 'element' they came under and from that guess at their sun sign. For instance:

Earth (dry palms, few lines) – Taurus, Virgo or Capricorn.
Water (moist, lots of lines) – Scorpio, Cancer or Pisces.
Air (dry with clear-cut lines) – Libra, Aquarius or Gemini.
Fire (hot, deep lines) – Aries, Leo or Sagittarius.

★ ★ ★

PART SIX

THE MOVE TO A SHRINE VILLAGE
AUGUST 1988

My life was changing dramatically. After three years of 'courtship' my boyfriend and I were ready for the commitment of a shared home. I had been unsuccessful in my search for secretarial employment – over the hill at forty-five, I was forced to consider self-employment to earn a living. I already knew that I did not like working for other people, and my astrological configurations indicated that I would be better as an employer than an employee. I did not visualise having my own business but was forced to consider an alternative route when every job application was turned down.

Thank goodness nobody wanted me because I was soon to lead a totally fulfilling, if monetarily precarious, life. I was to learn the wonderful lesson of self-worth and experience the heady joys of coping and overcoming all kinds of hurdles and obstacles.

I could only attempt work that I was already capable of. In my last home I had tried earning some money with bed and breakfast. While this was not enough to earn a full living, we thought that with the addition of a candle work-shop from which to sell my candles, the two combined occupations should do the trick. We therefore looked for suitable property with enough bedrooms for B&B and outhouses for the candle making.

Kent, my boyfriend, suggested looking in Walsingham, a delightful North Norfolk mediaeval village famed for its pilgrimages to the Shrine of Our Lady since the 11th Century. History relates that the lady of the manor, Richeldis, had a vision in an auspicious dream with a visitation by the Virgin Mary who instructed her to build a shrine, a replica of that in Nazareth. After its construction, royalty came to visit the new shrine, and before long pilgrims walked bare-footed, with cockleshells in their hats to denote the purpose of their journey, from all over the country to pray to Mary, now referred to as Our Lady of Walsingham.

An abbey and friary were built to house the many pilgrims and soon a bustling holy village was in full swing, catering for the thousands – and so it continues to this day, pilgrims arriving by the coach load to pray at the, now, two shrines (one for the Church of England the other for the Catholics) and to visit shops groaning with holy artefacts.

We imagined that amongst all this hustle and bustle of religious activity, B&B and candles ought to go down well.

We were lucky enough to find just the place – a run down, almost derelict old house with a stable and ruined outbuildings. Something really strange happened to me while I was viewing the property from the garden. I was surprised to have the feeling that Mary stood beside me and that she wanted me to live in the village. This was an unexpected thought for me, as I had long ago been disenchanted by the Church. My beliefs had understandably changed due to the bombardment of psychic activity and I could no longer believe in the organised religion I had been taught when younger. Apart from that, the denomination in which I received religious instruction did not revere Mary in the same way as in the High and Catholic Churches. I saw her role only as an ordinary mother of a supernatural son and was surprised when I realised she was so highly venerated in the village. It was odd for me to feel her presence so clearly in the garden.

1988 was the year when interest rates soon doubled and recession set in. People not able to keep up with mortgage instalments lost their homes, redundancies occurred and it was a difficult time for everyone. We had purchased our cottage at the onset of the recession and soon had to re-mortgage to survive, which was very worrying. Two incidences happened, however, which made me believe we would get through the troubled era.

All the walls of the cottage were heavily layered with old wallpaper and, after we had painstakingly scraped it off, we reached the bottom level to discover old newspapers pasted as a liner on to the original plaster. Unfortunately, due to the strong glue, we were frustrated by only saving small scraps, which revealed fascinating snippets of ancient news or adverts. I eventually found a date on one of the newspaper scraps. Surprisingly, it was dated 9th August 1888, exactly one hundred years prior to the date we moved in – what a find! It seemed like an omen that all would be well. It was not until the 12th February of the next year when we were grappling with the wallpaper in the upstairs hallway that we discovered another dated scrap of newspaper. Astonishingly, it was dated the 12th February 1889! Again, it was dated exactly one hundred years apart to the day we found it. No longer just a happy coincidence, I was totally convinced that this was Mary's way of letting us know that we would not lose our home. We did survive the recession.

In later years, when we decided to sell the cottage and convert the barn in its garden into a new home, I found a small piece of newspaper, black with dust, tied to a frame of some sort that had been hung from a beam in the barn loft. How strange to find it dated 12th June 1862. My daughter's birthday was 11th

June 1962. Yes, a day out, but still quite miraculous. I wondered what made the person originally tie it there? It served no purpose, but finding it also made me reinforce my belief that we were doing the right thing at the time with the new project. However, I am pre-empting my story....

During the cottage renovations, an electrician found under the attic floorboards two pages torn from 'The Astrological Ephemeris' dated 1800. A strange discovery in a shrine village where astrology is frowned upon, especially, I would think, in the eighteen hundreds. All the more curious, too, that I am an astrologer and use an ephemeris. It was a warming thought to know that an astrologer had lived in my cottage all those years ago.

My thoughts about Mary, or Our Lady of Walsingham, increased after I read in a publication that there had always been a 'lady' in the village since pagan times and probably long before. I wondered if she was one and the same person throughout the ages, but the next dream made me wonder more.

★ ★ ★

I dreamt that I was in a dark, primeval forest, kneeling on ground thick and spongy with fallen leaves. Huge trees rose high into the grey sky, their branches black and stark.

I was kneeling on the ground, aware that a lady stood in front of me. There was no sunshine; all was dark, sorrowful, brooding and silent.

I was overcome with the feeling of such enormous grief that I howled this torment into the soil. The tangible *huge* anguish, however, was not my own. I wept and howled the pain, the gut-wrenching misery, that kept on coming, right from the core of my being and sank with my tears into the depths of the earth. During this awful wailing lament, I was aware that the woman, garbed in a long gown, was waiting for my experience of the pain to finish. Eventually, when the awful grief had been poured into the soil, I looked up to regard her more closely. I asked her name. She did tell me, but sadly, I was not able to remember it when I woke up. I *knew*, however, that she was some Nature Goddess or Deity.

I also *knew* that she had allowed me to feel the grief of the Earth, of this planet, that is rapidly being destroyed by humankind. The place I was in was a dead place. Was it a place of the future, showing what it will be like if we do not stop the destruction of our planet? I was shown the terrible grief of a dying world.

I wondered if Mary had been that goddess, or nature deity in a previous incarnation. Why did she let me feel that anguish? That my awesome experience is entered into this book might give readers cause to reflect that our planet is becoming unstable – that we are being led to an inevitable loss of all life. How is it possible that a few people could be usefully effective in stopping the terrible decline? It would be good to think that 'eco-warriors' and politicians could work together to find a harmonious solution – but is that a possibility?

★ ★ ★

THE FIRST MIRACLE –
UP, UP AND AWAY

Kent and I worked hard to get the cottage habitable and ready for paying guests. I had been host to paying guests before so knew a little of what to expect, but my eyes were opened in astonishment to some of the goings on that we encountered in our home. A vicar and a prostitute who left their room in complete disarray after a drunken debauch – she sold her story to a seedy Sunday tabloid – gay priests who took exception to my shower, Charismatic Catholics who accused me of witchcraft, a lady who believed she had a tree growing out of the top of her head, and a gentleman whose leg was burned internally from a minor case of spontaneous combustion!

My life was hectic, cooking breakfasts, changing, washing and ironing bed linen, cleaning the house before and after guests, getting in food stores, preparing evening meals and getting out into the candle workshop by ten o'clock in order to make and sell my candles to passing tourists.

Looking back, I do not know how I coped, especially as life was not made easier by an incontinent wolfhound pup, a Houdini-inclined rescued lurcher who threw herself with abandon through window panes, parcels of beautiful kittens produced by a snobby pedigree silver tabby named Doreen – she of amazing black eye liner, who enjoyed a port and lemon at the pub next door. Sparky, the grey cat who had received the amazing healing was still with me together with a sibling, Bartholomew, from a later litter. To complete the menagerie was another cat named Dorothy.

I had to get some assistance and employed a nun, Sister Anne, who belonged to the Order of The Little Sisters of Jesus. Anne suffered a life-long genetic disorder of neurofibromatosis and related scoliosis. She was tiny, her spine was crooked and she was seldom without pain. I adored her. Unlike many of the religious people in the village whom I had met, she was not at all blinkered in her beliefs and we could talk about spirituality until the cows came home. She helped me with the candle making, and I would get so upset when sometimes parents dragged their children away from her because she looked 'different'. She had to put up with the stares of unkind people but she never complained that life was not fair.

Sister Anne confessed that before she died she had a dream she hoped to fulfil – a trip in a hot air balloon. At that instance, I knew with the same certainty that I had when I magicked the Halloween baby years before, that I would achieve that desire for her. I could not afford to pay for a trip but was convinced that somehow I would make it happen.

I found myself in the paper shop purchasing a copy of Country Living. I did not normally buy the more expensive magazines, as the budget would not allow it, so felt very guilty at the unwarranted expense and wondered why I had made the purchase. I read through the magazine with enjoyment to find my eyes riveted on a competition. The prize for the best entry was *a trip in a hot air balloon for two!* At once I realised why I had been led to buy the magazine. This was for Anne and I knew I would win the trip for her.

I did not tell her what I was planning, but when informed I had won the prize, I will never forget the look of wonder and excitement on her face when I told her that her wish for a balloon trip was being fulfilled!

The big day dawned and I cannot say I was particularly thrilled at the prospect of ascending the clouds in what seemed like a small and rickety dog-basket! Only the previous day I had read a newspaper article about some balloonists being burned to death on a crash landing – but I kept that information to myself. This was Anne's treat and, as we ascended into the skies, she was oblivious to fear and in a fever of excitement. She enjoyed the trip to the utmost degree, her beautiful eyes shining like fireflies.

The basket was so small that the three of us only just squeezed in and I thought how vulnerable we would be if we crashed, especially with the large gas bottle taking up most of the space and ready to explode into flames on impact. I noticed the pilot looking nervous as he listened-in to his radio control and asked if there was trouble.

"Not up here," he replied, "but winds have blown up below and we have to get through them on the descent."

The strong winds hurled us hither and thither as we descended and coming down we nearly crashed into a wood – but as we skimmed the treetops, I enjoyed the wonderful sensation of feeling like a bird about to land on a branch. Safely over the threatening trees and with the wind buffeting the basket, the pilot warned us we would have a bumpy landing. He planned to protect Anne by shielding her with his own body as she was so fragile, and I was told to brace myself for the landing by clinging to either side of the basket with knees bent to take the shock.

As the basket crashed on to the ground, it flipped over on its side and we fell with it. We were plummeted, inside the basket, across the stubble field, propelled sideways at a rate of knots by the strong wind. It was very scary, but I had braced myself well and was not hurt at all. However, Anne's screams were horrifying as she was thrown to the floor, squashed by the pilot who had fallen on top of her. When her screams were suddenly silenced, I thought she had died. So, too, did the pilot.

"Is she dead?" he asked me, his face pale.

"No, she's fine," I lied, "just do what you have to do." I knew that he had to turn off the gas flames or we would be incinerated and probably blown up as well – that newspaper report was fresh in my mind.

By now the balloon had deflated and was stable and the pilot had hopped out to turn off the gas and do other necessary things. I was able to turn my attention to my friend.

"Anne!" I spoke urgently to the prone, limp body. "Can you hear me?"

Silence.

"Anne!" I really thought she was dead and wondered what to do.

Eventually, with a little groan, Anne whimpered a response. So relieved to know she was alive, I asked her to see if she could move, but Anne told me that she thought her legs were broken. After a little while, she found that she could move and got shakily to her feet. No broken bones after all. She was soon dancing around the field, saying that the experience was worth the pain and was as happy as a lark.

I knew that with Anne's illness and the medication taken for it that she could bruise herself even turning over in bed, so I was very anxious about the effect this experience may have had on her. I told her to tuck herself up in bed as soon as she got home and not to come to work in the morning. By now the balloon crew had turned up, as had Kent, my partner, with glasses filled with champagne for us, which was a good ending for an almost perfect trip.

Despite advising her not to return to work, Anne came in the next day, her face beaming with happiness. Curiously, however, she did not have a bruise anywhere on her body. She told me she felt absolutely fine and really could not believe why she was not black and blue all over.

That was odd, but even odder was the fact that, while I had not hurt myself at all on the landing, I was, by some curious means, covered in bruises. Had, by some miraculous means, her bruises been transferred to me? Unlikely though it might seem, I do believe they had.

The balloon ride was certainly a trip of a lifetime that neither of us will ever forget and for more reasons than one.

★ ★ ★

SNIFFED OUT

When the Charismatic Catholics had their five-day convention in the village, it was a good opportunity for those with bed and breakfast establishments to cash-in before the winter set in. I was lucky enough to have a full house booked and looked forward to having some 'happy-clappy' guests with charismatic personalities. I put a lot of effort into making sure their rooms were attractive and comfortable and was just putting the final vases of flowers in the rooms when my guests arrived. I was rather disappointed at their dour faces that did not raise an answering smile at my cheery greeting. They watched me bring in the remaining vase of flowers as if I were bringing in a chalice of poison. They seemed offended with their rooms and after returning from an evening at their convention, astonished me by moving their belongings out, saying they could not possibly stay in such an anti-Christian house. A horseshoe displayed over the door, a book on herbs and my décor offended them.

I was deeply upset because I took pride in my home and put an awful lot of effort into making it comfortable and attractive for my guests. They were convinced that they had entered into a house of evil and, as their eyes bore accusingly into mine, I felt as helpless as the innocent women in mediaeval times standing before the Witch Finder General.

It was true, my beliefs were not as theirs, but I have never been anti-Christian, and while my décor might not have been to their taste, everything was clean and comfortable. While I held all respect for that which is good and right, they were not to know that. In their eyes I was a witch and to be avoided at all costs.

I have to admit that after they had gone I wept for hours at what felt like a completely unjust vilification. As a 'reluctant psychic' – one that has strange things happen out of the blue, but does nothing to call them – it seems I had been sniffed out as something revolting and dangerous.

Later on, at the instigation of the local Catholic priest who knew me well and liked me, the organisers came to my door to pay me for my loss of earnings. I asked them in and as they stepped over my portal they looked so scared, as if I was going to turn them into toads. By the time they had finished telling me how un-Christian I was, I would have done, had I known how! That they were extremely frightened of the 'dark side' was very evident. Well, so too was I, but it was very upsetting to realise that they believed I was a black witch and a danger to them all.

The next day, Sister Anne and myself repeatedly discussed what had happened.

At the height of our discussions there was a scrunch of footsteps over the gravel coming towards the candle workshop. As we looked up we saw a tiny dwarf man with such a cheery face, his full-sized wife, and their infant dwarf daughter. Hand-in-hand, they happily smiled and laughed their way into our workshop to admire the candles. How much love emanated from them – what a lovely family group!

Tears came into my eyes. It seemed to me that God had sent along these happy, loving people as a kind of peace offering, saying, "See these people – they might have reasons to be miserable, be the butt of peoples' stares and hurtful comments, yet they are finding happiness wherever they go instead of complaining and seeking evil like those people did yesterday!"

After the happy trio had departed, both Anne and I felt totally uplifted. Anne remarked, "If that wasn't a message from God, I'll eat my veil!"

We both laughed happily and pushed the thoughts of unpleasant people away from our minds.

It does, after all, take all sorts to fill our world, and it would be very strange indeed if everybody were the same.

★ ★ ★

Unhappily, this kind of thing happened to me quite frequently while I lived in the village. I wondered what it was about me that made the Christian pilgrims suspect I was a witch. As a psychic, I must have a different look about me, because I was 'sniffed out' on many occasions, and some ladies who stepped into my candle shop would make an abrupt turn, saying, "Oh, evil!" and scurry out again. Had I been a member of a coven or practiced some sort of witch-craft, I could have understood it, but I just did bed and breakfast and made candles.

I was often to feel primitive fear when I caught the accusing looks of those who would pin their projected dark thoughts upon me, and did not like it at all.

I even began to wonder if I had been in this village before, in a past life where I had been a 'wise woman' and suffered hanging in the Martyrs' field. I found out from a local, whose family went back generations, that witches had been hung there, way back in the past.

Perhaps I was being fanciful, but one day when driving along a lane, I passed a procession of pilgrims following their priest who was chanting psalms through a loud hailer, while a huge crucifix was carried aloft by two stalwart men. As I eased my car carefully around the devoted, I was surprised to find myself shaking all over and feeling physically sick! I could not believe or under-stand what was happening to me, but it would make sense if I had indeed been carted off to my death by a frenzied group of psalm-chanting Christians in a different life. Maybe I was picking up old vibes when that kind of thing happened, but whatever the reason, I was filled with primitive fear of the baying masses.

I have to say, however, that of the few negative fanatics that disturbed my days in Walsingham, there were so many wonderful people I met who more than outweighed the unpleasant episodes. I also came to realise that a place like Walsingham has unique qualities that draw to it both the good and the bad. So as well as the divinely spiritual, it draws the dark side, too. To people that are sensitive, it can feel very disturbing at times and euphoric at others.

★ ★ ★

One of the unusual things that happen in Walsingham are the 'miracles', especially after people have taken the waters at the shrine's well. I can claim knowledge of one of the miracles that happened to a member of a small party of sightless people who were led into my shop by their carers. Their progress was not assisted by one of my cats, Bertie, who as a kitten had enjoyed playing with the end of my father's walking stick. He could not believe his luck with so many white sticks to knock with his little paws. Luckily, it made the party laugh.

Giving one lady a carved candle so she could feel its shape, I asked if she was able to smell the aromatic oils it contained. She turned her sightless eyes towards me and with a smile replied, "Yes, I *can* smell the perfume." She went on to explain her sense of smell had been lost many years ago but, having drunk the waters on this visit to Walsingham, it had now returned! She believed it to be a miracle. The old gentleman accompanying beamed happily. "And the second miracle," he told me, "is that she has consented to marry me!"

How do such miracles happen? Is it the work of God, guardian angels, faith and belief or merely mind over matter? Many would say it is just coincidence, but – we now know that there is no such thing as coincidence, don't we!

★ ★ ★

A NEW VOCATION – REIKI

Fourteen years had passed by after my cat Sparky's miraculous recovery – you will recall I was instructed to heal him myself.

By now, my business had done well and I had been able to purchase a shop next door to our cottage. Sparky had appointed himself manager. I had never considered being a healer myself, but one quiet day when there were no customers in my shop, I found myself looking up at the ceiling and was surprised to hear myself say, "Okay, I'm ready to do healing now, what's the next step?" I felt astonished as healing was not something I had planned to do and wondered where those words had come from – literally out of the blue.

I thought about what I had just said. I still did not think that I had the qualities needed to become a healer, nor did I want to become one, but the way those words had just happened made me believe that they had been prompted by one of my guides. Apart from the miracle of Anne's balloon trip, I had not had any disturbing psychic occurrences in recent times. I had not had a disaster dream for years and, really, not very much had happened, nor had I wanted it to happen, on the psychic front. I had been frightened of the dark side, but as I thought about it I realised that I was not frightened any more. The only thing that worried me these days were the disturbing elements that came into the village in human form!

I thought of how happy I had become. My partner and I were very contented together and my business was ticking over nicely. I loved what I was doing. By now I had girls to help me and while I was only able to afford minimum wage for them, I felt good that I was able to offer them work in an area of low employment. Life was wonderful, I realised, but I still wondered why I had told the ceiling I was ready to heal. Maybe the time had come for more 'tuition' and exploration along my spiritual route.

I should have known better than to wonder because the very next day a man came into my shop and made a bee line for the relaxation tapes on display near the till. He muttered to himself, "Ah, just what I want for the healing workshop". He was so lost in his thoughts that he jumped when I interrupted him to enquire about the workshop. He told me that he was a vet and used something called Reiki healing on his patients. I had never heard of Reiki, but asked him for more information. He gave me the telephone number of a lady who ran the workshops.

When I phoned to enquire about Reiki, the lady told me that the easiest way to find out what it was all about was to go and have a short session with her. As I drove to her practice, I was a little apprehensive of the unknown and felt a bit scared, but also wondered how I would know if the Reiki worked, as I was not ill and did not need healing. How would I be able to judge?

On arrival, I was put at my ease and asked to lie down fully clothed on a massage couch, my head comfortable on a pillow and my body covered with a light blanket. The practitioner explained that she would rest her hands for three minutes in each of the different positions. If I felt any discomfort, I must let her know and she would stop if I wanted.

I did feel discomfort but I did not ask her to stop, as I wanted the experience. My head felt as if it were a pressure cooker with nowhere for the steam to escape. I wondered why it did not come out of my ears – the obvious place – but the pressure grew and grew. When she had finished, I realised that I needed to have full treatment to unblock whatever it was in my head, and so made an appointment for the next day.

As I settled down on the couch for the second time, I hoped the uncomfortable pressure in my head would not return. It did not. This time what I experienced was completely different and quite amazing. With my journalistic trait, I assimilated notes in my mind to record afterwards.

Though my eyes were closed, I saw the most beautiful colours at each different hand position. Beautiful purple, brilliant blue, green, yellow, all exquisite, pulsating, delicious, moving colours. When I saw the colour red, I could not decide its shade. It was not scarlet or blood red – more of an 'off-red'. I then distinctly heard a voice telling me, "It's burnt umber." I made a mental note to look it up in the dictionary on my return home. When I did, I found out that it was a natural earth pigment from Umbria, Italy.

After half an hour on my back, I was asked to turn over onto my tummy. I felt very relaxed and sleepy but my mind was still alert to what was happening to me – I did not want to miss any of the experience. When the practitioner's hands reached half way down my back, I found myself striding along a passageway towards an open door displaying bright sunshine outside. There was some kind of bamboo thatch showing over the top of the door lintel. Two Chinese men with long pigtails stood either side of the doorway, their hands thrust up their voluminous sleeves. Bowing respectfully to me as I passed to go out of the door, they replied to me as I spoke. At the time I remembered what I had said but, although I forget now, it was nothing important – merely passing pleasantries.

I knew that I was a man, and a man of reasonable means and position. I felt that I was a sea captain, perhaps having just conducted some kind of business deal.

I did not understand what had happened because I knew it was not a dream – I had not been asleep – but whatever it was it had been a 'real' experience.

When the treatment had finished, I told the lady about the colours I had seen. She smiled, opening a cupboard door to show me a large chart showing the body and its chakra points together with their colours. I knew nothing about chakras, so this was an education for me.

When I told her about the strange experience as a sea captain she smiled again and said "Oh, that would be a past life experience; it sometimes happens when Reiki is given." Well, that was food for thought indeed.

For the first time, I could readily believe that it is possible to slip back to a past life experience. It was not at all like a memory – it was Being and Doing as another person.

I had a similar 'flashback' at another Reiki session, where I found myself watching a little Chinese boy dragging a small handcart across rocks at the base of a mountain. It was only a glimpse, but very real.

It seemed a possibility that in a previous life I had been a sea captain trading with China. This brought to mind the fact that I had never liked oriental willow-patterned china. Ever since a small child, I'd had an aversion to it, and now it began to make sense. In my past life, I had probably shipped hundreds of crates of cheap willow-patterned china to various ports of calls. Like anything seen in bulk repeatedly, the mystique soon disappears. I reasoned that I had brought my dislike of willow-patterned china with me to this life. Strangely, since that realisation, I no longer have an aversion to it, even enjoying some in my kitchen.

After such unlooked-for experiences, I was keen to be initiated as a Reiki practitioner. I had realised after my sessions that it is not necessary to be unwell to benefit from Reiki. I felt so relaxed and wonderful after the treatment.

It seemed like I had been led to Reiki healing by my guides and felt quite sure that this is what they intended me to do. It seemed the time had come where the boundaries were shifting. Up to now, I had been receiving some kind of tuition that, while amazing and at times frightening, did not actually seem to have a real purpose other than make me realise that things are not what they seem – and alienate me from some people. Now I was being led to a 'human' healing group where maybe I could learn to be helpful to others. I still had no real interest in doing this but knew that I should carry it through.

I discovered that to be attuned into Reiki is an expensive business. The winter months brought scant pickings in the shop, but even though I had no spare cash, I nevertheless enrolled for the three-day course, believing that I would somehow acquire the fee to pay for it. I was sure my guides would help.

The energy built up at the course was quite amazing. It was so strong that it gave us all headaches, which dispersed once we began to give healing to each other.

During part of the exercises, when we were asked to imagine a cloud of energy over our heads, something unexpected happened to me. When I imagined my cloud, I also saw a flash of visionary lightening and with it came the inspired knowledge that the title of my book should be 'The Magician's Daughter'. How apt. I was, indeed, a magician's daughter, my dad having being a stage 'magician' – what a fabulous title for a book. I also received confirmation that I had acted 'as a child' when asking my Indian brave what my book should be about. I had eventually been able to work it out without his help. *(To recap, after the manifestation of the Indian brave had told me to write a book, he began to fade. I had then asked him what I should write about. He had replied, "As a child" and disappeared.)*

I had taken a selection of my candles to the course, confident that I would sell enough to pay my fees. To my embarrassment, I did not sell any at all but, ever positive, I took along some sample astrological charts the next day, hoping to earn the money that way. That did not work either. I was mortified, having to admit I could not pay my dues. The organiser (who had given me the Reiki healing) said she would pay the Reiki Master herself and asked that I pay her back as soon as possible.

I was not let down by 'them upstairs'. The day following the course, a customer came into my shop saying that she did not know the reason for being in my shop, but that her car had 'just brought her'. She spent the exact amount I needed on candles and astrological charts.

Her name was also Valerie and she was, amazingly, a healer and, after being informed that she had just paid for my healing instruction and initiation, she was delighted. The debt was so obviously cleared by the intervention from both her guides as well as mine, orchestrated to perfection and proving my faith in them was justified.

I asked Kent, my partner, if I could practice my Reiki on him. While he is not interested in spiritual matters, he does not disbelieve that strange things can happen. He was not particularly interested in the Reiki but was quite content that I 'had a go' on him.

At that time, the thing he most wanted in his life was a motorbike but could not afford one. After I had completed my session on him, he sat up, astonished that he had just been on a motorbike ride on a bikers' favourite road in Kent – lots of bends – he said the experience had been very real and had not been a dream. It seemed that he had received what he needed most at the time – a virtual reality bike ride.

The more I practiced Reiki on people, I realised that everyone had a completely different experience – and what was right for them at the time.

I could not see that I would ever do healing 'for real' and did not anticipate taking the other two Reiki degrees. My tutor had told me that I would know when the time was right and I did not feel it was yet.

* * *

Chakras: according to Tantric philosophy and yoga, a chakra is a point of energy in the astral body. There are seven primary chakras and colours, associated with various parts of the body – emotions, desires, thoughts, powers and health. The alleged energy of the chakras are not scientifically measurable.

SPARKY'S REVENGE
1998

I could list many stories about Sparky, but the one that most ably illustrates his intelligence and ability for revenge happened when our pedigree cat, Doreen, became pregnant. Sparky disliked her from the start but seemed incensed by this pregnancy and frequently attacked her. During one devilish assault, I pulled him away from her and gave him a light smack on the bum. I had never before smacked my animals, but I wanted him to realise the seriousness of his crime. I had watched mother cats clouting their offspring to make them aware of their misdemeanours and then, after the discipline, grooming and cuddling their children to assure them they were still loved, so I felt Sparky would understand.

Clearly, I had breached some rule of cat-etiquette, because Sparky was outraged by my action and, after glaring at me with slitty eyes, he stalked off with enormous dignity and ignored me for over a week.

When he deigned to enter the shop, then housed in an old stable in the garden, he followed the grey habit of an elderly nun and jumped nimbly onto one of the display shelves that groaned with candles and pottery holders. He stared at me, looking just like an evil-minded Ronald Searle cat. Sparky strolled along the shelf nonchalantly and, with deliberation, knocked stock off it as he went. I managed to catch what fell without loss and, as he continued his efforts of retaliation around every shelf in the room, I could not help giggling. The ancient nun, completely unaware of the drama unfolding before her, assumed that the cat was merely being clumsy – but I had watched Sparky daily thread his way through the shop displays without displacing anything. He *knew* that I could not swear at him in the presence of a nun and I suspect that he realised that God was his witness as he let me know what he felt of my previous actions.

Jumping nimbly from the last of the shelves, Sparky looked at me once more through venomously hooded eyes and stalked with enormous dignity from the shop. Turning back to stare at me, I knew he was telling me to never, *never*, treat him again in such a manner. I gave him a wink, trying to stifle my giggles in order to be respectful to the nun. Sparky disappeared around the corner to reappear later, full of purrs and smiles and keen for a cuddle. He had made his point and we were friends again.

* * *

When I acquired the new shop next door, Sparky was in his element. He had always taken a keen interest in sales, but soon promoted himself to manager and worked out a method of luring customers into the shop in order to make a sale. He sat outside the shop door, watching for people walking down the road. He would approach them, purring profusely, and curl his tail around the nearest leg while enjoying the attention. He allowed the people to stroke him for a little while and then walked to the shop, tail still hooked around the leg, almost pulling the person through the shop door. Next, he jumped up on the nearest display shelves, purring and gently head-butting the customers, weaving his way through the stock (never knocking any of it!) as he followed their progress, until they picked up something they wished to purchase. He then jumped up on the wrapping paper by the till, still making a fuss of 'his' customers, but as soon as the till 'dinged' and the money was safely put inside, down he jumped, ignoring his customers – sale made, what was the point – to stroll out of the shop and sit by the door awaiting the next possible punter to entice inside. He was a born salesman!

Sparky usually ignored all of Doreen's kittens, but he became curiously involved with one litter. The kittens' names were Little Dorrit, Dingle and Dexter and he forcefully removed them from Doreen and carried them off to a lair under the stairs where he tried to suckle them – without success. Thereafter, he let Doreen feed them, but otherwise cared for them himself – at the same time still attending to his managerial duties in the shop.

When the kittens were almost grown, Sparky clearly believed it was time they earned their living, for he surprised me by bringing them into the shop one day and proceeded to show them the ropes! He jumped up on the shelves followed by excited youngsters and seemed to be telling them what they should do. I had to catch a few displaced candles while they learned to safely traverse the crowded shelves, but they soon realised what was expected of them. They did their best to 'pull in the punters' but never mastered Sparky's expertise, settling for displaying themselves in attractive poses inside the portals and to approach and make a fuss of customers once they had entered. Maybe this is what Sparky had in mind, for he still patrolled the road outside waiting to lure in the unsuspecting customers while his three stooges laid in wait to flatter them once inside.

The cats made an attractive team and thoroughly enjoyed their jobs. They became a little melancholy during the winter months when trade was slow and there were no tourists around, but once spring arrived bringing visitors back to the village, they became very animated to be 'back in business' once more.

One day, the old cat was demanding my attention too much and, forgetting he was not a dog, I told him to sit – and he promptly obliged. I tried this on various occasions to ensure it was not just a fluke and he sat every time. Why on earth do we assume that animals do not understand?

We had a cat-flap in both the shop and the kitchen door, but Sparky preferred butler service. I would be busy with some chore or another to find myself looking towards one of the cat flaps. Sparky would be staring at it, willing me to open the door for him – which I always did!

I had a pressure pad under the shop doormat, which rang a bell in the house, over the sofa. Kent, my partner, was suffering from a hangover one day, which Sparky seemed to know annoyed me. He therefore strolled from the house to the adjoining shop and sat on the pressure pad, ensuring that Kent's head really thumped! What a cat!

Sparky eventually died – a huge loss to us all – and I buried him at the side of the shop door, together with a rose and a honeysuckle in remembrance.

★ ★ ★

My health had not been good and I was constantly exhausted. On a couple of occasions when I had closed the shop to rest on my sofa, I felt a cat jump up and begin to knead my legs. I looked to see who it was but there was no cat in sight, though I could still feel him. I knew it was Sparky, come back to give me some healing as I had done for him when he was such a poorly little kitty.

★ ★ ★

AURA HEALING AND TREATMENT, NATIVE AMERICANS AND A SPIRIT BEAR
1999

I attended a jazz concert in King's Lynn and was seated high up in the balcony, some distance away from the stage. The music was fantastic and the singer, dressed in a white suit, his hair parted in the middle and plastered down like a 'thirties' jazz singer, seemed to enjoy himself hugely. I noticed a bright white light jumping around him in time to the rhythm while he was singing and at first thought it was a trick of the lights, but as soon as he finished his song, the light shrank back around him until I could no longer see it. When he stood to sing once more, bright light pulsated about five feet around him. I was not sure whether this was his aura or his creative energy, but whatever it was, it was fascinating to watch and clearly showed his enjoyment of singing.

I had often seen a similar golden glow or light around people that I presumed were auras, but I never saw any colours, which disappointed me.

My shop attracted lots of healers and 'alternatives' and I had many interesting conversations with such people who told me that since their childhood they have always seen coloured auras surrounding people, describing the colours as shimmering outlines that changed with the mood or health of the owner.

I was very drawn to one lady, Melanie, who told me she was an aura healer. I had no intention of asking for a treatment but, nevertheless, heard the words coming out of my mouth, arranging a session with her. Clearly, this had been set up by my guides.

As I drove to keep my appointment with Melanie, I wondered why I had felt so compelled to ask her for treatment. I was curious about what she would do, having no idea or any preconceptions of what aura healing consisted of.

After my arrival, she asked me to sit in a chair and stood about six feet away from me, her hands directed towards me. Not knowing what to expect, I was completely surprised to feel my throat 'clicking' as if a cap of about two inches was being cranked open. It then felt as if something was circling around in my throat area. It did not hurt, but was a strange sensation. Taken aback, I involuntarily exclaimed, "Oh!" Melanie smiled and said, "Yes, it's amazing, isn't it!" I still knew very little about chakras but, in retrospect, it was clear that my throat chakra had been cranked open.

Melanie then asked me to lie down and make myself comfortable on a sofa. I felt very relaxed and closed my eyes but, wanting to know what she was doing, chinked my eyes open every now and again to check. She was gently patting the air around me, sometimes softly putting the tip of a finger on my body. At one point, when I knew she was behind me, I felt other hands being placed on my legs. I opened my eyes and, though I could still feel the hands, there was nobody there. I closed my eyes again with a sense of awe, knowing that what I was feeling was a spirit healer. I did not feel at all alarmed.

Then, to my surprise, I felt myself as a very old Native American. As well as feeling myself as that person, I was able to look down from above my body to see myself lying down. I was very old with a much-wrinkled face and my thinning hair was braided into two long plaits. Despite my old age, my hair was not grey, but a dull, 'tired' black of old age. I could not tell whether I was female or male but, because of the lack of hair ornaments, believed I was female.

When the session was over, Melanie told me she realised what the link was between us. She had felt it when we met and was not surprised that we had been drawn to each other. She told me that during the session she had seen us both in a past life as Native Americans. She was the shaman and I was the ancient grandmother of the tribe, named 'Grandmother of the Dreaming' – an apt name, I thought, bearing in mind that I was still dreaming in this incarnation. Clearly, I had been a dream visionary then as I am in this life. She told me that we had been great friends in that incarnation. Having just seen myself lying on the sofa as an ancient Native American, I could easily believe what she told me. I certainly had not expected such results from the session and could see why my guides wanted me to have the experience. Apart from receiving the vision, I felt wonderful and very relaxed.

I booked two more appointments. At the second session, I lay on the couch to feel myself drifting into deep relaxation as before, peeping every now and again to check where Melanie was standing.

Feeling very relaxed at one stage, with my eyes closed and hands clasped over my chest, I was surprised to feel the large paws of a huge bear resting protectively over my hands. I could feel the texture of the bear's hair and feel the length and strength of its long claws and wondered why on earth a bear had turned up who seemed to be protecting me. Having learned by now to 'go with the flow', I waited to see what happened next, keeping my eyes shut to retain the vision.

The bear's paws rested over my hands for some time, then, to my amazement, I felt the bear's head in place of mine! It was so real that I thought for one crazy moment that I had turned into a bear! I could feel huge bear incisors in my own mouth and, because the feeling was so very real, I was compelled to click my teeth to see if I really did have bear fangs, but thankfully realised my own were still in position! It was an amazing and strange experience, not at all frightening and seemed quite 'natural' and real. I did not understand, though, why a bear had been with me in such a gentle, protective manner.

Melanie explained to me afterwards that the shaman of old used to wear animal skins for protection when they were performing sacred ceremonies. She thought that perhaps I was having a past-life experience, or perhaps I was under the protection of her own 'imaginary' bearskin that she donned occasionally. However, that possibility did not seem the one to me as the bear had been 'real' flesh and blood – not an empty skin. Melanie then told me about totem, or spirit animals – something I did not know about – and that the bear had brought himself to my attention to show he was my protector. This was all new and interesting information and left me with a lot to think about. I certainly had not expected such amazing experiences when I went to have my aura healed!

★ ★ ★

July 1999

Soon after these wonderful experiences, I came to hear of a Native American shaman named Wan-an-nee-che, who conducts workshops across the UK, giving talks on Native American philosophies and way of life, so, keen to meet him, I organised a workshop at my home. His talk was fascinating, including an explanation about totem, or spirit animals. The Red Indians (as we named them before political correctness) called themselves the 'two-legged'. Because the four-legged animals were on this planet before themselves, the 'two-leggeds' thrived from taking lessons from the wisdom of the animal kingdom, noting what they ate and what they avoided and how they behaved. They noted the wisdom from each species and admired them for what they taught.

Wan-an-nee-che told us that when an animal chose to give us their protection, or 'totem', we would know by the sign it gave to us. He told us, therefore, to watch out for signs from the animal world. For instance, if we particularly noticed an animal cross in front of us, to think about what message it might have for us. He also told us to look out for gifts – perhaps a bird's feather noticed in an unusual place – something not evident in everyday life could be taken as a sign.

I had already had more than a 'sign' from my bear – I had 'physically' felt him but, noting that Wan-an-nee-che had a pack of animal totem cards on display, I decided to select one at random. Should I pick out the bear it would be my final proof – not that I needed it. Choosing a moment when people were focussed elsewhere, I selected a card at random from the pack, to discover it was that of the bear. I already knew that my spirit animal had, literally, been in touch with me but that was a thrilling extra affirmation. I felt very blessed.

I was still thinking about Wan-an-nee-che's talk the following day, especially about totem animals and their gifts. Wan-an-nee-che had told us to look for a bird's feather, which would be a special gift. I thought sceptically of all the birds' feathers I have seen on walks – birds are moulting all the time – they cannot all be a special gift, a token or a sign. That was my logic talking, but I made a resolve that when I took my dogs out for their walk, I would look for a special feather and wondered how I would recognise it.

The May morning was fine and sunny and, as I walked, I searched in vain for feathers and never a one did I see! I found that quite astonishing and, after a while, gave up, forgetting my quest to enjoy the scenery. My two lurchers, Tilly and Lily, sprinted round the field and the sun shone down, warming my body. I strode along, watching the girls racing at the top of the ridge to my left, admiring their speed and grace. I was also admiring a cluster of purple bell-like flowers growing in a beautiful haze, making a glorious foreground to the speeding dogs. My eyes were on the horizon and I had not glanced at the ground in front of me for some time, sure of my footing in a place I knew well. It must have been my sixth sense that made me stop suddenly. Looking down at my feet, I could see that resting between them was a beautiful magpie's feather! Here was my special gift and when I was least expecting it.

Not long after this, I had determined to go and pick some fresh spring flowers for the local Catholic priest who had been my champion during my upset with the Charismatic Catholics. He was now very ill and immobile with motor neurone disease. I had a very soft spot for him and knew that he had enjoyed being part of nature when he was mobile. I made him a posy from cow-parsley, bluebells, grasses and leaves. Watching the dogs run in the distance as usual, I stopped suddenly to see a bright yellow snail shell between my feet. I have never seen such a beautiful, unusual shell. I picked it up carefully, knowing this to be a gift for my friend, then walked on. Twice more I stopped involuntarily to find a pretty blue speckled eggshell and then a dainty feather between my feet. I cannot think how three such beautiful finds came to be so near to each other at the centre of a path, but I knew they were gifts for the man who could no longer stride along looking for his own treasures. Maybe the gifts meant that even if he could only move like a snail, his soul could fly like a bird. Certainly, to me it showed that something spiritual was shifting to allow me those finds.

★ ★ ★

PAST AND FUTURE LIVES

September 1999

When an acquaintance told me about a past life therapist, I booked a sitting. I was not sure whether I liked the idea of 'forcing' a regression instead of having it happen naturally – as it did for me when I 'became' a sea captain while receiving Reiki – but, as the therapist had 'come my way', felt it probable that my guides had sent me this opportunity and, therefore, I should take it.

Since the sea captain experience, I had given the idea of past and future lives a lot of thought, coming to the eventual conclusion that it was highly likely that we had more than one life on this planet.

I do like to search for other possibilities, however, before I come to conclusions, and another explanation I conceived about past life experiences was that *maybe* if one is in a receptive trance-like state, it is possible to 'tune in' to another person's past life. An example, I thought, was that the air is full of radio and television programmes as well as emails and web sites, and we are able to click a switch and either see, hear or log on to all sorts of visions, voices, music and data. Maybe the 'essences' of past lives are floating around the universe and sensitive people can 'switch' into them when in the right frame of mind in a similar way. I felt that this was a possibility, but my conclusion was that we have had past lives and we will lead other lives in the future. A good reason for ensuring that the planet stays green – it will not be nice reincarnating to a burnt world devoid of plant and animal life.

At the session, the therapist told me to breathe deeply and imagine a light inside my head circling around and around. Feeling somewhat cynical, I could not see how I was going to slip into a past life just by imagining my head lit up inside. She told me to visualise my guardian angel and then to see a door. To my surprise, I saw a wooden door, or gate, in the side of a grassy hill. Suddenly, I was filled with fear and began to panic. She told me to open to door but I was so afraid that my tears began to flow and I told her I could not open the door because I was too frightened. She reminded me that as my angel was with me, no harm could come to me and that I was in the here and now – what I was looking at was only a memory. So, with tears pouring down my face, I opened the door. Revealed in the gloom, I saw steep steps leading down to pitch darkness. The immediate walls and curved ceiling that I could see were dark, dank and cold. I shivered uncontrollably and really did not want to continue.

"What do you see?" prompted the therapist.

"Nothing," I replied, "It's so dark!"

"You have the light in your head, switch on the beam and you will be able to see," she instructed.

Somehow, I was able to illuminate the scene and there, sitting in chains at the bottom of the steps, was an emaciated old man, almost skeletal, his clothing so ragged that his pallid skin showed through. Clearly, he had been incarcerated for a long time. His hair was long, wispy and white and I knew that I had been that man. I also knew that he had been imprisoned for radical thoughts – to do with witchcraft, or spiritual beliefs that were not allowed in his time. The woman asked me what I was seeing and she told me that I could free the man – take off his chains. I was able to take away his shackles and he disappeared as a white light through the ceiling of that dreadful place towards a star.

The word 'oubliette' kept repeating in my mind – but I did not think it could be one as I understood they were dungeons with no access other than a roof hole where prisoners were thrown in and left to rot – the dungeon I was viewing was accessed by steep dank steps. I wondered if the man was French? My impression was that he had been left to rot in the dark.

The vision ended and I thought this would be the end of the regression, but the lady guided me through to another incarnation.

I found myself watching a lion at an arena. I was a stocky Roman soldier and, as I looked down, I could see my arms with black hair sprouting over them. I wore some kind of leather tunic. I felt a certain feeling of self-importance; I was not very bright – and was certainly brutal. I do not think I was participating in any gladiatorial games – I seemed to be merely observing, maybe as a steward on duty, waiting for something to happen – which it suddenly did. The wretched lion leapt across the space and lunged at my throat and that was that. My life as a Roman soldier was over and that vision ended.

The therapist then took me through a third and final visualisation where it was nighttime. I could see a Gypsy caravan where a dark Gypsy man sat on the steps, illuminated by light from a campfire in the foreground as he whittled at something with a knife. It was peaceful and sparks drifted from the fire up into the branches of a nearby tree. My perspective changed and I saw a small child around two years old. The child had a mop of blonde hair. The Gypsy man's knife suddenly became very large and I thought that he killed the child. I did not see it happen. I thought that I was that child. The vision was over.

As an experiment it was very interesting, but I was not sure that these had been real past lives or my brain obliging me with some interesting data.

Two curious things happened not long after these regressions.

My partner and I took a short trip to Ireland to visit friends who took us to visit an old castle. I enjoyed investigating all the nooks and crannies, peering over the battlements, imagining myself as a mediaeval maiden looking out for her knight, and trod carefully down the steep winding steps inside turrets, trying to imagine what it was like in days gone by. I then spied a doorway on the ground floor and opened it. I felt my hackles rise and became filled with apprehension. It was the entrance to the dungeons and, while not exact, it was very similar to the one in my vision. I felt too spooked to go down and explore. I knew that this was not the dungeon of my vision but, nevertheless, the similar architecture showed me that my vision dungeon was an accurate portrayal and my regression, therefore, could have been valid.

I have read that people often bring through to their current life their unresolved issues from previous lives, which can result in many health and relationship problems, strange phobias and unexplained illnesses. These can often be discharged after a regression. Even birthmarks and recurring dreams can be traced back to an earlier existence.

For years I had been unable to sleep without a window open. I liked to have fresh air in my room, even if the room was freezing, and would feel claustrophobic and uneasy if it were closed. I did not see it as a problem until I visited the United States and Canada where some hotel rooms we stayed in had no opening windows. One night, I felt so ill that I thought I was going to die, despite the fact that I knew the air conditioning was working. I was overcome with such huge fear and panic and could barely breathe. I looked so bad that my partner was seriously worried – as was I as I gasped for breath.

Since my regression as the prisoner in the dungeon, I have no more problems and can now sleep with a shut window. Maybe subconscious memories of having being incarcerated in a pitch black, stinking, airless dungeon had come through with me in to this life, to be dispelled by the memories. It is a possibility. Being entombed alive in an Egyptian pyramid (previously mentioned) could bring about that kind of phobia too!

* * *

I was talking to a medium at the Festival of Mind, Body and Spirit. There were many clairvoyants plying their trade, but I was drawn to a large lady with skin as black as ebony, hair a plethora of plaits encrusted with colourful beads, and a huge, ready smile. Her beautiful, Rubenesque body was swathed in bright colours. She was irresistible. One of the first things she said to me was (in a deep American drawl),

"Honey, you've been a pirate in a past life. In fact, honey, you've been a pirate in three lives and been made to walk the plank in each."

Her smile was infectious and I could not help but reciprocate.

"Honey," she continued, "in one of those incarnations, you just wouldn't jump off the plank and somebody had to push you off. That's why you go plum crazy when someone comes behind you and puts their hand on your back. That's why you're afraid of water."

I wondered how she knew this, or was she just making it up – but then I remembered, I do not like it when people come up behind me and sometimes, when I have been slapped on the back in a friendly manner, I have retaliated badly. But then, I reasoned, this must be a natural reaction – part of our primitive essential reflexes to stay alive.

Recollections flooded in. I have always been frightened of water and only learned to swim when I was thirty. I could not bear to watch people on a diving board and there is no way I would *ever* attempt to walk along a diving board or ever try to dive. Of course, a diving board looks just like a pirate's 'plank'. Well, I thought, *maybe...*

Then, smiling back at the big beam on the cheery medium's face, I also recalled how I had obsessively played pirates when I was a child (when I was not being a witch) and loved to read books about swashbuckling heroes as they roamed the seven seas. But, didn't everyone? Although I have never yearned to travel, one of the few places that has always been at the back of my mind as a beckoning destination is the Caribbean. As I thought of this, I mentioned it to the medium and she smilingly retorted, "Honey, of course you would like to go back there – that's where you plied your trade!" Her best argument so far, I mused.

This was food for thought, indeed, and I wryly recalled how piratical types had always attracted me – I easily went weak at the knees if I saw a bloke with a spotted scarf around his head, a glint in his eye and a ring in his ear – still do, come that that!

I thought about what the clairvoyant had told me and considered the possibility of having lived life as a pirate in a few incarnations but, not having experienced the 'reality' of being a Johnny Depp look-alike, think it more prudent to consider that suggestion as merely a *'well, maybe'*.

* * *

When I took my Reiki II initiation, I had a vision of what I believe will be a future life. As in many of my dreams or visions, I seem to be an observer. In this vision I was deep underground in a man-made cave-like area. 'Driving' past me was a 'vehicle', which although it was not running along tracks, seemed to be on a set course of some kind. There were four pretty women in the open vehicle or 'trolley', and they were chatting happily together, the best of friends. I realised that they were on their way to work. I also realised that they were all identical. They reminded me very much of Doris Day of the Fifties' films era. As I watched them disappear into the distance, I recall realising they were clones and that they had been produced for specialist work. By having identical characters, and presumably thoughts, they would be united with their work efforts and work fast and efficiently as one. This was a shocking idea, but the more I thought about it the more advantages I could see – but, in effect, they would be human robots. *I dreamt this before cloning was a current, debatable issue.*

★ ★ ★

I had another dream of a future time where I was sitting in the audience at an opera. The diva was warbling on stage and I knew that I was an identical of her – a clone. I looked the same, was also an opera singer, but my thought was "I could do better than that." I knew I was part of a cloning system for opera singers. I felt no problem with it other than feeling that I could have sung better than the one on the stage. This thought process disproved my theory of the Doris Day clones thinking and acting as one for a utility project. But maybe that is how it will be. Future science will produce either multiple thinkers like the cloned look-alikes or individual thinkers like the opera clone and myself.

★ ★ ★

I have never been an opera fan, nor have I ever wanted to go to an opera, but in an earlier dream I had the virtual reality of actually singing opera – I met every note high and low and it was the most exhilarating and wonderful 'real' experience I have ever had. My breathing was a work of art, I warbled, I trilled, and while the singing was incredible, the 'feeling' of my voice working so divinely was what was so awesome. I was aware in the dream that I could not sing in real life, yet here I was, being able to do so. Reaching all those notes while singing an aria was a totally amazing experience. While in the clone dream, I was *thinking,* aware I could sing better than the diva on stage, but in this dream I was *doing* and experienced every nuance of faultless song as pure reality. It was marvellous.

CHILDREN'S PAST LIVES

I never noticed my children talking about past lives – probably because it was not something I knew or believed in at the time – so I missed any clues that there might have been. I did not attribute the Gypsy dancing and Egyptian episodes with my daughter to past lives but to the other influences occurring at the time. I think that if they had been linked to other lives, it would have happened differently.

My granddaughter, Tatiana, however, at the age of four, gave me pause for thought on one occasion.

She was leaving the crèche she had attended since a baby, about to begin at a new nursery school. One of the little girls from her crèche was going to attend the same school, so I remarked to Tatiana, "It's good that your friend will be going to your new school as well, isn't it?" Tatiana looked at me and said in a very matter of fact way, "She used to beat me when I was a baby." Thinking this an odd way to describe bullying, I asked, "Do you mean she bullied you at the crèche?" "No," retorted the little girl, a trifle irked at my misunderstanding, "I *said* she used to beat me when I was a baby. She died when she was fifty-six, you know." At four years old, I doubt whether a little girl would know about dying or ages so I presumed that this was a reference to something that happened in a past life. I did not question her any further as the moment was over and she was chattering about something else.

My daughter informed me that Tatiana had mentioned (again in a very matter of fact manner), "When I used to be your mummy, my name was…" and gave an unusual name that sounded Roman. Not the kind of thing a small child would make up unless a past memory of another life had suddenly popped into her head.

A friend of mine, taking her own small granddaughter for a country walk, noticed the little girl waving to a ploughman. "Do you know him?" enquired my friend. "Yes, he used to be my friend, before," replied the little girl.

I have read many fascinating books about children's past lives and there seems to be one thing concurrent with all the anecdotes, in that all the children give their little bits of information in a very matter of fact manner, then carry on as normal.

THE MAGIC WELL
2000

I had confided to the builder who was doing some work on our home that *one day* I would like to have the well unblocked in the garden. I told him that a strange man with piercing eyes had come into my shop, muttering, "So much *Power*, so much *Fire!*" as he circled me like a spitting cat. He then hissed, "I've heard about you," and edged backwards as if I were about to turn him into stone. When nothing dire happened to him, he then uttered that in mediumistic circles across Britain, it was prophesised a third healing-well would be discovered in Walsingham. I could not help wondering if it would be my well. I also wondered what he had heard about me!

When I returned from work the following day, I was alarmed to find that the lawn was covered with an exciting array of old bottles, ancient pots of paints and all sorts of rubbish as well as the frame of an old Vespa scooter – all evidence that the well-excavation had already begun. The builder twinkled charmingly at my outburst at this unauthorised work. "You did tell me that you wanted it done."

"But not yet!" I wailed, bemoaning what it would be costing me.

I faced a dilemma. It seemed silly to get him to throw back all the rubbish, so told him to hire a skip and get rid of it. As he had hoped, I decided to let him continue with the excavations – which cost me a ridiculous amount of money that I could ill afford – but of course, I was very excited to watch the progress, as the wily builder knew I would be.

A somewhat portly young man was roped around his middle and sent into the well to dig out the rubbish. It was hard work for him, with nothing but a trowel and a bucket on a rope. It was dark too, so I provided him with candles in sconces nailed to the walls. After a few days of hard work, I noticed how he had changed in appearance. He looked so happy; he was slimmer and altogether looked a new man. When I remarked on this, he agreed, and told me even his own mother had not recognised him when he had walked in the door. He told me that there was such a lovely atmosphere in the well that it made him feel really happy. I wondered if this was the first miracle working!

I was quite aware that builders like to wind people up and I assumed that mine were no different. They all swore that they could feel a wonderful, spiritual atmosphere in the well; I took what they said with a pinch of salt but I could not deny the change that had taken place with the young man doing most of the work.

When the water level was finally reached, it was very exciting. A pump was needed, as it was impossible to excavate all the earth at the bottom without first pumping out the water. As it gushed from the pump, it was all brown and muddy to begin with, but then became crystal clear. Despite thoughts of botulism from all the rancid rubbish accumulated down the ages and evidence of rats that had been found, I decided to have faith and taste the water. It was delicious – and I had no ill effects afterwards. I was really pleased the builder had beguiled me to continue with the excavations and I planned to turn the garden into a public space where people could come and enjoy the tranquillity and taste the waters.

A CHRISTENING

The excavations were not quite finalised and ladders were still propped inside, tied together with bits of rope and baling twine and certainly not health and safety friendly.

While I was out, a friend and her mother were visiting Walsingham and, as they approached the village, the mother, for the umpteenth time, pestered her daughter on the advisability of having her young son christened. They decided to visit me, so the builder told them I would be back soon but, in the meantime, would they like to visit my 'miracle well' (the man was a PR artist!). The couple were thrilled to peer down into the mysterious depths. The mother, a devout woman in her late sixties, insisted on climbing down the rickety and precarious ladders and so descended the forty feet to the bottom, hoping to have a visitation of Our Lady. Dipping her hand in the muddy waters, she scooped a mouthful to her lips and ascended up the ladders in elation. This gave her giggling daughter the excellent idea of having her child christened, there and then, with the Walsingham waters. The quick-witted builder said he would 'officiate' and, after washing the day's grime from his hands, held the baby carefully and wetted its head with the well water, making up appropriate words to fit the occasion. How I wish I had been there! I also wished I had the grandmother's courage to climb down into the well!

As the builder obviously was not ordained, the 'ceremony' could never be regarded as official, but it satisfied the mother's less orthodox beliefs and sense of wacky fun and also, in some ways, satisfied the grandmother.

While the excavations to the well were under way, other building works were still going on to the house. On one occasion, I was standing with the builder, our backs to the well, discussing how I wanted him to build a log shed. Suddenly, I felt dizziness sweeping over me and had to cling on to the builder for support for a while. The feeling did not last for long but it was a strange sensation. Never prone to dizziness, I wondered what had caused it but did not for one moment think that it had anything to do with the well – after all, I was facing away from it, not even thinking about it, and certainly not looking down into its depths. What was curious, however, was that a lot of people who came to view the 'miracle well' during its excavation told me that they felt dizzy on the approach. I put this down to the newly released elemental energies – like genies from a bottle. Maybe the water elementals were relieved to have all that rubbish taken from their home – maybe the Mary-Goddess was pleased – whatever it was, it was tangible, not just to me, but to others as well.

The first people to ask for some of the waters (sent round by the builder at work on the front of the shop) was a desperate elderly couple who had left their middle-aged, mentally handicapped son in his wheelchair on the pavement. I gave them some of the water in a bottle and went with them to say hallo to their son.

As they returned to him, he was smiling.

"Gracious," exclaimed the mother, "he never smiles – look, he's even laughing now!"

I said, "The waters must be working already then," and the parents agreed – it was a minor miracle to them. That couple had come to ask for the well water as a last resort. They looked old and careworn but I noticed, as they pushed their son up the hill, that they had a new spring to their step and, no doubt, hope in their breast.

I did not know if the well had miracle qualities but it had done that little family a lot of good.

There is already an official well in Walsingham where a priest blesses the water daily for the flocking pilgrims. I did not intend my well to replace the religious one but I thought that my garden and its well would provide a pleasant and extra attraction.

★ ★ ★

DOWN UNDER

I had been hard at work making candles all day. I had been playing a cd of authentic didgeridoo music non-stop, as I liked it so much. At the end of the day I felt very tired and went to bed early. As soon as my head hit the pillow I heard some exciting drum and didgeridoo music coming from the garden – totally different to the cd I had been listening to during the day. For a moment I thought that the music must be coming from the pub next door, which often had live groups pounding out loud music, but then remembered that the pub had been sold and was now a private house. I lifted my head from the pillow and the music ceased. As soon as my head was back on the pillow it returned. Such a wonderful heart-throbbing beat came from the drums, such haunting, spine tingling sounds from the didgeridoo.

I had reached the stage in my life where I no longer questioned any strange experiences and now knew that sounds could be heard clairaudiently, so laid back with closed eyes to enjoy the 'magic' music.

I soon found myself transported elsewhere, dancing in a circle with a cheeky little man who grinned at me happily. I did not see others dancing with us, although I was aware that they were there and was similarly aware that we were all dancing under the night sky with an open fire burning close by. I was only truly aware of my partner and the music. The little happy man partnering me had such a cheeky face, with blue dotted patterns spiralling down his cheeks from his eyes. His hair was cropped very short and looked blonde, though I could not see clearly in the night's gloom. I thought his hair might also be covered in ash.

Although 'I' was dancing with this man, the real 'me' was wondering what was going on. I knew that I was not dreaming but enjoying participating in a vision, so while I was experiencing the pleasure of the dance, I realised that I must be viewing the scene through another person's eyes.

I was perplexed about the music, believing that it must be Aboriginal because of the didgeridoo but wondered about the drums – I knew little about the indigenous tribes, but did not think that they played drums. I also felt confused about my partner's appearance because his features looked European. I noticed that when he smiled at me with such a cheeky grin his white teeth were quite small – rather like a child's milk teeth. He certainly didn't have the indigenous looks or colouring of the Aboriginal race.

Because the rhythm of the drums was like that of passionate heartbeats and our movements more sexual gyrations than dance, I wondered if I were in the midst of some kind of fertility rite or ceremony. I enjoyed the music and the dance for some time until everything stopped suddenly, rather like the violin music so many years before, and the vision disappeared.

Back to normality, I realised that the music had been coming from the area of the newly completed well but I could not see any link between my vision and the well, other than the fact that Australia is underneath us!

I thought about my cheeky, happy little partner with his blue spiralled patterns on his face and realised that New Zealand Maoris have blue tattoos, while the Aboriginals paint theirs in white, so the vision was a puzzle.

I really wished I could understand why I had experienced such a tangible 'physical' vision. I did not have to wait long for an explanation.

A beautiful young lady came into my shop a few days later, with black hair swept high on her head, decorated with colourful flowers twined through the tresses. She looked like a wood nymph and I could not help exclaiming how wonderful she looked. She charmingly thanked me for the compliment in a New Zealand accent. As soon as I realised her nationality, I used the opportunity to ask her if she knew about Maori music. I was delighted when she told me that she was half-Maori, half-Native American and also a psychic, so I launched into the story of my vision and the music. The girl immediately reached into her bag and copied out an email address of some Maori elders in New Zealand. She suggested I contact them to obtain more insight and information into my vision.

As always, I was overwhelmed with the amazing synchronicity of cause and effect and I was soon in correspondence with the Maori elders via email, who felt sure they knew what my vision was about. Apparently, a museum in Scotland held the bones of both Maori and Aboriginal indigenous people wrongfully taken away from their country by explorers and put on display with other artefacts many moons ago. Recent conferences had been held between both Aboriginal and Maori delegates with officials in this country, in which agreements were made that the bones of their ancestors could be respectfully collected and returned to their rightful lands. Many joyful rites and ceremonies had taken place to celebrate the occasion. The Maori elder believed that because I was so 'sensitive' I had picked up on one of these ceremonies.

The mystery was also solved as to the appearance of my dancing partner. I was informed that because of mixed blood there are many European-looking Aboriginals, some even with blonde hair, hence the looks of my dancing partner in the vision. Because of their fair skin, white paint does not show, so they use blue paint or tattoo ink.

I can still see that young man's happy face and wonder if some day, if I ever travel to Australia, I might meet him. That would be interesting!

I wonder if I would have still received that wonderful vision if I had not been listening to didgeridoo music throughout the day.

★ ★ ★

CLAIRALIENCE: CLAIRAUDIENCE

Clairalience: *(Clear smelling) Sometimes known as clairscentience. Smelling things that have no physical source.*

This has happened to me a few times, although I have never really been sure that it has been a psychic experience or 'mind over matter'. For instance, I once saw a dirty old tramp walking along the road. I was in my car at the time but I remember thinking, "Coo, I bet he stinks!" and then the car filled with the stench of an unwashed body and clothing. On another occasion I was watching a television film about fire fighting. The firemen were engulfed in flames on the film when, suddenly, I smelt burning in the house. I rushed out following the smell of smoke, thinking that it must be something burning in the kitchen, but there was nothing. I think that probably my brain was triggered by what I had seen, so I do not really think that they were true clairalience experiences – but then, what is a true experience? What I could smell was very real.

When my well was being excavated, I checked on the contents of the skip as some of the old rubbish from the well was worth keeping – bottles and so on. On one occasion I experienced the most delightful perfume of flowers wafting around me for just a short second. There were no flowers in bloom at the time. I fancifully wondered if it had something to do with a nature deity standing near me, pleased that I had unblocked the well.

As a Reiki-Seichem Master I give initiations and quite often the girls I am instructing ask me if I have some kind of perfume-puffer, as they can smell strong perfume wafting around them. One smelt roses, another lily of the valley and a third, frangipani. I know that they have been given a gift of flowers from their guides for taking the course.

* * *

Clairaudience: *(Clear hearing) The power of hearing things not normally present to the senses. Hearing voices, music and other sounds that do not have a physical source. This can include hearing voices of those on the 'other side' (deceased people), our guardian angels or spirit guides, our higher selves, or God/ess. This can also include hearing voices/music/sounds that are actually echoes of the past – this happens a lot in haunted buildings. The locations for this sense are on each side of the head, just above the ears.*

This is what happened when I first heard The Voice, warning me about the accident and, after that, the Gypsy violin music.

Another time it happened to me was when I was friendly with a girl I believed to be sweet and caring, so when I heard a voice warning me, "Be careful of her – she's the jealous sort!" I did not take any notice, believing I was imagining the voice. I should have known better, for as it happened it turned out to be true, the girl's sweet looks belied a jealous and vindictive nature and I had cause to regret ignoring the voice.

As related earlier in this book, I also heard the voice in my dream telling me to have the whitest puppy, which would be devoted to me – and this certainly became true.

199

Another time I heard a voice saying, "You must take more exercise." I knew that I should because I had become overweight and, due to the nature of my work, had little spare time and if I had, I felt too tired to even walk the dogs. Because of that lack of exercise, I became diabetic with its host of complications and cannot blame anyone but myself, especially after my 'heavenly' warning.

A further incident is quite curious. I wanted to stock some Indian saris for my shop but could not find a source. My wish had obviously been picked up through the ether – these days I do not regard anything as chance – because a man came into my shop one Sunday, carrying a dusty rubbish sack with him. He asked me if I was interested in scarves and opened up the sack and out tumbled a mass of brightly coloured, twinkling saris onto the floor! I suspect he thought I was a crazy when I told him that he must have arrived by magic, but it did seem little short of a miracle to me that something I really wanted had turned up so conveniently without any effort on my part. The shop looked lovely with the addition of the beautiful saris and I made sure I kept some of them for myself.

Fast asleep in my bed a few nights later, I woke suddenly to hear a voice saying, "To welcome ka into your home, hang up some of the beautiful saris at your windows."

I wrote the message down in my bedside notepad to ensure I did not forget, wondering what this meant. Although I had never heard of ka before, my intuition knew how it was spelt and also that it was associated with Egypt, so it did not take much research for me to discover that ka (from ancient Egypt) was the soul or spirit of the departed. It seemed important to the person who gave me the message, so I draped some of the prettiest saris at my windows as a welcome to those crossed over, as requested.

★ ★ ★

DOG ANECDOTES

I mentioned earlier that we had an incontinent wolfhound pup. He grew into a gentle giant who, thankfully, grew out of his toilet problems. My partner and I decided to get a 'rescue' dog from the RSPCA to keep him company. As we entered the dog compound, I burst into tears as all the dogs began to leap up and down, barking to attract our attention. They knew a 'good home' was at hand and yearned to be taken out of their incarceration. I resolved to be strong and to make sure that my heart did not rule my head. I passed by dogs that were too noisy or bouncy and felt bad at their dejection when they realised they had not been chosen. While I was looking at one dog, I felt something touch my knee. As I looked down my heart *pinged* in recognition. This was the one! A dull-coated little lurcher, who reminded me of Sam, our ballerina dog of years ago, had managed to force her slim paw through the cage wiring. She was probably the most unattractive of all the dogs in the compound but she was the one for me.

My one concern was that she might kill our cats, so when I voiced the problem, the handler said, "Well, let's see." She took us all out into the yard then sallied forth to bring back one of the homeless cats and put it in front of the little lurcher. I felt very concerned for the cat, but being wise, it remained still and the dog just wagged her tail. Reassured, we made all the arrangements and were soon the lurcher's new owners. Her tail wagged happily as we took her away from the 'prison' she had been incarcerated in for most of her life. She was not pretty enough to have found a home easily.

I cuddled the little orphan on the car journey home, telling her all about her new family. To my surprise, I noticed that her dull coat quickly turned a shiny black – obviously she was pleased with the arrangement! Happiness is clearly the clue to a dog's shiny coat. I remembered Sam's dull coat of unhappiness with the new owner that shone as soon as I picked her up to take her home again.

We christened our new member of the family Orphan Annie and she became the devoted companion of our wolfhound, whose name was Cu Chullen, after the Irish king.

Annie and Chullen formed a team, seemingly on a mission from God, to bring happiness to Walsingham's many visitors in wheelchairs. Chullen would stand by the side of the chairs, his huge head the same height as the occupant's, and gently lick their faces. Annie, much smaller, would carefully wriggle up into their laps and cuddle-up to them. It was clear that those singled out by the canine couple gained so much pleasure from this attention. It was obvious to me that the dogs wanted to help people so often overlooked by others and from the happy smiles of wheelchair occupants, Chullen and Annie's work was well appreciated.

I always drew up astrological charts for all of my animals and had noted that Chullen had his Moon in Taurus. Amongst other things, this can indicate that the 'native' of the chart likes gardening in some form and appreciates flowers and growth. I wondered how this would show itself in a dog. I could hardly attribute Chullen's natural delight in digging holes to Moon in Taurus, but did notice that he liked to smell the perfume of flowers. I thought maybe they had interesting cat smells on them. However, when I saw him reaching up to smell a rose on top of a bush, I realised he really was appreciating the scent. He also loved to smell newly mown grass, inhaling, eyes closed, with obvious joy

Taking the leashed wolfhound to the shops one day, my arms were almost torn from their sockets when he noticed the florist's open hatchback car loaded with fresh blooms and dragged me across the road to plunge his nose into the middle of the flowers. The florist screamed in alarm to see the huge beast rushing towards her until she realised he only wanted to relish the perfumes. As well as appreciating flowers, he liked to pick his own blackberries and sloes from the hedgerows.

After Chullen's eventual death, Annie was distraught, so we decided to get another dog to keep her company to take her mind off her grief. We ended up with two lurcher pups, but before we obtained the chosen two I prepared astrological charts for various other puppies we were interested in. One lurcher had Mars in Aries and other warrior planet combinations and I realised that his joy would be to fight all the other dogs in the neighbourhood, to kill anything on legs and certainly not sit by the fireside. We later met his new owner who confirmed the bad character of the pup – he killed all the chickens in the area, chased all the cats and fought all the other dogs – which proves that astrology has its uses!

The charts of the two lurcher puppies that we eventually brought home fitted in with our little family well and brought Annie out of her misery.

Two years later, when we were walking them all on the vast sandy beach at Wells-Next-the-Sea, we noticed some horses galloping along the edge of the waves. A large wolfhound just like Chullen followed behind them. Annie's ears pricked up and she raced across the sands to meet her man, only to realise as soon as she got to him that it was not Chullen. Dejected, she returned to us with such sorrow in her eyes that we had a few tears running down our own cheeks. The poor girl had not forgotten him, but the young dogs soon perked her up, racing around her in circles until she could not resist joining in the fun.

I have to add that the event of Chullen's death was very sad. To block my grief, I tried not to think about him. As I was driving one day to the supermarket, I felt one of my hands actually resting on the back of Chullen. He used to stand by my side, leaning against me while I would rest my hand on his back. The feeling I was receiving as I drove along was like that. I could feel his silky hair between my fingers as if it were happening in reality. However, what was unusual was that it seemed I had a third arm and hand that was resting on him and 'feeling' his silky coat, while my 'normal' hands gripped the steering wheel as I drove.

I MEET WITCHES

Religion: *Belief in, recognition of or an awakened sense of a higher, unseen, control-ling power or powers with the emotion and morality connected with such: rites or worship, any system of such belief or worship, devoted fidelity, monastic life, a monastic order, Protestantism.*

Witch: *A person, esp. a woman, supposed to have supernatural or magical power and knowledge esp. through compact (mutual bargain, agreement; a league) with the devil or a minor evil spirit; a hag, crone; a dangerously or irresistibly fasci-nating woman.*

Sorcery: *Divination by the assistance of evil spirits; enchantment, magic, witch-craft.*

I have mentioned before that the shrine village of Walsingham drew all sorts, not just Catholics and Church of England devotees. The 'alternatives' were just as profuse and, contrary to what the members of orthodox churches assume, 'alternatives' also believe in God, Jesus and Mary – their religion or beliefs encompassing the spirit world and reaching out in different directions. I do not know why it seems to be conveniently forgotten that the three wise men were astrologers, that the Old Testament is peppered with stories of prophets foreseeing the future from precognitive dreams and that Jesus with his miracu-lous healing could be described as a shaman.

I was constantly reprimanded by churchgoers for selling 'New Age' music and even bottles of essential oils and crystals. When I queried why, they could never explain, except to say that it went against the teachings of the Church. I honestly could not understand this – the music was gentle and relaxing, with sounds of nature incorporated, composed for relaxation. The essential oils had been distilled from flowers, each having beneficial properties. Crystals, too, were maligned. I could not understand this, as they grow naturally and contain beneficial energies. Some wristwatches are charged by quartz crystals and in the pioneering days of radio, 'crystal radios' were the forerunners of what we know today. What is their problem?

I was interested to hear what the pilgrims said to me. Some were scathing and rude, others genuinely worried as to my welfare and some were downright pleasant and interested in the 'alternative' ways, but I really enjoyed speaking with the healers, the pagans, the Wiccans and witches that came into my shop. They were the ones with the gentle smiling faces who did not accuse, be rude, or wish me ill. They were the ones who hoped for world peace, did not sneer at others' belief systems; they were the ones who wanted to help others, regard-less of colour, creed or beliefs.

One such couple came into my shop one day. Like I have often been 'sniffed out' on various occasions for being 'different', I too had a nose on me! I suspected, so I asked them if they were witches. They admitted they were. I felt a bit scared – I can be just as afraid of people and what they might get up to as all my accusers can of me! I asked them if they were white witches or, er.... They smiled and said, "Let us put it this way, if we wished harm on anybody or made negative spells it would come back to us, so we don't – it's as simple as that." White witches then. Spells? Not so sure about that.

After an interesting conversation, they invited me to a 'moot' at a Norwich inn, where I could meet other witches and pagans, swop ideas and have general discussions. I agreed to attend, being genuinely interested in what might occur, but felt apprehensive as well.

It was a dark gusty night when I drove to Norwich and, as I entered the pub, leaves whirled in the door with me. I was very nervous. How stupid of me, but it just shows how the unknown can make us suspicious.

I recognised the couple from the shop and also a piratical man whom I greeted as an old friend, then confusedly wondered at my response, as I had never met him before. Had we together hoisted the skull and crossbones flag on a pirate ship in a previous life?

The group of people were very nice. Nothing spooky about them at all. They did not let me into any of their secrets or beliefs, so I was rather disappointed until the couple I had met in my shop started to tell an anecdote about what happened to them recently when they were trying to conjure up a fire elemental, a salamander. My ears pricked up. They said that they were in the centre of a pentacle in a darkened room. The dog was in his basket in the corner. They had gone through the appropriate protection procedures when suddenly the dog began growling in alarm. They then saw the red eyes of a summonsed salamander that darted around the room and tried to enter the pentacle.

I was horrified. I wondered why on earth they wanted to manifest a creature from another dimension. It clearly worked, however. What else could be 'brought through' from other places? They did not say what happened to the salamander. I wondered if they had brought it with them and got rather hot under the collar at the thought. Animals liked me. I hoped it would not decide to come home with me when I left – it might not make a nice pet!

I had enjoyed my evening but not the drive home. The wind had really risen and heavy gusts rocked the car as I drove. Norfolk roads are empty at night and I felt very alone. Swirls of rattling leaves hit the windscreen and I kept looking over my shoulder to see if red eyes were regarding me from the back seat. I arrived home safely without mishap but resolved to keep my psychic activities as they were – coming to me naturally, without pentacles, spells, incantations and invitations to elementals. No, not for me, definitely!

I learned a lesson that night. That it is possible to summon up creatures from another dimension. Not a good idea, I would have thought. I wondered if that medium I had met years ago had summoned up her golden trumpet – I felt now that it could have been a possibility.

THE WHITE WITCH OF WALSINGHAM

"I always say to myself," said the smiling pilgrim as she stepped into my candle shop, "that I *must* go and visit that lovely White Witch of Walsingham." Her smile widened as I made to demur. "No, it's no use you denying it – I *know* you're a witch!"

In the candle shop, my customer, fiddling absentmindedly with the crucifix around her neck, continued smiling at me as she leaned heavily on her stick. "Well, I'm right, aren't I, you *are* a witch?"

"I *suppose* so", I replied, "but I don't like the word 'witch' – it conjures up broomsticks, evil cackles and spells over a cauldron. Maybe 'wise woman' or 'mystic' or even 'seer' would be more appropriate." She nodded with satisfaction, then passed an enjoyable time choosing items to purchase, her faith unhindered by the proximity of such as I, which left me pondering upon the reason for being 'found out' in this most holy of holy villages.

I happily made candles in the back of my shop – which was filled with the wonderful mingled perfumes of the essential oils that the candles contained. The aromas wafted up the road on steam from an extractor fan, beguiling the nostrils of passing pilgrims and bringing them in threefold. With no money for swish shop fittings, I used imagination and utilised what I had. An old cast-iron bed in the window made an artistic display case, over which were provocatively draped beautifully embroidered priests vestments – on sale or return for a pilgrim who imported them direct from nuns in Krakow. New Age music plinkle-plunkled in the shop while my three purring cats wove their way with delicate expertise amongst the candles stacked from floor to ceiling. Ethnic clothing swung from hammocks and artfully constructed paper and reed chickens peered out of the colourful and pleasing confusion. I undoubtedly created an eccentric image, which I suppose, in retrospect, was enough for the suspicious to point their fingers. However, through the years I was forced, after many unwanted brushes from 'beyond the veil', to admit to myself that I had indeed got 'something' and that it frightened a lot of people – myself included! I was, therefore, an alien amongst the hoards of Christian pilgrims, and while I did not proclaim my enforced beliefs, I was certainly sniffed out. I often felt like the innocent women accused of witchcraft during mediaeval times.

I have a mole above my lips, which would have got me into trouble during the Puritan years of 1646. Matthew Hopkins (The Witch Finder General) would have had a field day with me. Suspect witches were arrested and their clothes torn off in public in a search for 'supernumerary teats'. Any moles upon their body were, in Hopkins' view, the undisputed mark of the Devil. If these moles were insensitive to pain and did not bleed when pricked with a knife, the woman would be proclaimed a witch. In order to fuel Matthew Hopkins' fanaticism he made sure any knives used had a retractable blade that disappeared into the handle, so the naked witches could be well and truly tortured, then burned, drowned or hanged. Those were dark days indeed for innocent women, whose knowledge of herbs and healing helped many, and I am afraid echoes of that kind of ignorance still hold sway today.

Later in life, my belief in 'magic' was to be reinforced because of extraordinary 'supernatural' things that happened to me, but because of the realisation there was a dark side, I thought it unwise to become involved or meddle for fear of unwanted intruders. I parenthesise the words 'magic' and 'supernatural' because my conclusion is that such occurrences are perfectly natural, happen to many people and should not be viewed as anything other than a gift from those unseen helpers along our spiritual paths.

I felt no need to become a Wiccan or pagan or other such, and I certainly did not feel the need to join a coven. Dancing naked at full moon and performing strange rituals did not seem necessary. If I was to be anything, I was on my own. Maybe some could call me a 'hedge witch' – a loner – but doesn't that sound like some old hag in tatters caught up in hawthorn while searching for henbane?

As I reminisced while the nice pilgrim tried on a kaftan, I recalled that at school I was rather an outcast. My views were different even as a small child and they set me apart from others. I found myself in the role of comforter to weedy children in distress and even the terrifying school bullies came to tell me their problems. As I grew older, strangers who spoke to me told me how much better they felt afterwards. A few kind words, I realised, went a long way and were, I suppose, my beginnings as a healer.

While I had always thought of myself as a Christian, by the end of my fifteen year stay in the beautiful mediaeval village of Walsingham, I realised the suffocating confines of accepted religion could no longer contain my soaring, widening beliefs.

So, how would I describe myself? Certainly not as an initiated witch from some strange coven. Not as a crone who mumbles spells and tries to conjure up ravens from the dark. I am just a natural, like many others who get glimpses of other dimensions, who can channel healing, help others and are 'taught from above'. Someone who has – and indeed, still is – journeying along her own spiritual path, led by visions, intuitions, dreams and incredible experiences. If that is what constitutes a witch, then maybe I am one, as I had originally planned to be when I was a child. However, I prefer the more acceptable job description of 'Wise Woman'.

The till dinged satisfactorily and my customer left happily, escorted to the door by Dingle, Dexter and Little Dorrit, all purring loudly. I had to face up to the inevitable. I did have gifts, which meant that other people would class me as odd, different, witch-like – but actually, I perceive those gifts as a natural part of our integral make up, ones that we have cast aside because in the Middle Ages they were classed as 'un-Christian'.

★ ★ ★

CLAIRVOYANCE

Clairvoyance: (as defined in the dictionary) The power of seeing things not normally perceptible to the senses: second sight: divination – from the French word 'clair' clear, 'voir' to see. Clear seeing. Having 'visions', seeing images (still or moving) on the inner screen of the mind (eyes can be opened or closed). Also includes seeing auras, apparitions, angels, etc. In other words, seeing beyond the physical. The area of the body that receives the psychic impressions for this sense is located in the centre of the forehead (the third eye).

Judging from people I have spoken to or books I have read, many clairvoyants have seen and spoken to spirit people from a very young age and have taken it for granted. I do not remember 'seeing' anyone or anything when I was a child or having friends from the Spirit World – the first manifestation I saw was when I was in my forties and was the Indian brave who appeared and told me to write this book. There have only been three other occasions since.

My dream world, however, proved to be the chosen way for my clairvoyance to show itself – and I mean chosen *for* me not *by* me. The fact that I seldom have clairvoyant dreams these days is evident in the way my 'progress' has taken a different route, but I am now experiencing many visions via the Reiki healing process. I do not 'see' while my eyes are opened but while they are closed, and then the visions begin. I understand now the term 'the third eye' or 'the inner eye'. The visions are seldom of long duration but, nevertheless, virtual reality and breathtaking are the colours that I see. Nothing in this world compares. The fact that I have access to such beautiful colours makes me believe more than ever that there are other worlds for us yet to explore, and perhaps this world we live on is just a 'kindergarten' where we journey along this world's highways trying (hopefully) to lead a useful life and get the rules right of an obscure game as we go.

I came to the conclusion many years ago that the world is a stage and we are mere actors upon it – and that we chose our parents, our role and lifestyle *before we were born* in order to learn lessons while living a life not experienced in previous incarnations.

Clairsentience: *(clear feeling or clear-sensing) 'Feeling' things about people or situations that we otherwise could not know. People who are strong in this ability often talk about having 'gut feelings' about things and are usually very sensitive to the energies and emotions of other people. Negative energies can often cause a wrenching or queasy feeling in the abdominal area. This sense can also warn of problematic situations - having a 'bad' feeling about something. This sense is located in the solar plexus.*

★ ★ ★

SOME MORE ABOUT REIKI

My Reiki instructor was correct when she told me that I would know when the time was right to take my Second Degree in this healing process. By now she had become a Reiki Master and I asked her to give me my initiation.

My Reiki One was taken with about thirty other students, this time tuition was given on a one-to-one basis, which I much preferred. In Reiki Two, the student learns various symbols which accelerate the healing process and which can be used for distant healing. I am always sceptical until facts are proved and I did wonder how healing could be sent across distance. My tutor lay down on a couch on the other side of the room and instructed me to send the healing across the room to her. I went through the procedure, very doubtfully, but when I had finished was surprised to see her relaxed state stiffen and her eyes open wide in surprise. She told me that it was very evident to her when I had finished and was even astonished herself that the experience had been so tangible.

A day or so after my Reiki Two initiation, a house agent phoned me on a business matter, mentioning that she had very painful shoulders and could not move her neck. I asked her if she wanted some distant healing and she said, "Yes – anything to free the pain!" I told her to stay seated after our phone call and to relax for about twelve minutes. I did not tell her what to expect because I did not know – this was very different from doing distant healing on my teacher a few yards away. I hoped the procedure would work but still doubted my abilities, despite my teacher's positive response.

I received a thank-you card from the estate agent the following day, telling me that she had felt great heat playing over her shoulders, then the pain disappeared and she could once more move her arm freely. Well, that was a very convincing beginning for me.

I began to give more and more Reiki treatments, each time being astonished by the results and my clients' varied experiences during their treatment. I keep notes of what they tell me and now have some very interesting data.

I had no intention of taking the Masters Degree and giving tuition. I did not think I would be capable of that, but I eventually felt it was time to take the degree, even if I did not wish to give tuition. I guess my guides were nudging, as usual.

Reiki tuition does not come cheap. I could not afford my Reiki Master's Third Degree fees of £1,000 however hard I tried to save. I wished I could find someone who came cheaper and, via one of my customers, I found another Master. However, she told me that she gave Reiki-Seichem, Seichem being another compatible energy, sourced from Ancient Egyptian teachings. As it had 'come my way', I was all for it, but first I had to be initiated into Reiki-Seichem and the lady agreed to come to me and do the first two degrees at my home.

While I was in a nicely relaxed state during the initiation, I thought about my lovely horse, Tiffany, and 'saw' her looking through the french windows, like she used to when she was alive. Then she materialised through the glass, turning into a unicorn as she came, shrinking in size to an animal about the size of a large goat.

The unicorn disappeared after a little while and I was then aware of two black bear cubs mock-fighting and rolling around the floor in play in front of me. It was lovely to watch them and I realised that whilst I had previously had the *feeling* experience of my spirit bear's protective paws over my hands while his head covered mine, here I was *seeing* some cubs playing. I had been aware that my first bear had been a brown, or grizzly, bear, but these were a different species. I wondered if all bears were my totem.

For about a month or so after this assumption, whenever I closed my eyes at night time I would see a series of different bears, confirming my belief that I came under the umbrella collection of all species of bears. When I came to this ultimate understanding, I saw no more bears, which was a shame as I so enjoyed seeing them. But this was usually the way of my tuition. Once I came to a positive understanding of something, then that particular 'something' stopped and other lessons began.

I wondered about the unicorn. They are supposed to be a mythical animal but I have always believed that all rumours have a basis in truth. Maybe this animal came from another dimension, from the land of magic and healing. I did not understand the reason for its appearance but it was wonderful for me to see it, along with the bears, and felt very blessed.

I eventually took the Master's Degree, and while I did not plan to give initiations myself and teach the art, was glad I had got this far and that it felt 'right'.

After the many bear 'sightings' had stopped, whenever I settled down in bed at night and closed my eyes I would see a series of animals, night after night. Apart from otters, I could not name the others, their habitat not being in the UK. I wondered why these animals showed themselves to me and the thought came into my head that maybe these were animals doomed for extinction. After this I saw no more animals, which confirmed the daunting thought that through man's intervention our planet is going to lose so much and that I had seen a preview of those in decline at the moment.

We know that our planet is being abused and so much flora and fauna is rapidly declining, but what can we do to help save the animals? Without birds and animals, what a sorry state this planet will be. TV documentaries do their best to inform and wildlife sanctuaries and zoos are doing their best to help, but it is not enough.

Mankind is creating its own demise by upsetting the balance of nature. What mankind forgets, or does not realise, is that while our present lives are not affected, our future lives will be. Do we want to return to a naked planet where survival will not be easy?

★ ★ ★

HYPNOSIS

A doctor friend of mine was interested in giving hypnosis and, because I trusted him, I was keen to give it a whirl. All went well and I found myself in a beautiful state of relaxation. On the third session he took me back to the age of five. I became very distressed so he took me away from that time. I did not know why this had happened but clearly my mind did not want to remember.

One of the exercises he gave me while under was to imagine a cat coming through the door. Try as I did, I could not conjure up that visualisation. Even in my trance state, I was thinking too logically to be able to summon up a non-existent cat. However, while I was trying to do the visualisation, I was aware that I could 'see' two Siamese cats sitting in the passageway on the other side of the closed door. After the session, I told the doctor about them and realised that he did not have Siamese cats – I had seen his pet when I arrived at his house and it was a fat common-or-garden black and white cat. The doctor smiled at me. "But I *used* to have two Siamese cats, which I had to re-home because I was allergic to them." In my hypnotic state I had clairvoyantly seen his previous pets.

I visited another hypnotherapist to see if it would help me to lose weight (it did not) and during one of the sessions something interesting cropped up. I had specifically asked him not to take me back to the age of five after my distress when under hypnosis previously – but he forgot my instructions. Taken back to that age again, I immediately panicked. I felt sick, began sobbing, threshed around and cried out, "She must never know! She must never know!"

The hypnotist quickly bought me back from that time, but it was clear that something 'bad' had happened to me at that age. It probably was not serious – except to a five-year-old child – but I suppose my mind had decided it was best for me to forget and did not want any interference. It proved to me that a hypnotist could not 'control the mind'.

* * *

Hypnosis: *(Dictionary definition) A sleep-like state in which the mind responds to external suggestion and can recover forgotten memories.*

THE SECRETS OF THE UNIVERSE

Many years ago, in the deep of the night when I could not sleep, I was attempting to understand the meaning of 'it all'. I became enveloped in something awesome and was shown *all knowledge*. I was given *total understanding*, my mind encompassed *all and everything* and I was as one with the whole of the universe. I glowed with enlightenment and finally slept.

I was more than euphoric when I woke in the morning, remembering that I had been given knowledge from the universe, but once I tried to recall it – it had gone. My memory of it had been wiped clean and I remembered nothing, nothing at all – except that it had happened. It was then that I realised the knowledge is there for us all, but not in this lifetime.

PART SEVEN

UPPING STICKS AGAIN
2002

I had not thought to move away from Walsingham. We had converted the barns at the back of the shop into a lovely home and, after living amidst brick, rubble and dust for so long, were about to enjoy the luxury of attractive surroundings when the bombshells dropped. First, my partner was told he was to be made redundant in six months. Second, I discovered my shop was about to fall down. Because it was a listed building, we had to have it demolished and rebuilt, adding on to our already substantial mortgage. With no other jobs on the horizon, we were forced to put our home and my shop on the market, which broke my heart. I loved what I did – despite the few who accused me of witchcraft – and had believed I could work there happily until the day I died.

For a little while I felt very sorry for myself, until I thought, hey! Things usually happen for a reason and perhaps 'them upstairs' thought I was wearing myself out working seven days a week making candles and serving in a shop when I should be doing something else. I perked up after that and after a year's agonising wait, our home and my shop were sold and off we went to pastures new. I looked forward to having time to myself where I would be able to work on my book and get it finished. It was long overdue and I wanted it completed – clearly my guides thought so too!

I had wanted another old house but prices were too high for us, not being in a position to apply for another mortgage. We made offers for various houses we did not like and which were really not suitable, and were turned down on all of them. I wanted to be near to my parents, as they were in their nineties and would soon need my help; I also wanted to be nearer to my children and grandchildren.

Everything seemed to be orchestrated from 'above'. At the last moment, we found a home that was exactly ten minutes from both my parents and my children. It met other factors that we needed and really could not have been more suitable. To make it even more miraculous, the house was empty with no chain and belonged to a friend of mine who allowed us to bring in as much furniture as we liked prior to completion, which made the process easier. It really seemed like a wand had been waved.

* * *

OF PARROTS

Perhaps because of a past life as a pirate, or maybe because of a fascination for Long John Silver, I had always harboured a desire to own a parrot, so when I saw a handsome young African Grey for sale my interest quickened. His hatching day was the fifth day of October, one day after my partner's birthday and two days after mine. This seemed to be a sign from above – I can excuse any indulgence if I have a sign! I subsequently bought the parrot and named him Mr Flynn.

I was able to draw up the parrot's birth chart so I could assess his character. Mr Flynn, despite being a gentle Libra, had quite a lot of Scorpio in his chart. In humans, this brings 'the sting in the tongue' and acerbic phrasing, but with Mr Flynn it manifested as the 'sting from the beak'. He really cannot stop himself from biting – and he bites really hard, even though he looks apologetic and says 'bad boy'. He's sometimes known as Fingers Flynn!

Unfortunately, when I let Flynn out of his cage for the first time, he was so scared that he flew straight into the windowpane, falling stunned to the floor. I anxiously picked him up. Insult added to injury, he screwed his head right round and sunk his big curved beak into my fingers. Ouch! It was so painful! This was the beginning of the end for me as far as Flynn was concerned. He connected me to fear and pain and I was on his number one hit list as Mrs Very Nasty. Every time I let him out of his cage, Flynn bit me so badly when I tried to get him back in again, that it was clear I was the enemy. In the meantime, he was billing, cooing and bonding with my partner, Kent, and a love affair was established. Parrots, when they bond, do so for life, so I knew that my chance for friendship with Flynn had gone.

Fingers Flynn, clearly a very intelligent parrot, soon notched up an immense vocabulary and kept us hilariously entertained, but I was saddened I had to keep at a distance – he dive-bombed me and even wearing a hat for protection, I felt too vulnerable to be around when Flynn was loose. I had no thoughts of getting another parrot even though I used to view them in the pet shop quite often. One day, however, I noticed another pretty African grey whose hatching date (shown on the cage) was the same date as our move from Walsingham to our new home. As if lit up in flashing neon, this announced 'a sign' to me and I became the owner of a second parrot. I paid a deposit for her and purchased a flat-pack cage that was soon loaded up into my vehicle. I planned to pick the parrot up the following day, once the cage was ready for her.

As I drove back towards home thinking about the little parrot and our bank balance that could ill afford such indulgence, I noticed a vehicle overtaking me. My eyes were drawn towards its customised number plate; I could scarcely believe what I saw. In large capitals, I read – POLLY! Together with the corresponding birth and moving dates, this second 'sign' indicated that the little parrot was for me. I could now excuse the expense after the go-ahead from above!

When naming my animals, I always found that the names came out of the ether for them, and while I had yet received nothing for this parrot, was sure that a name would come to me in the night, which it did – a strange one too – Dimity. I was puzzled because I thought that dimity was some kind of material, not a name so, in the morning, I looked it up in the dictionary immediately to discover that it was, indeed, a material, defined thus: *'A stout white cotton, striped or figured in the loom by weaving with two threads. Derived from the Greek DIMITOS twice and MITOS a thread. Twice* is obviously the operative word – or *second.* The *second* parrot! I was awed to realise Dimity's name had been chosen for her by a guide who understood Greek! After so many coincidences, signs or synchronicities, I felt sure that little Dimity would soon bond with me – and, of course, she did. As gentle as Flynn is ferocious, she sits on my shoulder, nibbling my ears and crooning, is easy to handle and is a little darling. Not as intelligent as Mr Flynn, she is a slow learner and maybe Dim by name and Dim by nature might apply. However, she has loving in abundance.

After Dimity had settled in our home, we placed Flynn's cage beside hers. The two parrots eyed each other up and down with interest, performed a few acrobatics to impress the other and shuffled along their perches towards each other.

Flynn – who had heard us call our new family member by name – said, "Hallo, Dimity!" and she, hanging her head coyly replied, "Hallo." What an excellent introduction! One day, while performing intricate acrobatics on her swing, Dimity missed her footing and fell to the bottom of her cage. Mr Flynn bent forward towards her and enquired in a worried tone, "Are you all right?"

The two birds provide us with endless amusement and the house echoes with their mimicry. Mr Flynn, especially, seems extra telepathic, knowing as soon as I have decided to go out, when he will begin to say, "Bye-bye, see you later," before I have even risen to fetch my bag or car keys. He laughs uproariously, joining in the general family hilarity until we are weak from mirth. He loves it when I drop something noisy in the kitchen and is 'in with an oath' before my mouth is open, but if any of us, pets included, have a slight accident, he is quick with his query, "Are you all right?"

Both the parrots love to imitate coughs and sneezes and have a field day when we have colds. Flynn knows the food timetables and begins to call the cats and dogs, imitating meows and woofs until none of us know what's going on, while Dimity practices her 'peep-bos' and polite "Hallo, how are you? Pleased to meet you." Mr Flynn has learned some French and likes to alter it to suit himself; "Bonjour, comment ca va? Bonj, mate, ou est la gare?"

I could fill many more pages with amusing parrot anecdotes but must keep to the book's route. Every step of my life has proved to be a learning curve and I learnt something unexpected from my parrots.

I learned that they are individuals, that they are intelligent and that they have different degrees of intelligence, just like us, just like other animals. I learned that not only can they mimic our voices exactly but they also seem to understand the words they have learned. Mr Flynn is able to use his vocabulary to construct sentences. He seems to have a wicked sense of humour. He is able to pick up my thoughts telepathically. He knows when I am sad and will whisper instead of shriek. He knows when he is naughty and calls himself a bad boy.

Dimity, while not so intelligent, is gentle and caring. They are young birds yet and their characters and personalities will be more apparent to me as the years go by.

I previously learned from my animals that we underestimate them – I learned this too from my chickens, but my parrots taught me that – telepathy apart – they can socialise with humans and conversational interaction is possible.

A NEW BABY

I was soon busy in my new home with lots to do – I had not even set up my computer to get to grips with the book – when my daughter, who had recently produced my second grandchild, Zachary, asked me if I would look after him during the week. I have to admit I felt thwarted in my attempts as a writer, but finding myself immersed in nappies, prams, bottles and a wonderful little baby, I discovered a new thrill in being a 'mum' again. I had such fun as the little boy grew up and we formed a wonderful bond together. I was too tired at the end of the day to write, so the book was put to one side yet again.

I have to admit that, with my knowledge of the existence of past lives, I wondered if this little boy would show any signs of remembering a previous life. His eyes, when newly born, certainly had the look of an old soul but other than that, while he was in my charge, I did not notice anything that could relate to previous incarnations.

What did astonish me, however, was the fact that he understood what I was saying at only a few months old. I used to push him around the village in one of those old large, high prams. I propped him up with lots of pillows and talked to him as I pushed him along. Sometimes I would get a senior moment and forget where I was going next. On one occasion, I was muttering to myself, "Oh, where am I supposed to go for goodness sake?" when I felt two little gimlet eyes boring into mine. The baby – about nine months old – was staring at me with a little smile on his face and pointing down a road that was the forgotten route. I thanked him and off we trudged, but my mind was whirring. I had no idea that babies could understand what was said to them at such a young age and be able to help out by gesticulating!

★ ★ ★

MORE HEALING

After my little grandson left my care to begin a new life at crèche, while missing him tremendously, I had my time to myself at last and looked forward to working on the book in earnest, but clients were coming for Reiki and I found myself agreeing to give Reiki One initiations. I was very nervous with the first couple of students, but my confidence grew as I devised a proper structure for my lessons and tuitions.

With a student due that morning to receive the first lesson and attunement I ever gave, I lay relaxing in the bath, praying that my spirit guides would help me and that everything would go well. Deep in thought, I was suddenly aware of the face of an old Native American. Wrinkled, kindly. As soon as I was aware of him, he disappeared. I knew that this was my healing guide letting me know he was there for me. I asked him what his name was. The reply was 'Hiawatha'. This made me laugh, for I knew this was a fictional name. I also realised my guide had a sense of humour. I asked again and received the name 'Big Snow'. I thought at first what a strange name – maybe I was imagining all this. But then I thought some more. My understanding of the naming system of Native Americans is that the names refer to something relevant that happens when they were born. Parts of America have harsh winters and, therefore, my guide must have been born after a deep snowfall. It made perfect sense.

My tuition work was increasing and I was getting more clients for treatments too, as well as interest shown in astrology lessons, so my days were structured for healing and courses and the book was put aside. I felt, however, that what I was learning, esoterically, was of equal importance and, almost daily, I received more insights to be included in the book.

I think the most momentous occasion for me was when I saw fairies just after I had initiated a girl into Reiki One. I always get my students to give me a treatment afterwards so that I can be sure that they are able to pass on the energy. While I was on the couch receiving treatment from my initiatee, I was surprised to notice a group of fairies watching the procedure through foliage – within the room. The fairies did not resemble Walt Disney Tinkerbells in pretty pinks and blues. The 'Wood Folk' – I *knew* this is what they called themselves – were the colours of nature, blending in and almost a part of the foliage through which they were making their observations. Their faces were not ugly but neither were they pretty. They had quite fleshy noses and features. Their rosy cheeks looked like berries. In retrospect, they resembled folklore gnomes. Their expressions were emotionless, almost bland, but it was obvious to me that they saw me as clearly as I saw them. The image soon faded but, as I lay on the couch, relaxed and happy, I felt complete awe at what I had just witnessed. I also *knew* that the wood where they lived was in the same space as my Reiki-Seichem room, but was in a different, or parallel, dimension.

Throughout this book I have used italics when using the word 'knew'. This is because the 'knowing' is so final that it does not need to be questioned. I did not really know another way to describe the feeling. Recently, while watching John Edwards, the American TV medium, I noticed that he mentioned 'the knowing', and this validated the understanding of my own 'knowing'.

Claircognizance: *(clear knowing) Having knowledge of certain situations, people or places without having any information to facilitate such knowing. This can be things of the past, present or future (premonitions). A common statement from people who are strong in this ability is "I don't know how I know, I just know." The location for this sense is on the top of the head (the crown chakra).*

I have also used the word 'synchronicity', which will crop up a few more times.

Another example of this for me was when, after coming to my conclusion about parallel dimensions, I discovered a book called 'Supernatural' by Graham Harding. After its purchase, I was interested to discover that the author researched parallel dimensions (through the medium of hallucinogenic drugs). It would appear from his research about the similar half-man-half-animal representations in cave paintings across the globe, that Harding believes they indicate that, since the dawn of time, shamans have visited, via the mind, parallel lands where 'fairies', mythical and folklore creatures and even 'aliens' are located. Reading the book convinced me that many of my own experiences might have come, not from 'far out in space' but maybe right where I am sitting, although in another dimension, another time space.

★ ★ ★

I was perfectly happy with the process of Reiki-Seichem that I was giving but when I met a tutor for Spiritual Healing (National Federation of Spiritual Healers), I thought I ought to explore this route too. Spiritual Healing only deals with auras and is not the 'hands-on healing' that is Reiki. I have to say that mountains did not move for me as I learned this method of healing. As I cannot see auras, the exercise seemed a little futile but, unexpectedly, I found that on some occasions, my hands were stopped from going further towards a body (the same thing that occurred when I did the healing on my cat Sparky all those years ago). Despite never feeling anything at all when the healing was done to me, my 'clients' at the classes said they felt the healing heat coming from my hands. That encouraged me but I still did not feel at home with the method.

I had a truly amazing moment at one of the classes, however. I was going through the healing process on a volunteer, believing I was not suited for this type of healing. I glanced up at a neighbouring student busy at work 'healing' his volunteer, to actually see beams of golden light vibrating from his fingers towards his 'client'. Clearly, I was seeing the healing energy as it came from his hands. It looked like a torch beam. I looked further around the room and saw the same golden light coming from another person's hands, directed from her fingers towards her client's body.

I was grateful to my guides for allowing me to see this. It proved to me that the healing is just as 'magic' as any other. I prefer, however, to give Reiki-Seichem treatments, but it is good to know that I am capable of giving the Spiritual Healing if it is more appropriate.

The time came, sooner than I thought, when Mr Flynn bit Dimity's tongue and she bled badly. She was so in shock that she did not want me to hold her so, instead of Reiki, I gave her the Spiritual Healing. She calmed in no time and came closer to me to receive the healing energy. Her tongue quickly stopped bleeding and she was back to normal by the next morning.

★ ★ ★

When I give Reiki, something miraculous takes place. Almost always I get 'a feeling' in my hands, which I have learned shows where a problem lies in the body. My clients always feel the heat coming from my hands – though I seldom feel it myself – and while not uncomfortable, sometimes they say it is almost too hot to bear. This heat shows that the healing energy is going where it is needed.

Sometimes I feel my shape changing. For instance, I sometimes feel myself getting much shorter with stocky legs and know that what I feel is the arrival of an aboriginal healing guide. Sometimes I feel much taller.

Once I felt myself getting overly tall and my head seemed to grow very high and elongated. My client informed me after the healing that she had seen me in her mind's eye as a tall man wearing a very high hat, like those depicted on Egyptian tombs. My guess is that an Egyptian Seichem healer was helping at that time. Obviously, I do not physically change shape but just feel the differences.

Sometimes my clients tell me that they have felt extra hands on their body. I have experienced this myself. I have to explain, however, that during a Reiki treatment a person only gets what is right for them. Those who would be frightened by such an unusual feeling (spare hands) will only perceive total relaxation and a feeling of well-being and receive nothing 'other worldly'. Every person is at a different stage of spiritual development and Reiki seems to accommodate all.

★ ★ ★

Every time I give a Reiki treatment I learn something new. A lady contacted me in response to an advert of mine. She told me that while she did not want to take Reiki tuition, she was desperate to try anything in order to alleviate her daughter's suffering and wondered if I could help. She explained that her daughter had become mentally and physically handicapped during birth due to the incompetence of the medical staff. Consequently, by the age of twenty, Amanda, as I shall call her, had a child's mind, had never been able to walk, was wheelchair-bound and suffered from sores that would not heal. I explained the Reiki process and that, while I was sure that treatment would help in some way, I could not guarantee that it would be what she hoped for.

I never tell people that Reiki is a cure-all because we do not know what Spirit has in mind for us. We also do not remember what we agreed to come into this world for and if we have agreed before birth to receive a lifelong illness or suffering for the purpose of learning and experiencing, then the Reiki will not make a difference – though on some level it will bring comfort.

I was a little apprehensive before my client arrived. I had not dealt with a situation like this and, while I trusted my guides to give me assistance, my mortal logic was bothering me.

When my client arrived in her wheelchair, I took to her immediately. Both her parents needed to be with her to lift and care for her and I could see the strain that years of looking after their daughter had etched on their tired faces. I often wonder how such parents cope with the stress of lifelong care.

As soon as I began the Reiki-Seichem treatment, the parents told me how surprised they were to see how relaxed Amanda had become. They told me that she *never* relaxed, so this was a good sign! Amanda's mother sat by her side and held her hand while her father sat on the other side with a hand on her leg. Clearly, they wanted their much-loved daughter to be comforted by them in what was a strange situation for her – one that her limited intellect might not understand.

During the hour's treatment, I noticed that all three were lulled into a complete state of relaxation. I could see that the lines of worry and weariness were being smoothed from the parents' faces. I realised that because they were both in contact with their daughter, they were also receiving the healing energies. What a wonderful thing – and also three for the price of one!

Afterwards, they both told me how amazing they felt. The father said that this was the first time he had been able to relax and forget his worries. They were both re-energised and revitalised by the treatment. Amanda enjoyed her visit and the treatment and was thrilled to meet all my pets. I kept in touch with Mum for a while, and she told me that the sores were gradually healing over.

★ ★ ★

The time came when I had my first animal client. Again, I was apprehensive as to how I would cope. I had given Reiki to my own pets when they were ill and it always worked for them, but I did not know how an animal who did not know or trust me would react.

In brief, the gorgeous black Labrador I treated was a naturally boisterous dog, usually barking loudly and continually at visitors. Its owner could not believe how quickly her dog calmed down for me, desisting in the usual frenetic barking. She had never known it happen before. In all, I gave the dog four or five treatments and, after the first time, she was so pleased to see me and obviously keen for the Reiki-Seichem treatment, automatically lay down in front of me as soon as I arrived so that treatment could begin. The dog had been under veterinary treatment for a cancer condition and staff at the clinic were amazed at her obvious and rapid improvement when she returned for a check up.

After each session of Reiki-Seichem treatment was completed, the owner's other dog always nosed her way in so that she could have some healing too!

★ ★ ★

What does Reiki mean and how does it work? Reiki is a Japanese word, which means universal life force or energy. Buddhist and Tibetan monks took years to learn the techniques many thousands of years ago. These days, some Reiki Masters do 'on the spot' initiations and, even worse, initiations over the phone to participants eager to get on the Reiki bandwagon. I do not agree with this rushed method, giving my own students two days of gentle tuition and treatments with plenty of written information to back up what I have told them.

The decision to be a healer is not one to be taken lightly and needs serious thought as there is a lot of responsibility attached to the work. The tuition and initiations, or attunements, should also not be taken lightly by Masters.

The treatment is given by the practitioner placing their hands in a series of positions on the patient's body, leaving them there for about three minutes. There are a number of symbols, which can be used to accelerate this energy. The energy flows through the practitioner into the patient and heat, and sometimes even cold, will be felt coming from her hands. It is very simple but effective and, for some reason, an hour's treatment feels like only ten minutes. Something strange happens to time, I believe, when giving or receiving Reiki-Seichem.

The word seichem comes from ancient Egyptian healing that brings another harmonious energy.

* * *

SYNCHRONICITY AGAIN

I have mentioned synchronicity throughout this book. I understand this was a word invented by Carl Jung to explain the many 'coincidences' that happen throughout life. He had received precognitive dreams himself and other 'supernatural' experiences and, as a scientist and psychologist, tried to apply logical reasoning to explain such events. I illustrate next, with another anecdote, how synchronicity works.

I had placed an advertisement in a psychics' magazine for the aromatherapy candles I produce, empowered with Reiki-Seichem healing signs and symbols. In response, I had a telephone call from a woman living in Wales who (after telling me she was not interested in the candles) asked me if I could help her, as she was troubled by a number of distressing low plane spirits that were 'possessing' her. I felt out of my depth in advising her, but instead of dismissing her as deluded, as many would, told her that I knew what she was going through because of my own experiences.

Having only recently completed the spiritual healing course, I felt my tutor would know what to do, so I telephoned her for advice on how to help the woman. It transpired that my tutor had friends whose work was ridding people possessed by entities, or 'attachments' as they describe them. These friends *had only just moved to Wales*.

I was able to effect the introduction and the distressed woman eventually telephoned to thank me and tell me that things were going well for her.

Synchronicity is that kind of 'coincidental' cause and effect. Why did that woman pick me out of a selection of many magazine advertisements, and at that particular time when I had only recently met the tutor whose friends worked at removing 'entities' and who had just moved near to the unfortunate woman?

Her guide obviously knew what he was doing in the pulling of heavenly strings, but it seemed to me quite amazing how the synchronicity worked.

Another sort of synchronicity is shown when new inventions are discovered. Often the same breakthrough is made at the same time on the other side of the world. I think it must also happen with names, as I have, since naming my parrot, heard of new baby girls being named Dimity! Yet another example is when my daughter bought an antique book, as it had caught her eye, in some obscure place. She showed it to my father, who thumbing through it, pointed to a picture of a little boy in a toy car. It was himself as a three-year old! He had a similar photo, taken at the same time, in his own archives for validation.

★ ★ ★

Talking of discoveries on the other side of the world reminds me that over the years I had lost touch with my friend in America – the one whose baby I predicted. As I was nearing the last stages of writing this book I so wished I knew where he was when, out of the blue, I received an email from him. He told me that he had often wondered where I was since my various moves and hoped to find me.

While he was scrolling through book publishers' names on the web, to his surprise my name popped up in relation to a book entitled 'Ahead of Time – the Mystery of Precognition' by Dennis Bardens. I was completely unaware of the book's existence. My friend was able to track me down via this information and when he told me about the book, though now out of publication, I was able to obtain a copy.

I had been interviewed many years ago by the journalistic author, a specialist in psychical research. His book contained a whole chapter headed 'The Seer' about my psychic abilities via precognitive dreams. Dennis Bardens had researched thoroughly into the events I had dreamt about, obtaining dates and extra data that I had not known about at the time. As well as discovering that I was now officially a seer, I was also in contact with my friend once more. Yet another of life's wonderful 'coincidences'.

VISITORS FROM THE OTHER SIDE

A lot of my animals have returned to me in dreams. Heartsease, one of my dogs, had gone dippy in her old age and had to be put down, poor dear.

In my dream, she trotted into my room, tail wagging, her white hair washed and fluffy, jumped nimbly up onto the bed and wriggled down in-between my partner and myself, telling me, "I'm almost well again." After making herself comfortable, she curled up and slept. During her lifetime she was never allowed to sleep in our bed, so it was curious that I dreamt that she did on this occasion. The dream was so vivid that I am quite sure this was a real spirit visit from Heartsease. This gave me the insight that when an illness has been severe, healing has to take place to individuals in the Afterlife, before progress can be made to further their journey.

★ ★ ★

I have dreamt on two different occasions that my maternal grandparents visited me in the night and stood side-by-side next to my bed. They did not say anything to me but emanated love and they looked serenely happy together and united. This surprised me because they did not seem to like one another very much in life! It was so good to see them and also good to know that they came to visit me to ensure that I was all right. There was no question in my mind that this was a proper visitation.

FEBRUARY 4th 2005
THE MAGICIAN MOVES IN AND ON

I moved both my parents into my own home. Dad was ninety-two and dying and Mother was ninety-three and unable to cope any more. They had done a sterling job at being independent, but now it was my time to take care of them.

I think I can easily say that this was the most difficult task of my life. Both old people were disorientated. Dad was hallucinating and looked like a skeleton, lying bed-bound in their room. Mother was distraught and difficult. Both were malnourished and even with carers coming to help, I did not know how I could continue coping with such a difficult situation.

One night, I was at my lowest ebb, weeping into my pillow and asking for some kind of help to cope. I felt so alone and so incompetent. I was gradually aware that a hand was placed comfortingly within my own. I turned to see a young Native American male kneeling on the floor beside the bed. As soon as I had acknowledged he was there, he was gone, though I could still feel his comforting hand in mine for quite a while. I no longer felt alone. It was a wonderful feeling. It reminded me that we are never alone and that our spirit guides are always with us.

On 16th July 2005, my father, the magician, died. He had a long struggle and I went through quite a number of harrowing 'death bed scenes' before the final one. The week before his death, while in hospital, he entertained the ward with 'magic' tricks – an entertainer to the last. The last week of his life was spent in a lovely nursing home near to us. He could barely talk, only managing to croak the words, "Why?" On the morning of his death, I had taken my mother to see him but realised that while his body was still alive and labouring, he was 'not in it'. I took her back home and, feeling exhausted from the long battle, lay myself on the sofa and fell asleep. I woke at two-thirty pm, feeling a kiss behind my ear from a young man, like my dad used to give me when I was a little girl. A few minutes later the phone rang. It was the nursing home telling me Dad had died at two-thirty. That kiss had been from him.

My daughter, out jogging, 'saw' my dad, her grandfather, as a young man. She had also previously wondered what he meant by saying, "Why?" This time he was able to finish the sentence. "Why does it take so long?" (to die). This was just shortly before his death. Afterwards, she said she could feel such a sense of euphoria from him as he was released from pain and old age. She told me the feeling was so tangible that she could not feel anything but happiness at her grandfather's release from his mortal life.

A month or two after the death, I had a vivid dream about Dad. He was young again, wearing a pinstriped suit – as he used to as a young journalist. He was bent over, reading a book in his den. He turned toward me when I exclaimed in joy at seeing him, and I rushed to embrace him, but stopped, saying that as he was a ghost, my arms might go through him. He looked a little surprised at what I said because he clearly felt quite normal. He was very happy to see me and while we did not 'physically' touch I did *feel* embraced. We talked a little – I do not recall what about, but I do remember that he told me, "I'm around a lot." – meaning in spirit.

I returned to my parents home the next day and went into his den to stand where he had been in my dream, in front of his bookcase. I had already removed what I felt were the important volumes, but I found that my hands went directly to a book I had not considered before. When I extracted it from the shelf, I discovered it was a typewritten manuscript about my grandfather – a Fleet Street journalist and editor himself. It was his story of life in Fleet Street when he was a young man, of his meetings with Edith Cavell, Oscar Wilde, Emily Pankhurst and a host of what are now historical people. What a find, and one that would have been overlooked but for the dream.

I later told one of Dad's friends about my dream, who surprised me by saying that he had also had a vivid dream in which my father appeared to him as a young man – this was unusual in itself because this friend did not know him until he was in his late sixties.

When I spoke to my uncle about the two dreams, he told me, in amazement, that he had also had a vivid dream in which his brother had appeared and, like his appearance in our dreams, that he was young again. I do not think that between us we needed much more evidence that he had visited us from beyond the veil!

It was clear to me that from the moment of my father's death, he had been able to assume the age he wanted. He looked to me to be about thirty years old.

My daughter told me that she tried to get in touch with my father about five months after his death without success, but instead, his sister came through, who told Lucinda that her grandpa was no longer 'around' as he was 'off' visiting other places, making journeys of discovery. My daughter was aware of a tin of violet sweets while she received the message – my uncle later confirmed that at the family home there had always been tins of violet sweeties to dip into.

This message rang very true to me. My father was a very enquiring man, wanting to know how everything worked and liked to delve into all sorts of things. As a journalist he was constantly travelling around looking for stories – he was seldom at home because he was always questing after this, that and the other. As he was like this during his life, I did not imagine that he would be any different after death! While I was so pleased to be visited by him after his passing, I was surprised he came as I really did think he would be 'off and away' in excitement, without a backward glance!

Believing that my dad had now 'gone on further', I did not expect any more visitations from him. As I said earlier in the book, I do not want my friends and family on the other side to hang around just to support me. I would prefer that they went on to do what ever they have to do – though of course it is a very welcome surprise when they do show up. I know that they are not lost to me and that when I die myself I will meet them again.

It was with surprise, therefore, a week or so after my daughter's experience, to find my father leaning over to kiss my hand. It was as if he was really there. The feeling soon dissolved but I was astonished at how real the experience had been. While bed-bound and slowly dying, he had a lovely habit of kissing the hands of carers, my mother and myself to show his gratitude for all the help he was receiving. I am sure that he was thanking me for looking after mother, now aged ninety-four, who still lives with me.

It seems probable to me that once in the Spirit World, our loved ones can explore the various levels, the halls of learning and whatever wonders are on 'the other side', doing whatever they have to do to progress themselves – or, if they prefer, to just relax and loll around, eating grapes from celestial couches – but that they are still able to pop back from those levels to check on their loved ones on the corporeal plane. Maybe those 'levels' are not far off out in the universe, as I had assumed, but very near to us in another dimension.

Corporeal: *Dictionary definition: having a body or substance: material, not spiritual.*

FEBRUARY 2006
GUIDES

I had almost completed the final draft of this book when I had an urge to sit down with pen and paper and make a list of my guides. Unlike professional mediums, apart from the occasions I have referred to, I am not aware when my guides are with me or what they actually do. It seemed a good idea to clarify them, so sitting myself down, I listed who I thought my guides were, what they do to help me and what qualities I believed they brought me. This is the result:

'The Voice' *Role:* Advisor; gives me verbal advice in extreme cases. *Qualities:* gives me an ability to see what others should do but I seldom give advice (in case it is the wrong advice) except in extreme cases. Like my guide, I seldom intervene, unless I feel strongly enough.
Native American Brave *Role:* Instructor; strong, enigmatic, a warrior. *Qualities:* gives me courage and strength in adversity. Also gives me the ability to instruct, teach and discipline. I am usually mild, but can be fierce if pushed!
Gypsy Lady She was seen by a medium at a psychometry session. *Role:* gives insights when I read palms, gives me help (probably with astrology, too). *Qualities:* gives me a love of colour, nature, the need for freedom and the yearning for outdoors. May be a distant relative.
Big Snow (Native American elder) *Role:* Healing guide. *Qualities:* gives me humour, compassion, understanding, patience, the ability to heal, understanding of nature, respect for people, animals and the planet.
Young Native American male Came when I was in despair: *Role:* comforter. *Qualities:* compassion, care and understanding of others in despair.
Aboriginal healer *Role:* takes over when I am healing. *Qualities:* healer
Bear (Spirit or Totem animal) *Role:* protection. *Qualities:* gives me strength in adversity, tenacity, gentleness, ability to work alone, love of nature, tendency to put on weight (!) Need to hibernate (!)
Fox? *Qualities:* instinct for survival, tenacity, love of nature, loner temperament, intelligence.

Horse? *Qualities:* fear of unknown things, ability to bend one's nature to others, strength, willingness to work for others.

Writing this down was quite an eye-opener for me. I had always thought that mediums had one main guide with maybe a couple of auxiliaries. To have six 'human' guides and at least one, and maybe two other, animal guides seemed quite excessive to me. I queried the fox and the horse because, while I was able to connect minds with them in reality, as referred to earlier on in the book, I do not know whether that automatically gives them their role as totem animals or guides to me. I do feel an affinity there, so believe that they are probably my occasional animal totems while the bear remains the main totem.

Having completed my compilation, I then had an urge to go on the web and 'look for my spirit guide'. I had no expectations of some magical message but as the urge was strong, I logged on.

It came as no particular surprise, therefore, when the first site I looked at informed me that most people have around six spirit guides and gave exercises on how to contact them. It also referred to a book that I was currently reading. To me, that gave me the affirmation that my urge to write that list had, indeed, been a task set up by my guides. It was certainly a clarifying exercise and one that I would recommend.

I do not know whether guides are supposed to bring their 'qualities', as I have listed, because, after all, we should have them in our own personalities, but maybe when a particular guide is around and helping, those qualities are magnified, giving us extra strengths.

* * *

Compiling the list that included 'my' bear reminded me of a television documentary I recently watched about black bears. The film showed a huge mother bear after having just given birth to her baby. I was astonished at the gentleness with which she handled the tiny scrap – her giant clumsy-looking paws with huge talons protruding from them did not look as if they were designed for delicate work and yet they obviously were, as she carefully manipulated her baby to her breasts with such tenderness. I was reminded of the time I had been aware of my spirit bear's great paws laid across my own hands in a similar gentle, protective way that I had not thought possible.

Tiffany, my horse, had similarly shown me that she, too, could be effectively gentle when she carefully avoided treading on tiny chicks in her stable, as well as the time she meticulously groomed the tiny kitten as it sat trustingly on the gate.

* * *

MARCH 2006
THE WOLF MAN

I had a strange dream whereby my long departed dog, Pansy, had picked up my parrot Dimity in her mouth and I thought that she had killed her. Although blood stained, the parrot seemed all right, none the worse for her encounter with the clumsy dog – like Benjamin Bunny was not hurt when Pansy brought him home so long ago. After cradling Dimity for a little while, she recovered enough to climb up onto my shoulder, where she likes to perch. The dream then changed and I found myself looking through some windows that seemed to be in a large ancient manor house or mansion, beautiful and mellowed. I was not aware of what the room looked like, but I sensed wood panelling, 'faded grandeur' polished wood floors with ancient Persian rugs, comfort and all the genteel trappings of such a house. The windows jutted out in an oblong and held square leaded lights. The view outside was glorious, very green, gently rolling hills dotted with old trees – like the uninterrupted acres of a 'country seat'. The colours of the countryside and sky looked 'different' to ours. Across the close-cropped sward loped a pack of five or six wolves. They looked magnificent.

There was a knock at the door. Because I had Dimity on my shoulder, I did not want to open the door in case she flew off, so I looked out of the window where I could see a man standing at the door. The wolves by this time were frolicking around him. He smiled at me through the window and I knew he was 'The Wolf Man'. His face was handsome with a subtle wolfish look. As he smiled I noticed that while his teeth seemed canine, they did not appear unattractive or wrong. His lupine eyes slanted a little. I do not remember his clothing well, but it seemed to be of greys and browns – trousers and either a jacket or a jumper of some sort. He was speaking to me but I could not hear him through the window.

I was not frightened of him or his wolves but I knew that he came from a place of myths, another dimension – and maybe that 'other' place was what I was viewing from the window.

I did not understand the dream when I awoke. I recalled that I used to have terrible nightmares when I was a child of answering a knock at the door to find mad wolves snarling and snapping at me, their mouths foaming, revealing gums drawn back over their fearsome teeth. I would try to shut the door, but never could.

Maybe The Wolf Man was telling me that there is nothing to be afraid of in the Other Worlds, and that I can open the door at any time without fear. That is a comforting thought.

* * *

RECOGNITION OF ASSISTANCE FROM PARALLEL WORLDS

After giving a Reiki-Seichem treatment to a client, we were discussing spiritual matters and I told her my story about the disembodied voice that saved my life when I was eighteen. The lady looked at me with wide eyes of astonishment as enlightenment came to her about an incident in her own life.

She told me that many years ago, when she was driving along a twisting road, she found that her car 'took itself' quite gently from the road onto a nearby grass verge. She was very calm and just let it happen. Seconds later, from the other direction around a corner, a large lorry appeared, lost control and skidded across the wrong side of the road *where her car would have been.* Once the lorry had righted itself, the lady, still feeling quite calm, drove back onto the road and continued her journey – but it was not until I told my own story that she realised what had happened and that supernatural control had taken place and saved her life. *This is exactly the reaction I hope this book will achieve* – that the anecdotes about my own experiences will jolt my readers into the awareness that a similar thing had happened to them – and that they had brushed it aside as coincidence. This realisation will bring the understanding that we all *do* have unseen presences around us, guiding us through our lives, letting us know they are there for us and helping when necessary. In our modern, logical world it is easy to forget this.

Hopefully, this book will encourage you to take notice of the coincidences that come your way and to listen to your inner voice, your intuitions, to heed dreams and visions and to be aware that these are given by beings on another level, allocated to help you along the pathways of this life.

★ ★ ★

IN CLONCLUSION

I so often wondered why I should I be singled out to experience so many paranormal adventures. I concluded that it can only be for me to pass on those experiences, together with the subsequent knowledge and, yes, wisdom that I gleaned – to let other people realise that there *are* things that go on outside the dimension we know and that we *are* contacted and helped from places that we cannot see. We just need to be receptive, more aware of those inner intuitions.

We have been conditioned to believe in only what is logical and explainable, but we should cast aside that conditioning.

It seems from my experiences that we are here on this planet to *learn* – not just academic lessons from school, but to learn personal growth, compassion and understanding of others and, above all, to gain wisdom – all part of a spiritual path.

It should not matter if we decide to take a different route to others because none of us are the same, but if we do not seek growth of some sort then we are wasting the time given to us in this life.

Don't let us waste our time and energy on petty complaints and annoyances or hark back to the past to what *was* or *might have been*. It only creates negative energy and stops progression. If our life seems harsh, then purposely look for something good in every day – a bird song, a smile, a sunset. It can *always* be found and generates optimism that in turn generates positivity.

No one person can change the world for the better but every person is capable of making a difference, however small. Make sure it is a good difference!

As I progressed through life, I discovered that anything I learned of worth came from within. This made me consider the source of such knowledge and deduced that 'someone unseen' was tutoring me – which would indicate that if this happens to me, then it can happen to *you* and to others as well.

★ ★ ★

I retrospectively realised that the paranormal events that began for me with disaster dreams were necessary because of their impact and precognitive content. I could not ignore them. My belief system had to change. I was understandably terrified with the dark forces I had to deal with, but I did cope and it made me strong. For some time I worried that I was going insane but too much proof that my 'mysticism' was real and not imagination eventually put a stop to that thought and I became more and more confident.

I now believe that those difficult and frightening experiences were 'tests' – 'examination' times, or even initiations that the shaman would have gone through in past times. I got through the first and difficult stages with flying colours and was rewarded with gentler tuition. Everything I received after 'the dark times' was of a different and wonderful nature.

I no longer fear that 'the Devil and his minions' are out to get me – though I realise I should never drop my defences! At one time it felt as if I had been courted by the Dark forces as well as by the Light, but it is something that I had to deal with. I guess each person's experiences are different according to their need, capabilities and karma.

★ ★ ★

Maybe it is not necessary for all people to follow a spiritual path in this life. Maybe for some, their purpose in this life is to generate money or perhaps be an entertainer. Each person has a different role to play. If everyone were busy lighting candles, burning joss sticks and going into meditations the world might grind to a halt. We can only surmise at the grand plan, after all, and follow our intuitions regarding ourselves.

Because of my interest in astrology, I realise that we are given our potential at birth – but we would have already chosen our parents *prior to birth* for the correct lifestyle for the conditions we had agreed to experience this time around. Arrangements would have been made for the exact time of our birth to ensure correct astrological alignment of the planets overhead – that bring differing talents to 'make the world go round'.

It would not be effective if our world were overloaded with artists daubing in attics or designers creating amazing designer gowns if there were no financial wizards to generate the necessary commercial interests. Equally, if we were all born to ponder the meaning of life by sitting on top of a mountain, nothing else would get done – there are not enough mountaintops anyway.

The twelve zodiac signs provide the balance of talents and that seems to me like part of a very 'grand plan'.

Not everybody needs to wonder about esoteric mysteries. How would we get our houses built, plumbing fixed, broken bones set, children taught or, indeed, the opportunity to just enjoy life watching our television?

We are all different, and rightly so, but whatever our vocation, our lives would be enhanced if we listened to the 'inner voice' that we *all* get from our unseen helpers, our Higher Self, our Guides and loved ones in Spirit that we so often allow our intellect to ignore or overrule.

★ ★ ★

In the early years of my psychic adventures, I could never find any books to explain what was happening to me. I have since read many that show my experiences are not unique, that these things are happening all the time to other people. How I wish I had known that at the time.

What does seem unique about my experiences, however, is that, strangely, I seem to have received a wide spectrum of paranormal experiences instead of having been given a 'specialist subject' to carry through.

It seems to me that professional mediums have seen and communicated with spirit people since childhood and can easily tap into the Spirit World or other dimensions – call it what you will. They specialise in one aspect and have built up their strengths in that quarter to help people through their Guides and Angels. I do not consider myself a 'proper' medium – more a reluctant psychic! I cannot tap into mysteries willy-nilly. They come out of the blue when I least expect them, real and significant, but not something I can tune into naturally. I cannot be an oracle to order – though maybe one day I shall learn to do so.

So, why have I been picked out for such attention? Why did my Native American brave tell me to write this book? It seems obvious to me now, even though it has taken a lifetime of experiences to reach this stage. I have been given the task to show ordinary people like myself that they, too, should look for the extraordinary in their lives. My theories and beliefs after forty-six years of astonishing encounters with the unbelievable will be the basis of another book.

Meanwhile, I realise that Life is a glorious mystery and hope that what I have written within this volume will encourage readers to 'notice' the hints offered along Life's highway. Once '*They*' notice that *you* notice their hints and subtleties, you will be teased with more and more fascinating insights.

★ ★ ★

Oracle: *Dictionary definition: a medium or agency of divine revelation; a response by or on behalf of a god; the place where such responses are given; a person with the reputation, or an air of infallibility or great wisdom; an infallible indication; a wise, sententious or mysterious utterance.*

Karma: *Dictionary definition: (Hinduism and Buddhism) the moral quality of a person's (or animal's) actions regarded as determining the nature of a future existence or incarnation; the concept of such transcendental retribution; the theory of inevitable consequence generally; fate, destiny.*

233

★ ★ ★

Magic: What exactly is it? The dictionary definition states: the art of producing marvellous results by compelling the aid of spirits, or by using the secret forces of nature, such as the power supposed to reside in certain objects as 'givers of life' – a secret or mysterious power over the imagination or will.

I know that magic exists. It has come to me naturally and that is how it should be. I do not believe that I should try and 'compel the aid of spirits' or 'use the secret forces of nature' to either conjure anything that does not happen naturally, or try to change the course of events – though maybe I did a couple of times. I do not think that anybody should. If we deliberately meddle with the unknown, we can only cause problems but that does not mean we need to be unaware that magic is happening around us all the time.

I do not believe that my esoteric adventures are yet over, I am sure more 'tuition' will come my way.

I feel very privileged to have been sent down such a thorny road, overcoming the terrors and pitfalls to discover peaceful byways as well as my own truths.

I believe that my words will be helpful to many, falling as seeds in a fertile meadow to flower in colourful abundance for those who wander in search of their own particular truths along the pathways of Life.

This flowery analogy is a good place to remind you to follow the old adage 'sow and ye shall reap'. A thistle seed begets more thistles that can be mighty prickly and uncomfortable. Wish ill on others and it will return to you – 'What goes around comes around'.

Always keep a notebook by your bed to record dreams, and one in your pocket or bag to note down any 'coincidences'– even if they do not make sense at the time. Dreams often need to be de-coded – the sleeping mind is very clever.

If anything happens that frightens you, remember that fear cannot physically hurt you and it can be pushed aside. Shout or laugh at your fears to drive them away. You will find hidden strengths.

As you learn to heed the intuitions and messages, maybe the purpose of them will become clear. Your life will be enriched when your senses are attuned, bringing untold pleasures and the lives of other people around you will also be touched.

It is not always necessary to understand why these things happen, but it is important to acknowledge that they do.

The sixth sense is an ability lying dormant in everybody. I ask that you rescue your latent sixth sense from its dusty wrappers and give it a good polish – your life, like mine has been, will then be truly enriched!

Footnote

My full name is Valerie Gordon Anckorn.
The talented cover illustrator, Jason Holt, told me that if I wanted to have
the name 'Anckorn' on the cover, the chicken would have to go.
I chose the chicken!

Jason Holt can be contacted for commissions via e mail:
disgusting_dinosaurs@hotmail.com

RECOMMENDED READING

Yesterdays Children – Jenny Cockell – Piatkus   ISBN 0-7499 –1246–4

Past lives, Future Lives – Jenny Cockell - Piakus   ISBN 07-499–1608 7

Indigo Children – Lee Carroll & Jan Tober – Hay   ISBN 1–561 70–608–6

An Indigo Celebration – Lee Carroll & Jan Tober – Hay
ISBN 1–56170–859–3

Ahead of Time – the mystery of precognition – Dennis Bardens – Hale–D
ISBN 7090 – 4507 – 7

Children's Past Lives – Carol Bowman - Element ISBN 186204354x

Return From Heavan – Carol Bowman – Harper   ISBN 06–10 30 44–9

Coming Back – Raymond A. Moody JR.MD - Bantam   ISBN 0-553–29398–2

The Four Elements – Margaret Gullan–Whur - Rider   ISBN 0 – 7126–1429 x

More Lives than one…? Jeffrey Iverson – Pan   0330 252569

Supernature – Lyall Watson – Hodder   ISBN 0340 188833 2

The Final Message – Rael – Tagman Press   ISBN 0-953 0921–1-9

Elohim's nursery – David Medina – Regency Press

The Twelve Houses – Howard Sassportas – Aquarian Press
ISBN 0 – 85030 -385-0

Planets in Aspect – Robert Pelletier – Para Research. Inc   ISBN 0914918-20-6

An experiment with time – J.W. Dunne – Faber

Dancing with the Devil as you channel the light – David Ashworth – Crucible Publishers   ISBN I – 9002 7330 36

Supernatural – Graham Hancock – Century   ISBN 1–8441–3681–7

Spirited – Tony Stockwell – Hodder Mobius   ISBN 0-340-83354-8

Destiny of Souls – Michael Newton Ph.D. – Llewellyn   ISBN 1-56718-499-5

Journey of Souls – Michael Newton Ph.D. – Llewellyn   ISBN 1-56718-485-5

Same Soul, Many Bodies – Dr. Brian Weiss – Piatkus   ISBN 0-7499-2541-8

Essential Reiki – Diane Stein – The Crossing Press   ISBN 0-89594-736-6

Valerie Gordon's shop:

BOUDICCA'S TREASURE TROVE
21b High Street, Heacham
Near Hunstanton
King's Lynn PE31 7ER

Tel: 01485 579 376

Opening hours: 10a.m.- 1p.m. – 2 p.m.- 4p.m.
Half days Thursdays and Saturdays (closed 1 p.m.)
Closed Sundays

New Age shop with handcrafted aromatherapy and
ornamental candles made in Heacham.

Ethnic swirly skirts and sparkly tops – Reubens women
catered for too. Sparkly cushions and throws, scarves,
baubles, bangles, beads and bells, wind chimes,
crystals, books, - including The Magician's Daughter! –
essential oils, relaxation cd's, candle holders,
lots of incense and incense holders.

Astrological charts and readings
Reiki-Seichem treatments

Two-day courses for
Reiki-Seichem and Beginners Astrology.

come and visit – but best to phone first
as book signings etc. might interfere with
shop hours.